JUMP COMMANDER

JUMP COMMANDER

In Combat with the
505th and 508th Parachute Infantry Regiments,
82nd Airborne Division in World War II

MARK J. ALEXANDER and JOHN SPARRY

CASEMATE
Philadelphia & Oxford

Published in the United States of America and Great Britain in 2012 by
CASEMATE PUBLISHERS
908 Darby Road, Havertown, PA 19083
and
10 Hythe Bridge Street, Oxford, OX1 2EW

Copyright 2010 © John Sparry
ISBN 978-1-61200-091-6
Digital Edition: ISBN 978-1-93514-951-4

Cataloging-in-publication data is available from the Library of Congress
and the British Library.

All rights reserved. No part of this book may be reproduced or transmitted in any
form or by any means, electronic or mechanical including photocopying, recording
or by any information storage and retrieval system, without permission from the
Publisher in writing.

10 9 8 7 6 5 4 3 2 1

Printed and bound in the United States of America.

For a complete list of Casemate titles please contact:

CASEMATE PUBLISHERS (US)
Telephone (610) 853-9131, Fax (610) 853-9146
E-mail: casemate@casematepublishing.com

CASEMATE PUBLISHERS (UK)
Telephone (01865) 241249, Fax (01865) 794449
E-mail: casemate-uk@casematepublishing.co.uk

Contents

Acknowledgments		7
Introduction: A Word from the Author		9
Prelude: First Jump		12
Chapter 1:	Learning to Fight	14
Chapter 2:	Preparing for War	30
Chapter 3:	Early Days in the 505 Parachute Infantry Regiment	48
Chapter 4:	North Africa	57
Chapter 5:	Sicily: From the Jump to Biazzo Ridge	73
Chapter 6:	On to Trapani	90
Chapter 7:	Return to North Africa and Preparations for Italy	103
Chapter 8:	From Salerno to Naples	111
Chapter 9:	To the Volturno: The Battle of Arnone	120
Chapter 10:	Duty in Naples	140
Chapter 11:	Northern Ireland	154
Chapter 12:	England	161
Chapter 13:	D-Day: June 6, 1944	174
Chapter 14:	La Fière Bridge and Causeway	193
Chapter 15:	Montebourg Station	199
Chapter 16:	Westward to the Douve: The Battle of St. Sauveur-le-Vicomte	212
Chapter 17:	The 508 Parachute Infantry Regiment	219
Chapter 18:	Hill 95	226
Chapter 19:	Recovery, Holland and the Bulge	234
Chapter 20:	Return and Transition	244
Chapter 21:	You Can Take the Paratrooper Out of the Fight, but…	253
Note to Veterans		264
Editor's Note		265
Notes		267
Bibliography		281
Index		283

To my grandmother, Mary Alexander. She was the rock that gave my grandfather strength while he was overseas. Today, she is still the foundation of our family. And to my wife, Kelly. Your love and kindness are the wind in my sails.

ACKNOWLEDGMENTS

I WOULD LIKE TO THANK my grandfather's friends and fellow World War II veterans for their service and for kindly sharing their experiences with me. They put their lives on the line when it mattered most, and I will always be grateful. I would particularly like to mention Jack Norton, Chet Graham, Don McKeage, Otis Sampson, Robert "Doc" Franco, Dean McCandless, Spencer Wurst, Virgil McQuire and Wilton Johnson, whose conversations and correspondence have added to Mark Alexander's story. I would also like to thank Bob Murphy for his help in checking an early manuscript for errors, and generously supplying photographs.

While writing this book, I very often pushed aside things that needed attention around the house or in life. My wife Kelly was amazingly understanding and encouraging throughout the long process. I'm quite sure there were times she felt I would never finish, and without her love and support, I wouldn't have.

Mary Alexander, my grandmother, is the best writer in the family. Reading her memoirs gave me great insight into the kinds of things that really interest readers. Whenever I slowed down or found myself completely stalled on the path towards finishing the present book, talking to her always helped. Her wisdom, strong moral character and good sense of humor kept me grounded.

I must thank my agent, Gayle Wurst, of Princeton International Agency for the Arts. She spent countless hours reading over versions of my extra-long manuscript, then directing and encouraging me on to great improvements. She also did a wonderful job editing the final copy. Without her, it never would have made it into print.

My publisher, Casemate, has a knack for finding truly compelling stories and bringing them to the reader. I am thankful to David Farnsworth and Steve Smith for choosing mine to be among their fine collection of World War II histories and memoirs.

I want to thank Phil Nordyke for his generous help with photographs and maps; Deryk Wills, who tracked down some wonderful pictures in British governmental archives; cartographer Mark Franklin for his quick and excellent map creations; Jim Blankenship for looking up soldiers' names and ranks; and Dan Roper and Barbara Gavin Fauntleroy for help identifying quotations.

Finally, a big thank-you to my parents and to my family in general. We have always encouraged each other to follow our dreams.

Introduction

A Word from the Author

In 2001, I began interviewing my grandfather, Mark Alexander (Col. USA, ret), in the hope of later putting pen to paper (or more accurately, fingers to keyboard) and turning his words about his experience in World War II with the 82nd Airborne into a book. I knew he had made three combat jumps and had led three different battalions in front line battle before he was seriously wounded late in the Normandy campaign. His was an amazing story, one that should be captured as fully as possible and, if everything worked out, shared with the world.

However, there were obstacles. We arranged to meet in his office, a fairly large room attached to the main house, but with a separate entrance. The walls were covered with 82nd Airborne memorabilia, and a few shelves held paintings he had recently completed.

As we sat down, I pulled a mini tape recorder out of my pocket, and placing it between us on the desk, hit the record button.

A look of mild alarm crossed his face.

"What's that?"

"It's a tape recorder, grandpa."

"Why do you need that?"

He may not have realized at first that I wanted to turn his war experience into a book. It's entirely possible that I kept that nugget to myself, not yet knowing if I would be able to follow through. The point is, he wasn't comfortable being recorded. I turned the tape recorder off and put it away.

Later that night as I went over my handwritten notes and tried to capture all that I could remember on my computer, I reflected back on TV interviews I had seen as a child. The president stood behind his podium answering questions while reporters furiously scribbled down every word. It seemed remarkable that they could capture enough to write a decent article. My writing was far too slow. Clearly I needed either to learn shorthand or somehow use the tape recorder.

Taping our conversations in secret was out of the question. I wouldn't betray his trust in that manner. Instead, I showed up for our next appointment with pen and paper. As we talked, I took notes as before. Every once in a while I would say, "Hang on a second, grandpa," pull the recorder out of my pocket, turn it on and repeat something he had said, turn it off, and put it back in my pocket. By the next interview, I stopped putting it back in my pocket and just sat it on the desk. It wasn't long before I was openly recording everything. He even kept the device a few times to capture things that popped into his mind when I wasn't around. This last idea didn't work out very well, because the buttons were small and hard to read. He usually spoke into it while it was paused or off.

Now we were really rolling. I tried to take a long lunch and interview him at least once a week. We did, however, still encounter a few other speed bumps. One was that he skipped over miles of detail. It wasn't in my nature to stop him in the middle of a story, and the first time I heard a new one, I certainly didn't ask questions. I wanted his mind to travel wherever it wanted. The details could be filled in later. I collected follow-up questions about a particular engagement or situation, and he would briefly answer, then go on with the same details he had given me the week before. Eventually I learned to steer the conversation back to the area needing better explanation and also to ask better questions.

My grandfather died in May of 2004, two weeks before I met some of his war buddies in Normandy, France, where they were celebrating the 60th anniversary of the D-Day invasion. I was sad of course, but it was a great experience meeting his friends and hearing how their tales intertwined with those of my grandfather.

I am the caretaker of http://www.505RCT.org, a website dedicated to the *505 Parachute Infantry Regiment*, in which my grandfather led the 1st and 2nd Battalions in World War II. Over the last year, I believe I have received over a hundred messages from people looking to know more about a family member who served with the 505. Our association, including some of the few remaining veterans, attempts to provide as much information as possible. Sadly, there is usually little or nothing to report. The soldiers who knew them best have often passed on or cannot be located.

Every veteran stepped up and served his or her country, regardless of capacity, and their stories should not pass with them. If you know a vet, I encourage you to talk to them about their service. If you are a veteran, it may feel strange to write down or record a portion of your life, but if you do, it benefits all of us. Please mention your buddies as well. A description of their personality can be as important, or even more important, than what they did. Did they have a good sense of humor? Could they play a musical instrument? Gems like these help people to know their relatives—especially those that they never had the chance to meet.

Those interviews in my grandfather's office opened a door, giving me a view of the drudgery and crazy adventure that was army life in the war, the adrenaline and responsibility of battle, and the holes left when friends died. I saw the shock of first combat, what it meant to look out for your men when it was almost impossible, and what happened if those in charge put their own needs first. Mark Alexander, my grandfather, eventually confided in me things that he hadn't told anyone else, at least not in decades.

Our talks were magical in a way. They allowed me to leave my world for a while and travel through a very uncertain and desperate time. I am lucky to have had them and I feel blessed that his story is available to the rest of the world.

Prelude

The First Jump

Major Mark Alexander stood in the open doorway of the C-47 aircraft carrying a stick of seventeen paratroopers over the open water of the Mediterranean. It was September 9, 1943, and he was about to parachute into Sicily in Operation HUSKY, the spearhead of American landings in the first wave of troops thrown against Hitler's Fortress Europe. This was IT, the first combat jump for the 505th Parachute Infantry Regiment, 82nd Airborne Division, and the first mass regimental combat jump in United States history. It was an historic moment, not only for Alexander and his regiment, but for the 82nd Airborne, the United States Army, the Allies and, indeed, the world.

Alexander peered into the darkness, checking the positions of the planes around him. He carried on his shoulders the responsibility of over 500 elite troops. Only eleven days earlier, Colonel James M. Gavin, commanding the 505, had unexpectedly relieved Alexander's battalion commander, moving Alexander up from executive officer to commander of the 2/505. He had to fight to get the staff, still loyal to their former boss, in line. Relationships had to be developed with regimental headquarters, and the air wing tasked with carrying his men into battle.

The paratroopers had trained extremely hard, most recently in the grueling conditions of North Africa, where they had battled dust storms, dysentery and disease, legions of flies and scorpions, the lack of fresh water, and unforgiving heat that regularly reached 130 degrees. The ground was so hard and rocky, only two training jumps were attempted. The first one resulted in so many broken bones that full battalion jumps were called off. Two men jumped from each plane in the next exercise. It was training for the raw pilots more than anything else.

The First Jump

Alexander had done his damnedest to ensure his battalion would all be dropped together, even if they were dropped in the wrong place, so they could fight together as a battalion. He'd extracted this promise from the commanders of the 64th Troop Carrier Group that would carry them into battle. Lt. Col. Tommy Thompson, their executive officer and an ex-fighter pilot, now was piloting Alexander's plane.

But were they flying together in formation? Studying the sky from the doorway, Alexander could see a few other planes, but not nearly enough to carry the entire 2nd Battalion. The men had chuted up just after 8:00 p.m., and were heading through a nighttime sky into their first fight. Untested pilots were liable to drift apart in the dark, and the fear of hitting another aircraft and crashing into the sea was certainly in their minds. With very few features in the water below to guide them, the pilots were navigating by compass and elapsed time, flying on an eastern course. To make matters worse, a windstorm had whipped up in the Mediterranean, blowing from the west and creating a strong tail wind.

The red light came on in the aircraft cabin, cutting Alexander's thoughts short. The co-pilot was signaling that they were ten minutes away from their drop zone, a few miles east of Gela. The 1st and 2nd Battalions were to jump behind enemy lines, seize a crucial road junction, and hold it until the 1st Infantry Division arrived. Alexander tensed, waiting for the flash of the green "go" light. He would lead his men out the door.

"The green light came on, but we were still way out over the ocean. If we went now, we would hit the water and drown before we could get our gear off. I blocked the door, and of course the men tried to push me out. They were that eager to get out and get the jump over with. Someone had stopped, and they thought he'd frozen from fear, so they just pushed all the harder.

"I yelled, 'Get back, dammit! We're still over the water! Get back!' I was holding on and talking to them as fast as I could. My orderly, Sanders, was the next guy in line. He could see the ocean too and tried to help me fight them off."

The men pressed harder. Alexander was losing his footing and grip. Parachute or not, if they exited now, they would die.

CHAPTER ONE

LEARNING TO FIGHT

CAN COMBAT LEADERSHIP BE LEARNED? Or is it something a person is born with? In the case of Mark Alexander, the answer to both of these questions is *yes*. General James M. Gavin, his regimental, and later divisional commander in World War II, recognized the combination of innate qualities and military know-how that drove Alexander to excel and always lead from the front. Alexander was "a superior troop leader in combat," Gavin wrote. "He is possessed with exceptional courage and performs brilliantly on the battlefield." [1]

Mark Alexander joined his local National Guard in Lawrence, Kansas, three months before it was activated on December 23, 1940. He was an athletic 29-year-old with an art degree from the University of Kansas and no military knowledge or training whatsoever. He entered the army as a private; two years and eight months later, he was promoted to lieutenant colonel. By June 1944, he had made three combat jumps and led three different parachute battalions in some of the hottest battles in the European Theater of Operations. Even in a time of war, it was highly unusual to rise through the ranks so quickly, especially for someone who began with so little knowledge of the military.

He did feel that he had an advantage, however. His childhood.

"I was a green guy when I first entered the army, but I was a fast learner. And I think combat came more naturally to me then it did to most people. You'll think this is crazy, but we used to play a lot of Cowboy and Indian when I was a kid. We played all those games where you've got to ambush the other guy. I was always the leader, and I picked up on a lot of things.

"On top of that, I had a little .22 rifle at seven years old, and learned to shoot and hunt rabbits, occasionally a duck. I think by hunting and doing things like that, I learned a lot more than a lot of others ever did in principle."

Mark J. Alexander was born to Edward Ethen and Ruby Alexander on January 23, 1911. He was a breech baby, and his mother almost died in the delivery. About six months later, he was christened Marcel James Alexander in the Congregation Church of Lawrence, Kansas. Mark was the second of four surviving children, who also included Harold (November 1908), Donald (June 1913) and Edwin (July 1920). The death of his infant sister, Donald's twin, is one of his earliest memories: "Virginia died of pneumonia at six months and I remember my mother crying for several days. As a child, I did not know what to make of it."

Like many soldiers in World War II, Alexander came to manhood in the hardscrabble years of the Great Depression. Brought up in the school of hard knocks, he learned many lessons as he rode the rails seeking work, labored at heavy construction jobs, and did anything else he could find to turn an honest buck (or a quarter). He emerged from these experiences as an astute judge of character and on-the-ground situations, a man who was always ready to listen to others, but above all had learned to trust his own instincts.

These traits were built on a strong foundation of small-town, middle-class, Midwestern values. His mother Ruby, who came from a family of farmers, was an exceptionally kind, hard-working woman dedicated to her family and social causes, who firmly believed in the practice of Christian charity. Alexander remembers many a day that out-of-work "bums" would knock on their door. Even in the depths of the Depression, when feeding four growing boys was particularly tough, Ruby Alexander "no matter what, would give the men a slice of bread with something to go on it, whatever was available." Her sons soon started to suspect that their house was mysteriously marked; itinerant hobos they had never seen before would skip the other houses on the block and head straight for their door.

Even years before the bubble burst in 1929, a solid job was neither easy to find nor hang onto, but Alexander's father Edward was a good provider who always seemed to land on his feet, even in times of adversity. Through adaptability and determination, he not only managed to support his growing family, he improved their social and financial standing, and emerged from the Depression as a respected business leader and pillar of the community.

This is not to say it was an easy trajectory, as Alexander's earliest memories reflect. "I was born in a small house on Elm Street, with an outside privy. Twice a week, Mother and Dad heated a tub of water on a kitchen wood stove, and we all had a bath in another tub on the linoleum kitchen floor. When I was about four, we moved to a place in North East Lawrence where we had about five acres and a two-story house with windmill well pumps and water tanks. For the first time, we had an indoor toilet and did not have to go out to the privy in the cold of winter. We also had a horse and buggy and a cow for milk for us three boys.

"When I was about five and a half, we moved to 508 Indiana Street in South Lawrence, two blocks from Pinckney School, which I entered at six years of age. About the time I finished grade school we were beginning the Great Depression, and Dad lost his job as an accountant for the Underwood Feed and Grain Mill when a son of the owner wanted the position. Prior to that, he had lost his job as an agent for the American Express Company when they closed their office in Lawrence.

"In 1924 we moved to Seattle, Washington, where Dad was employed as an accountant for a marine shipping organization. This was a temporary job. He later worked for an apple grower in Yakama, Washington. The whole family picked apples; we kids were not in school. At the end of the season, Dad was again out of work and we moved back to Lawrence.

"Our mode of transportation to and from Seattle was a soft-top, six-cylinder Dodge. Dad built cabinets for our food and cooking utensils and hung them on the running boards and rear end. We had two tents and most of the time camped out on our travels. I was 13 and Dad let me drive part of the time, but didn't trust Harold because he would not keep his eyes on the road and scared us half to death.

"When we returned to Lawrence, Dad found employment as the manager of the Lawrence Golf Club. I think it paid $125 per month and later $175 per month. He and Mother purchased a two-story home with a bath and a half and four bedrooms, about 1,700 square feet, for $4,000. It had been built by a Mr. Philips, who had gone through the Klondike Gold Rush and returned to Lawrence with enough cash to build a nice home. Dad held his management job at the golf course until about 1933, when he got elected as City Treasurer, a job he held until 1944 when he retired.

While Alexander's father was fighting on the job front, and his mother was striving to manage on a shoestring and bring up four strapping boys, Alexander was developing a reputation as a scrapper. This came partly because of his position in the family as the second-oldest boy, and partly because he was called "Marcel," a "sissy name" that got him into fights at school. But it also stemmed from bravery, stubbornness, or a combination of both, and an innate need to test his limits and those of others. Notably, he also had a marked gift for making allies of former enemies.

Two recollections, his first day at grammar school and that at junior high, aptly illustrate this character trait. "My first day at Pinckney School, I had a fight with Jimmie Moor and was sent home with a note for my father and mother. Later, Jimmie and I became good friends. In the fifth grade, there was an older bully who beat me up pretty good, but in spite of his pounding, I would not say *enough*. Later, this same boy took it upon himself to protect me from some other older boys.

"With the move to Seattle and back, I lost six months of school. At 13, I entered Lawrence Junior High School and promptly came down with scarlet fever and then pneumonia. I was ill for more than three months and was very weak when I returned to school. The first day at junior high, I'm the Alexander, so I get the front corner because they seat you alphabetically. The teacher called my name. I stood up, because that's what you did in those days. She called my name, Marcel, three times and I'm just standing there. She turned around and looked and said, 'Oh, I'm sorry, I thought you were a girl.'

"The guy behind me guffawed, and I hit him in the mouth. We started fighting and I get thrown out of school for a week. That was the first day of the school year."

Good old-fashioned sibling fisticuffs probably were the most frequent of Alexander's fights. A few occurred between him and his younger brothers, but he more often found himself having to defend them. "Another problem was that Don would start a row and then step out of it by saying, 'Well, maybe I can't beat you, but my brother Mark can,' and then I had a fight on my hands."

Significantly, Alexander did not pick on smaller, younger boys, but willingly challenged older, bigger ones. He also had a strong protective instinct toward those he cared about, and would rise up to defend them if he thought they were hurt or vulnerable. This brought him into many battles with his older brother.

"Harold and I used to fight. Particularly, he would do things that made Mother cry. One time we fought because he gave all the meat to the dog.

"I came home and mother was crying. I said, 'What's the matter?'"

"She said, 'I had enough meat for the week and now it's gone. Your brother fed it to his dog.'"

"Those were tough times. Generally, she had fresh meat the first night. Then she'd take the bone and make meat soup, and then we had sliced meat, what there was of it, for the week."

"So I said, 'Harold, come out in the backyard.'"

"Mother hated to see us fight, but we'd do it anyway. He was three years older and bigger than me, but I was more athletic than he was. So I learned to fight at an early age. Finally, when I was 16, I got so I could whip him. Then we didn't fight much any more."

Protective of his mother, Alexander could nevertheless defy her authority in a fit of willfulness, and he even on occasion stood up to his father. The family owned a piano and a violin, on which the young Alexanders were expected to practice. Putting food on the table was no small feat, but Ruby still insisted that her boys be educated. In her view, music was almost as important as the three Rs.

When Mark rebelled and refused to practice the violin, Ruby let him know he would be in for it as soon as his father was home. But Alexander had made his mind up he was done with music. His father came home and took the hairbrush to his son's backside. Mark refused to cry, and Edward swatted harder and harder until the brush broke. Disgusted, he threw it on the floor with a "god dammit," and never again struck his son. Mark never had to practice the violin again, either.

Although the Alexanders were more fortunate than many during the Depression, his family's struggles to make ends meet left an indelible imprint. Alexander was internally driven to be a high achiever, and in such lean times, this drive created an early awareness of the need to make—and pay—his own way in the world.

A local event, a potato-digging contest in the sandy soil down by the Kaw River, is the single best example of his capacities and character. "They'd plow the potatoes out of the ground and we'd come along and pick them up. They had a contest of sorts. It was men and boys and everybody looking for potatoes. I was 13 years old, and that day I filled 81 sacks. No one else had more than 70. The sacks were heavy. You had to half drag them. Each sack weighed close to 100 pounds.

"I beat everybody because I was actually digging for them. A lot of them only grabbed what they could see. It was soft sandy soil, and I'd get some that were still covered. The sacks were heavy, but although I wasn't big, I was strong. We were paid ten cents a sack. I made $8.10, and used it for clothes to go to school. As I remember, I also bought a new single-shot .22 rifle. That was a lot of money in those days for me."

In high school Mark was a middling student, excelling only at athletics. His first mentor, his football coach Mel Griffith, "profoundly impressed" him as a role model. Mark played defensive end, and the Lawrence team under Griffith's direction went unbeaten for three years. Griffith crucially taught Alexander the value and art of good teamwork, instilling in him a life-long interest in sports and a passion for athletic competition.

It was thanks to Griffith as well that Marcel Alexander changed his name to Mark, ridding himself of the "feminine" name his mother had given him because she wanted a girl. "Coach Griffith started calling me Mark. I liked that better than my christened name of Marcel, as I was always having to fight to show the rest of the world that Marcel was no sissy, and I was tired of fighting.

"One day I went home and told my mother, 'Mom, I'm going to change my name to Mark.'

"She said, 'Why do you want to do that?'

"'Because I'm having to fight all the time about this Marcel business.' And I said, 'I like the name of Mark.'

"She objected, but I told her that she had probably done me a favor inasmuch as I otherwise might never have learned how to fight.

"Finally she said, 'Well, if you insist on it.'

"From then on I was Mark."

Endowed with his new name, Alexander pushed beyond the limits of his family, school and community in his senior year of high school. It was 1929 and the Depression was still gaining momentum. He and three of his friends decided to see what riding the rails was all about. How tough could it be?

"The four of us wanted to see what jumping a train was like. Lots of people were taking train rides in those days. They were even riding when there wasn't any work to be had anywhere. They were going everywhere. All directions. One group would hear they were picking apples in Washington. Another one would hear they were picking grapes someplace else, or stacking wheat. They were always traveling back and fourth, trying to find some work."

Alexander was the instigator of the adventure, which included his best friends, the Poland brothers. "I had Bumps and Bill on it with me going through Kansas City. There was also a guy named Pee-Wee

Weidman. He wasn't so big, but he had done some prize fighting and thought he was pretty tough.

"The train stopped and this railroad bull came along with his lantern. The door was open, so he shined his lantern into the car and said, 'Hey you guys, get out of there!' So Bumps and Bill and I jumped out of the car.

"Pee-Wee said, 'I'm not getting out.'

"I said, 'Pee-Wee, you better get out of there. This guy's rough.' He had one of those lanterns with a battery in it that swung by its handle."

But he refused to budge.

"The bull said, 'Well, son, if you can't get out of there on your own, I sure as hell can help you.' He jumped up in the car and swung the lantern into Pee-Wee's head, cutting his ear about half way down to where it just hung there by some skin. We had to go to a first aid station to get it sewed back on."

Alexander also had a strikingly different, artistic side to his nature. A file of papers he saved from his boyhood contains animal pictures he had cut from magazines to use as models for drawing. About the time he took up riding the rails, he entered a contest at school that brought together his interest in art and sports: "In 1928, we had a contest for the design of a school mascot. I drew a picture of a lion's head and proposed the 'Lawrence Lions.' That is their mascot as of today."

It is difficult to know if artistic sensitivity was an inherited trait, or the result of Ruby's nurturing and determination to instill her sons with a sense of culture. What is certain, though, is that a penchant for visual art ran through the family: both Harold and Don, who was exceptionally gifted, shared Alexander's natural talent and artistic inclination. Later, at the University of Kansas, Alexander sold chrysanthemums at a football game, earning good money; he and Harold, also a student at the time, then combined forces to create a little business decorating for fraternity parties.

Alexander's artistic sensibility seemingly contrasts with his duke-it-out personality, but it helped him to become an astute observer of men, nature and the minute physical characteristics of the immediate world around him. This power of close observation later proved invaluable to his success as a commander of front line troops. A stay in Canada following his high school graduation, however, might well have put him in the Canadian military instead of the U.S. Army.

That summer, Mark and Harold stayed with their uncle, Charlie

Jeffries, and his daughter Nella. "They lived in Toronto, Canada, but we spent most of our time north of there on an island in Lake Muskoka, where they owned a large cabin." This branch of the Alexander tree possessed an abundance of wealth, and introduced the young Alexanders to new experiences that contrasted greatly with their life in Kansas, where there was never quite enough money to get by.

"Uncle Charlie developed and managed the Consumers' Gas Company of Toronto. They manufactured gas and coke from coal and delivered to the entire city. They owned the gas lines throughout the area. He paid for our trip. We went to Toronto by train and were met at the railroad depot by Uncle Charlie's chauffeur with a Rolls Royce provided by his company. We were dressed so poorly that cousin Nella, some 20 years older than I, took us to a first-class men's wear store. She bought Harold a white flannel suit and me white flannel pants and a sweater. That suit would later get me into serious trouble.

"We stayed a few days in Toronto and then drove to the island retreat. There was a motorboat and a canoe for transportation around the lake.

"I learned a great deal from Uncle Charlie and Nella. He was a very successful CEO, and Nella had been on stage in New York with John Drew and the Barrymores. She developed tuberculosis in her early 20s and had to retire from the stage. In Toronto, she was very well known in her work as director of the Canadian National Dramatic Festival. She had many influential friends at home, and often received visits from wealthy and sometimes famous guests. Nella got on us about our speech and manners. She and others set examples for me to emulate, and I even picked up a temporary British accent. It was fun."

Alexander was eager to learn, and straightened up nicely to fit in with this upper-class environment, but he couldn't completely stay out of trouble. "I had a date with Beth Campbell, the daughter of a charter boat captain, who lived on the mainland close to the hotel. There was a dance there about half a mile down the shore, but it was obligatory to wear a suit and tie. I waited until Harold went to sleep, borrowed his new suit, paddled in the canoe, picked up Beth and attended the dance.

"Afterward I took Beth home. I bid her goodnight, took a step backwards and fell into a boat slip. As I was going down, I remembered the suit and thought, 'Oh my god. Harold is going to kill me.' It shrunk about six inches when it dried out, and Uncle Charlie and Nella nearly shipped me back to Kansas. Fortunately, they got over it in a few days and forgave me.

"At the end of summer, after we returned to Toronto, Uncle Charlie took me aside one evening. He said, 'Mark, your father and mother have four boys. I don't have any. If you want, you can stay here and live with me, and I'll either send you to the University of Toronto or put you in the Consumers' Gas Company and push you as hard as I can.'"

"I said, 'Let me think about it.' So I mulled it over for a couple of days before deciding I did not want to leave my family. I turned Uncle Charlie down; otherwise I'd be a Canadian citizen and later would have likely served in the Canadian military. I was always grateful for the offer and for having had the experience of living with them."

Having tasted another life, Alexander returned to the States determined to better himself, but he looked around and found no real future in anything around him. Ruby had always been a very strong advocate of education, and Alexander came to see college as the only way to get ahead in life.

The University of Kansas, which Alexander always called "Kansas University,' was in his home town; it was thus less expensive for him than other colleges, and he could live at home if he came up with the tuition. He and Harold attended at the same time, and both had to earn their own way. Mark worked hard after high school to save money for his schooling, but initially he was rudderless, with no idea how to match his interests to a promising area of study.

An early leadership position for (then) Marcel Alexander, Vice President of the Junior Class.

Alexander in 1929, when he played defensive end on his high school football team, which went undefeated for three years. His coach was a role model and started calling him "Mark" instead of his birth name "Marcel." He liked Mark much better and adopted the new name.

"After staying out of school and working at any odd job I could locate, I enrolled at Kansas University in the fall of 1931 and spring of 1932. I was broke all the time, did not do well in school and dropped out. Working here and there at odd jobs paying 25 to 40 cents per hour, I saved a few dollars and enrolled again, taking 12 hours at the university in the fall of 1933. I had decided I wanted to major in geology.

Throughout this turbulent time, Alexander learned many things that would make a major difference in his military career. Enrolled at university as a geology major, he "liked the director of the Geology Department, Dr. Raymond C. Moore, who was also the State Geologist." The appreciation turned out to be mutual. Moore took Alexander under his wing, reinforcing the message of Coach Griffith that Alexander was worth the attention of the best professionals in their field.

The practical knowledge of geography and maps Alexander now learned also proved to be invaluable on the battlefront. This was especially true for reconnaissance patrols, which he insisted on personally conducting as a battalion commander to assess the terrain before attacking. "Dr. Moore gave me part-time work at the university developing a 20' x 10' base relief and contour map of the State of Kansas. It was basically a large, painted clay landscape of the state. He had a small photographic development laboratory next to his office and taught me how to develop black and white photographs. I developed a series of photos he took when he went down the Colorado River from its source, through the Grand Canyon and all the way through. They went in big wooden boats about 18 feet long and were the first group that ever did it. He was also recognized all over the world as a leading paleontologist. I learned a lot just watching and listening to him.

"In the summer of 1934, the Assistant State Geologist, Dr. K. K. Laudes, took me into the field to the Port Rock region of Kansas as a rod man, and I took notes on a survey of past rock formations. Later in the summer, Dr. Recides of the U.S. Geographical Survey joined us. They determined from the survey that there was a geologic dome in the area with an excellent prospect for oil. On the last day in the field, several oil company scouts tried to get Dr. Landes' notes, but he said he could only release them to everyone at the same time.

"At the dinner table that night, Doctors Landes and Recides told me I should lease some land. I told them I had no money and could hardly stay in school. They said they too were short on cash and made no effort to lease acreage. At the time, a professor only made about $5,500 per year, and both had families to support. I drove through the area four years later and there were oil derricks about as far as one could see. The big oil companies had scrambled for leases as soon as the survey was released."

Alexander's time in the field convinced him he did not want to be a geologist. "I was out there for about two months in the field and hardly saw anybody at all. I was more of a people person." He dropped out of school, broke, and decided to try his luck at finding work out of state. He was now 24 years old. "In 1935, I drove to Los Angeles with an older friend and worked at whatever I could find. I worked for an Italian maker of plaster of Paris religious objects and then in the interior decorating department of Barker Brothers, the big furniture store. When that job ended, I rode the rods back to Kansas."

Walking, hitch-hiking and bumming his way on the rails, Alexander went from Kansas City to Saint Louis and down to New Orleans, where he had lined up a job with the Dole Pineapple Company unloading cargo on the docks. When he reported to the Dole representative, he discovered the company's dockworkers had gone on strike. The whole lot, Alexander included, was out of a job.

He learned to adjust his tactics to the terrain. He scoured the area for work and scrounged up employment as a roustabout. "There was a whole line of guys, mostly black, that would go down in the boat, and come up with a big bunch of bananas on their shoulders. They told me to look out for snakes. A certain type of little snake would sometimes be in the bunches, and a bite from one was generally fatal. I was fortunate enough not to come across any."

He soon discovered that each dock had an unofficial kingpin. "Usually you'd have to give him 50 cents or something, and he'd tell you where there was a job. And of course he'd line up his friends with work. They were like little mafia heads. I became top deck foreman on a banana-hauling gang. They would take them from the boat, walk up a ramp and stack them in the car. I liked that job better.

"I also worked for a while as a bouncer for one of the local bars. One Friday night it was really packed and these two big steel workers were drinking together. One of them must have said something the other one didn't like, because they got into a fight. I only weighed about 150 pounds and these guys both looked to be over 200 each. I knew I had a problem on my hands, so I tried to time it and barreled into them. They both fell on the floor and started laughing. I lucked out on that one.

"There wasn't any more work in New Orleans than there was in

Learning to Fight

Kansas, so I rode the rails into Memphis, Tennessee. Other bums had warned me there were tough bulls there. I was walking down a line of railroad cars looking for the next train I would jump, when all of a sudden one of them steps out from behind a car, and *wham*. He hit me right on the neck just below the ear, knocking me down on my knees. Then he rammed a big colt .45 in my belly and said, 'Get your ass out of the yard, bum.'

"I'm not going to argue with a guy like that, especially if he has a gun. And the law is with him in the first place. I was trespassing. Apparently, some of the bums had been stealing and the bulls were mad. They were real mad. I had to find another place to jump on a train."

Riding back to Kansas through the extremely cold night, some of the other men in Alexander's freight car "peeled wood off the floor and made fires. When it looked like a fire was about to burn through the bottom of the floorboards, they moved it over onto an unburned area. The smoke was so thick that you would pass out if you tried to stand up for any amount of time." The doors were shut tight, and "the only way to get any decent air was to have your face right next to the floor."

Lying flat on the floor of the smoky train car, Alexander determined then and there to finish his education. He decided that a college degree, any degree, was a necessity. Once home, he took a series of manual labor jobs of increasing risk to pay for his education. "I worked at odd jobs for about six months in the fall of 1935, and got part-time work reading water meters at 35 cents per hour. Then I got a job on the road gang. There were 17 black guys and Alexander. I happened to know the foreman, or he wouldn't have put me on.

"We each had a big, flat-bottomed scoop shovel. Each shovel load of wet cement weighed about 30 pounds. They paid 35 cents an hour, and that first day I was determined to keep the job. So the first morning I worked like hell. I really pushed it in.

"We were building an apron on Highway 36 going toward Kansas City. Some other guys were on the wheel barrel, bringing it over and dumping it onto a wood platform. A truck pulled the platform down the road as work progressed.

"At noon, I was leaning against a tree, eating the sandwich I had brought along. An old, gray-haired guy came over to me and said, 'You don't mind if I sit down by you, do you?' I said, 'No, it'll be nice to have someone to talk to.'

"We talked a little and he said, 'Son, I want to tell you something.

You're setting the pace out here and you're killing us. You've got to slow down a little bit.'

"Of course I was working hard so I could keep a job, but I eased it up.

"Later, because I knew the foreman, he put me on dry sacks of cement, hauling it on a truck. I liked this job a lot better until I started getting sores all in my arms, picking up those sacks. Later, I found out how the black guys on the mixer kept from getting sores. One old guy said, 'Rub Vaseline all over your arms before you go to work in the morning. After you go home, just take a good bath.'"

This was the first in a string of jobs that revolved around construction. Alexander usually followed direction without complaint, but the minute he was ordered to do something unreasonably dangerous, he flatly refused.

"The grade along the highway was pretty steep. One day we lost our tractor man. He quit. The foreman came to me and said, 'Alexander, I want you to drive that tractor.'

"I said, 'I haven't got any experience on one of those.'

"He was insistent. I said, 'No, I'd probably roll it over. That's too steep a grade. A guy's really got to know what he's doing on a steep grade like that.' He got mad and fired me.

"He put another guy on it and on the third day he rolled it. He got all burned by radiator water down around his genitals. I knew him real well. He was kind of off psychologically for quite a while after that because it hit his genitals. But the company didn't care about that. At least I was smart enough not to try to drive that tractor on that slope.

"My next job was as a steel construction roustabout on the Kaw River for a company building a dam for an electric power plant. It was rough and dangerous work, but I was lucky to have it. They had a boat with steel pilings on it. We drove rows of interlocking steel pilings down into the riverbed. Each one was probably 45 feet long. They fit down tight and formed a cofferdam, where they could pump the water out and then pour in the cement. After the cement dried, we had to pull those pilings.

"They had a stiff-arm there that I would say was about 125 feet long, a crane. There was an eye in the top of each pile. We'd hook a cable from the stiff-arm to the pile. The crane would pull while a guy would stand on the boat down at the bottom and hit the pile with a sledgehammer. When he'd hit it, it would jump a little bit. You really had to hit it hard. It would only come up a little bit at a time.

"One of the pilings wouldn't come out. The foreman said, 'Alexander, stand up on top—we had a wood frame to stand on—and hit the piling from up there.'

"I said, 'No, I'm not going to do that. The block could come loose.' I'd seen them come loose before. That steel cable would whip so hard, it threw the block and tackle clear across the river. I said, 'A guy could get decapitated. No way.'

"He said, 'What's the matter? You chicken?'

"I said, 'No, I'm just not stupid.'

"He got another guy on it, and after four strikes with the hammer a bolt broke. It tore loose, went up, fractured his skull and knocked him in the river. It's a wonder it didn't kill him. Another guy and I had to dive and get him out.

"I worked for that foreman for about another week. He wouldn't speak to me because I wouldn't do that job. And because that guy got hurt and I know he felt bad about it. Of course I was the first guy out of a job when we finished that part.

"They didn't care if they killed you or not. The first go-round, if you got hurt they'd see to it you got a doctor. You got bandaged up and then you'd get hell getting any kind of settlement out of it. And they didn't care later if you lived or not."

Alexander saw time and again the effects of bad leadership. This served as another lesson that later easily applied to commanding soldiers. "On another job we worked with cribbing—big square logs about 40 feet long. There were 30 or 40 of these huge things we were bracing. They were held back by a big pin, and a carpenter was down at the base fastening the bottom one. He was in a hole getting the cribbing ready, so the floor could be added. He signaled the foreman to pull just a little on the pin, but he pulled too hard, too fast. Instead of removing the restraints on only the bottom log, which had been secured, a lot of logs fell down in there. Luckily, the carpenter was over in a corner, or he would have been killed.

"That old, long, bony carpenter came out of there with a crowbar in his hand and started chasing this foreman. 'You son-of-a-bitch, I'll kill you!' he said. He ran him around the parking area three times and finally the foreman got enough lead to get in his car and drive off. He didn't come back for three or four days.

"When we finished that job, they wanted me to paint the smokestack, which was probably 125 feet high. I painted the outside on a sling that was hooked on the upper rim of the stack. Then the foreman wanted me to paint the inside.

"I said, 'No, I'm not going to paint in there.' It was August. It felt like it was about 150 degrees inside that thing. I said, 'We've got to rig up a fan to blow the paint fumes out of there. I'm not going to go in there the way it is now.'

"He said, 'Okay, I'll get somebody else.' So I lost my job again. The guy who replaced me fell on the second day and broke his back."

All four of Ruby and Edward Alexander's children would serve in the military in World War II. Mark (at left) and Edwin (second from right) volunteered, joined the paratroopers and saw action in Europe. Don (third from left) and Harold (right) were drafted. Don put his artistic talents to good use and served at Fort Leavenworth as a mapmaker. Harold, who had a Masters of Science degree, did medical lab work in a hospital. All four brothers survived the war.

With money in his pocket, Alexander re-enrolled at the University of Kansas and completed his art degree in the autumn of 1937. Throughout, he remained involved in athletics. "I was a good hockey player and at one time or another was on the Kansas University track and swimming teams. I did a little boxing at 147 pounds. My normal weight was between 148 and 150, but I would sweat out and come down to 147. During our last tournament, I fought a long, skinny guy. It was three, three-minute rounds. I knocked him down twice, but he had this big nose of mine really bloody from that long arm of his. They called it a draw. I've got too much nose to be good at that."

Although he sketched and painted off and on for the rest of his life, Alexander chose not to pursue art as a career. "In my analysis, I was not

Learning to Fight

Above: Alexander was always very interested in sports and physical activity, including diving.

Left: Alexander practices archery as a youth camp counselor in 1938.

Below: Alexander as a counselor at Cheley Camp for youth in Colorado.

talented enough to make a good living as an artist. But I could teach, and I therefore enrolled in graduate school in the spring of 1940, intending to get a Masters in Education and Fine arts."

Alexander would never receive, or even get close to obtaining his Masters. The war in Europe was now in full swing. Hitler's Germany had invaded Czechoslovakia and Poland. France and Great Britain in turn declared war on Germany. The United States would eventually be sucked into the fray, but before that day came, Alexander would have big decisions to make.

In the long run, his lack of money turned out to be a blessing in disguise. It taught Alexander many key lessons that reinforced his natural desire to lead, and hence to have more control over his situation. One was to surround himself with people who were excellent at their jobs. Another was to trust his own instincts and make his own decisions.

But the most important lesson Alexander learned was the difference a leader could make to the well being of his men. By repeatedly putting their workers in danger, his bosses had pounded this in with a virtual sledgehammer. Alexander later commanded the respect and loyalty of his troops in the most critical of situations, in part because they knew he would never order them to do anything he would not do himself.

CHAPTER TWO

PREPARING FOR WAR

WHILE ALEXANDER WAS AT THE University of Kansas in 1938 and 1939, he developed a friendship with another student, Ed Renth, which would lead to a major change in his life. "We both worked out at the gym and I occasionally ate dinner at his home. Ed's father was Col. Ed Renth, the ROTC instructor for the university.

"Colonel Renth said, 'Mark, there's going to be a war for sure,' and he convinced me the United States would be involved. I didn't have any military training, but he advised me to try for a commission since I had a college degree. 'If you enlist in the National Guard,' he said, 'I can qualify you for competitive examinations coming up just before the first of the year.' If I passed the exams, I would be made an officer; if I did not pass, I would be in the enlisted ranks for three years."

The United States had just enacted the first peacetime draft in its history. Alexander's outgoing personality and natural ambition combined with his work experience to convince him to enlist. The school of hard knocks had taught him that men in authority were not to be trusted to make good decisions regarding the safety of those who worked under them. An officer would have a greater measure of control over his situation than an enlisted man.

Alexander signed up with the local National Guard, went to drill once a week, hit the books and took the test to become an officer. When the National Guard was mobilized, the 35th Division was assigned to newly built Camp Robinson, Arkansas. Its members were now full-time military. "We were in new frame buildings built on top of red clay, which turned into red mud when it rained. My initial assignment was in H Company, 137th Infantry Regiment, 35th Infantry Division.

"A few days later, I learned I had passed the test and they assigned me as a 2nd lieutenant on January 1, 1941." He was immediately moved within his regiment, becoming the heavy weapons platoon commander of B Company. At this point, almost all of his military experience consisted of weekly premobilization drills. Alexander knew it didn't amount to a hill of beans.

At last I have been assigned to B Company of Emporia [Kansas] origin, he wrote to his mother. *Old Captain Darnell [his commanding officer] is a gruff old boy, but I believe a good soldier. I hate to leave H Company as they have a grand personnel, but at least I'll learn something by this transfer. The one thing I'll miss is that I have sort of been depending on Lieutenants Mall and Cook for enlightenment on military set up. I'll now be on my own and must somehow make the grade.*

Have sure learned a lot about how the army operates within the last week. [...] I have been assigned to a heavy weapons school for tomorrow afternoon and every afternoon this week. Will learn to use the 60mm howitzer and 37mm anti-tank gun.

"I reported as a shave tail to my new company. One of the first things I did was gather my platoon. I said, 'Look, I'm probably the greenest lieutenant in the United States Army. I'm going to need your help.' I was fortunate to have a very good, experienced platoon sergeant. About a week later he came to me and said, 'All the guys like you and you're going to be just fine.' It was great to have their support. And the sergeant kept me out of any serious trouble."

Alexander possessed natural leadership qualities that showed themselves in sports, as a camp counselor and other social situations as he was growing up, but almost everyone around him knew more about the military than he did. He listened and absorbed as much as he could from his men, while also maintaining command. If he was offered suggestions or advice that he believed to be incorrect, he always heard the man out, but made his own decisions.

As he wrote to his much younger brother Ed, on January 13, 1941: *I am learning a great deal every day and only hope that I may be able to get ahead of the rest of this tribe of officers. My main trouble is that I have so much to learn about general soldiering that most of these fellows already know. However, I know well that I can beat at least the most of them at anything we do and I am determined to do so. [...] General Truman is to inspect us sometime today and we are really polishing up.*

I have been going to a school in physical training for the last few days, from 9 till 11 each morning, and have learned a few things that will help me. But for the most part I find that I know a hell of a lot more about physical education than these brass hats do.

Colonel Renth came in last night and I should soon be able to see him and find out just what I am to do down here.

Well brother, take good care of those folks of ours. I'm depending on you. And also, I am counting on you for a good showing in your studies. If it's worth doing, it's worth doing well.

The commander of the 35th Division, General Ralph Truman, was a cousin of (then) Senator Harry Truman, who would later become president. His division, like the others recently activated from the National Guard, was far from combat-ready. It had been 20 years since World War I and a lot of the same soldiers were still there. "Most were just too damn old to sleep out in the open and move fast with their battalion or company. A company commander is supposed to be able to run like the others and stay in condition with his men," Alexander later commented.

Now nearly 30, Alexander was far from young for a 2nd lieutenant, but he still was much younger than many of the other men. "The commander of my company, Captain Darnell, was 49 years old. Man, that's old for a company commander. Really old. That's the age for a guy who's about ready to become a general. A company commander should be in his 20s or 30s. Ideally, in his 20s."

Politics ran wild in the Guard between the wars, and many of the higher-ranking officers were there by political appointment. To rectify this, the army assigned a full colonel to each of the National Guard divisions for the special purpose of shaking them down. "In other words, they had a lot of power. They could say, 'That guy's too old. Transfer him.' They had authority to go in there and relieve people even over the commanding general's wishes. They almost controlled the division more than the general did."

The person assigned to the 35th Division in this capacity was Col. Per Ramee, a contemporary of Gen. Joseph

Ruby Alexander visits her son, Lt. Mark Alexander, at Camp Robinson, Arkansas, while he serves with the 35th Infantry Division.

Stilwell, who had graduated from the Academy with Stilwell in the class of 1904. "He knocked a lot of guys out fast and caused a lot of other changes to be made. But it was necessary." Alexander's 49-year-old company commander, Captain Darnell, was reassigned almost immediately. The division commander, Gen. Ralph Truman, was left in charge for quite a while, but finally replaced before the division was shipped overseas.

After Darnell was reassigned, two brothers controlled B Company. They had been in the National Guard since they were 18 years old: the oldest became the company commander and he appointed his brother as his executive officer. The new commander was a 1st lieutenant, but the position called for a captaincy. He had been in the reserves for about ten years. The executive officer was a 2nd lieutenant, a position that called for a 1st lieutenant, and had been in the Guard for roughly five years.

Alexander's physical conditioning and expertise as an athletic instructor stood him good stead in his early days as an officer. "I was pretty good at athletics of different types, so I gave the company their workout every morning before breakfast. I'd give them quite a bit of calisthenics, and then we'd run. I also, among other things, got charged with teaching them to throw a grenade. A grenade is fairly heavy. You have to throw it differently from a baseball or you'll hurt your arm. We didn't have practice grenades, so we used beer cans full of sand.

"I had them out there one day: I was facing one way and all these guys out in front of me were throwing from one side of the street, over the road and into a field. Just as I gave the order to throw, I knew something was wrong because about half the men were grinning. I spun around in time to see six or seven cans smash into the side of a passenger car that had quietly driven up the street behind me.

"I didn't say, 'Who did it?' because I knew I would never find out. I said, 'You bastards sure crossed me up. Don't do that again.'" After an investigation, a friendly Inspector General cleared Alexander of liability for the damage to the automobile. But he did have the privilege of making a report and writing out an insurance claim to cover the large dents left by the beer cans.

"One morning I was up in front of the company leading them through calisthenics and noticed everybody was looking over my shoulder. So I called them to attention and turned around, and there stood old Colonel Per Ramee.

"I saluted him and asked, 'Colonel, can I do anything for you?'

"'No, you're doing fine. Carry on.'

"I continued the workout and he was down there every morning for about a week, watching me give the exercises. Then on March 29, 1941, the division personnel officer called me to come up to division headquarters. When I got there he said, 'This is rather unusual, but Colonel Per Ramee has recommended you for 1st lieutenant,' and he pinned the bars on me. Normally this would take place at a regimental level and called for more time in grade.

"When the company commander found out I had been promoted over his younger brother, I was in the dog house. I got every shit detail that came along. I'd get officer of the guard every day including weekends, was on duty through holidays, and anything else undesirable." This situation went on for about a month and a half, and although Alexander did not complain, the word got around that he was in a tight spot.

The division personnel officer brought him in again. He said, "The Chief of Staff and I have been talking about you. We know you're having trouble in B Company. Your record shows you've always been very athletic. How would you like to be division athletic officer?"

"I said, 'Sir, I would like it *very* much.' So they made me division athletic officer, and I developed all kinds of programs: baseball, basketball, swimming, diving, boxing, wrestling and football."

Usually competitions were between companies and regiments, but sometimes Alexander took his teams to compete against civilian teams in nearby cities. One outing had his boys squaring off against boxers from a local YMCA in Memphis, Tennessee, whose boxing coach had a semi-pro team in addition to many other guys who just were learning to fight.

1st Lieutenant Mark Alexander before his face showed the hardships of war.

Preparing for War

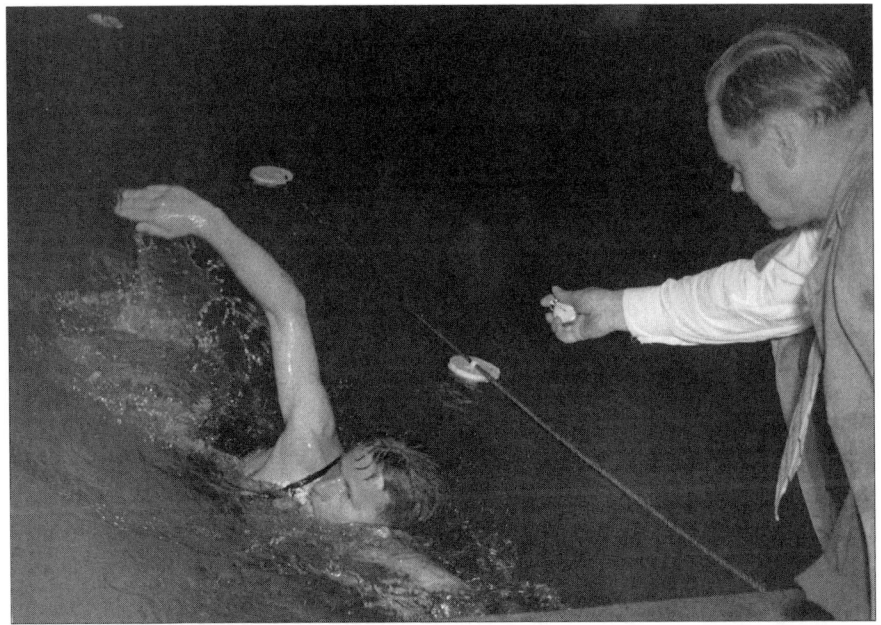

PFC Bill Snyder of Company I, 134th Infantry Regiment, 35th Division, originally from Lincoln, Nebraska, swims for a personal best in the 280-yard free style

Alexander (at right) congratulates the captain of a tournament-winning team

Alexander specifically stated that he had seven guys who were still learning the sport. "I said, 'Don't set my boys up against your top guys and beat the shit out of them.'" He was assured of a fair match.

"That son-of-a-bitch. They won every match except one, where we got a draw. I stopped one event because our guy was really getting the hell beat out of him. I was so damn mad at that YMCA coach. I said, 'You lied to me. You've got some semi-pros here fighting against my guys.'

"He wanted to set up another round of fights! I said, 'I wouldn't bring a team back here if you paid me. You took advantage of guys that were still learning to box.'" Alexander had other choice words for him that are not fit to print.

Serving as division athletic officer was far better than his position with B Company, but it was not a combat role. "I had been afraid that the division athletic job would put me in a side pocket when we were really getting some tactical action," Alexander explained. When his unit went on six weeks of maneuvers in the forests of Alabama in late summer of 1941, he was mostly stuck in camp. A letter home at this time expresses his strong desire *to go back into the field where I can learn so much more about soldiering. That is what I really need.*

Although Alexander was unhappy with his position, it had benefits that became apparent with time. In the immediate, it put him in card games against a future president. "When everyone was out in the field, there wasn't much for an athletic officer to do other than run errands for the division personnel officer and Chief of Staff. I got to know the commanding general of the division, Maj. Gen. Ralph Truman, and the general staff very well. Senator Harry Truman, the general's cousin, had been assigned by President Roosevelt to get the National Guard divisions into fighting shape.

Some of Alexander's tournament-winning boxers.

Boxers who accounted well for themselves against others in their class, but did not claim the top prize.

"Senator Truman came down a few times and he liked to play poker. Usually he'd stay two or three days and they'd have a few card games. If they didn't have enough players, they came and got me. I filled in three or four times and played cards with Harry Truman, Ralph Truman and the staff. The senator had a good sense of humor and was a pretty good poker player."

Before he saw the benefit of these new relationships, Alexander got stuck with a new, even less desirable job. "One night the Chief of Staff called me in and said, 'Mark, the General wants you to take over the division mess. It's in bad shape and he wants you to get it straightened out.' He knew that as an athletic officer I didn't have a lot to do right then with the division on maneuvers.

"I said, 'Sir, I'm new to this army and I've been an athletic officer for almost six months. I need field experience. Why do you assign me as a mess officer when what I need is to be with a competent unit in the field on these maneuvers? And besides, I have no ambition to be a mess officer.'"

Alexander asked if he could speak to the General himself about it. "You can take your chances," was the reply. This was somewhat risky. He knew General Truman from the poker games and a few other encounters, but not nearly well enough to ensure he wouldn't get his head bitten off. He caught Truman that night as he returned to his tent and made his pitch. The General was not moved. He told Alexander he had a job to do and he expected it to be done.

Alexander's first day on the job was a rough one. "We had big mess tents out in the field. I went down and had a look at my new command. It was dirty. It was lousy." The same day, "the division inspector general showed up. He started jumping all over me because it was such a mess. 'I've only been here for about eight hours,' I said, 'Give me a chance to get set.'"

The inspector was the type of soldier who wore jodhpurs and tall, shiny boots. He stated he would be back to check on progress in the kitchen, and told Alexander he had better have a garbage pit dug by evening.

"I made sure we had a regulation pit, six feet deep by ten feet by ten feet. The inspector came back after dark. He was looking for me, but I was staying out of sight. He got the mess sergeant, asked the whereabouts of the pit, and learned it was down by the edge of the woods. It was black that night. Real dark. I crawled out and said, 'Wait a minute, I'll take you down there.'

"The inspector said, 'I don't need your help. I'll find it.' So he walked off in the dark. A minute later, he started yelling and cussing. I knew what had happened right away and sent the sergeant after him."

Sure enough, the inspector had fallen in the pit. The sides were slick and he couldn't get out. His shiny boots, jodhpurs and the rest of him were covered with mess hall garbage. "And he never did call on me again. He never came back. He had established his reputation in the garbage pit."

Alexander's earlier plea for a position back in the field must have made an impression with the General. A letter on September 14, 1941 reports some potentially good news: *Three days ago the General came up to inspect the camp. He sent his aide over to tell me that if I made a go of it [with the mess] and got them straightened out and back to real soldering, he needed a H.Q. Company commander and I would be it. Or, if I wanted, he would send me to school. [...] It has been tough as hell as this damned rear echelon is made up of the non-combatant sections of the General's staff. They have been out of the field for so long they need a kick in the pants about every half hour to get them to do anything. Well, I'm driving the heck out of them and getting results. [...] It's so damp here, can't even get this ink to dry. Am feeling fine, tough as they make 'em.*

Alexander stayed with the mess until the division finished maneuvers. The brass was satisfied. "Well, maybe not fully satisfied, but it was such an improvement they let me alone." General Truman, good to his word, gave Alexander a week's leave, then sent him to infantry school at Fort Benning, Georgia. The next few months radically influenced the course of Alexander's military career, and permanently changed the course of his personal life.

Alexander reported to the four-month course with a group of 150 1st lieutenants and captains. As he wrote on November 2, 1941: *I am in class 18 of Basic Training, Co. E, 2nd Battalion. We have in this class officers from all over the U.S.A., four from Hawaii, five from Philippines, six from Puerto Rico. We unmarried men live in two-story wooden barracks. Not exactly exclusive quarters, but O.K. The married men live and eat off the post. So I am to be just about the busiest man in town until February. [...] This is a tremendous military post, there must be 50 or 60 thousand troops, engineers, parachute troops, air corps, infantry, anti-aircraft, and so on.*

"For the first time I was getting into what the army was really all about: weaponry, tactics, logistics, et cetera. I found the studies very interesting and we learned we were expecting to be involved in a war with Germany and Japan quite soon. Of course, we had no idea how soon."

In addition to his regular course of studies, Alexander was crucially introduced to the idea of vertical warfare. Fort Benning was the training ground for incoming paratroopers, and Alexander was fascinated by the new concept of dropping troops behind enemy lines. The paratroopers were an elite, all-volunteer branch of the army, and were paid far more than straight leg outfits. Alexander watched the men train, saw them running on base and "admired their esprit de corps." Fighting alongside the best of the best appealed to him, and he soon signed up. He continued his studies while awaiting transfer. [1]

In a confluence of life-changing events, Alexander attended a dance on base shortly after arriving at Benning, where he was introduced to a nurse named Mary Collins. She immediately caught his eye. "The first thing I noticed about Mary was her smile." He quickly discovered that she was also kind and had a good sense of humor to match her ready grin. Alexander asked Mary to dance—a significant act, as he did not dance well and usually tried to avoid it. Mary, however, took lessons at the Author Murray dance studio, and when her partner knew what he was doing, "everybody would move off the floor. She really knew how to twirl."

Mary's appearance was all the more alluring in that she wore a very special dress. Years later, she vividly recalled her "dream frock made of lovely white eyelet cotton; yards and yards of skirt that would swirl as I danced, a tight fitting bodice, and a ruffled collar. Black velvet ribbon was threaded through small white loops, twice around the waist and once around the skirt. When I slipped the dress on and looked in the mirror, I knew how Cinderella felt when her fairy Godmother waived her magic wand. Now all I needed was a Prince Charming. It was at a dance wearing this dress that I met my husband."

Alexander's first letter home describing Mary clearly shows he was smitten: *I met a little black-haired nurse who has the most desirable disposition I have ever known. She's little, black hair, Irish, her name is Mary Collins, she's cute, has a turned up nose, seems to do and like all the things I care for, has a wonderful personality, and backs me up on anything I want to do. She is the youngest of a large family and knows how to take as well as give. She worked her way through nurse's training school in New York and is very appreciative of the little things in life.*

Alexander and Mary enjoyed a whirlwind romance, dating regularly while he was at Fort Benning. There was, however, one problem: *You'll love this Mary I know*, he wrote home. *The catch is that Mary is a 2nd lieutenant in the Army Nurse Corps, and they have a rule that no nurse will be released from service for the purpose of being married. Well, perhaps it wouldn't be a good thing right now anyway, as I hardly know where I am to be tomorrow or the next day.*

Alexander's letter to his parents, telling them about Mary but alluding to his uncertain future, was written in February 1942. By that time, he had rejoined the 35th Division, now relocated in San Louis Obispo, California, as part of the western defense command. On December 7, 1941, Japan had launched its surprise attack on the U.S. fleet at Pearl Harbor, immediately bringing the United States into the war. "Within 24 hours, about 30 percent of my class was recalled to

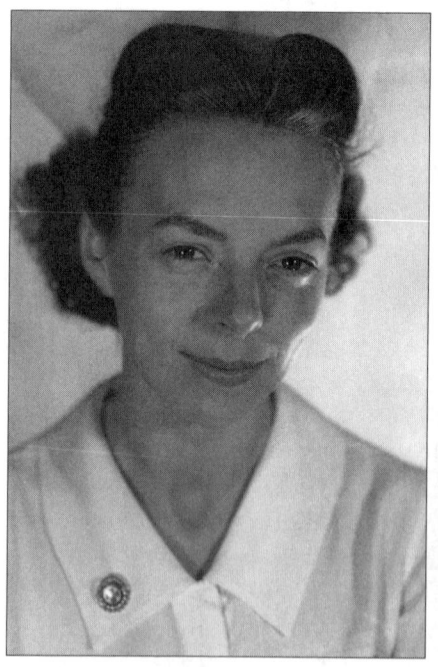

2nd Lieutenant Mary Collins, the woman who captured Alexander's heart.

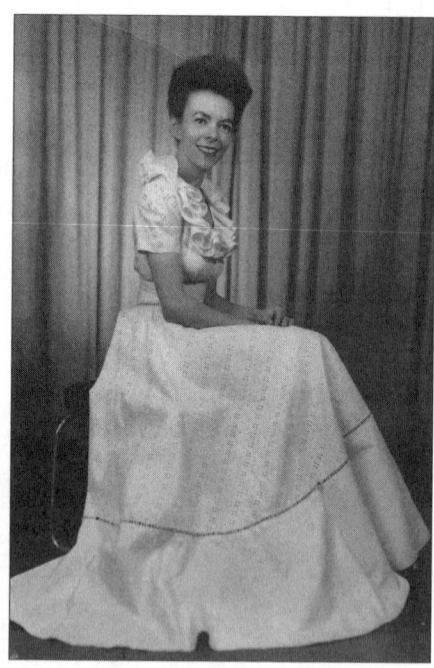

Mary Collins met her future husband while wearing this dress. "After we had been married and before he went overseas, he asked me to have my picture taken wearing the Cinderella dress. I did and became his pinup girl for the duration, replacing Betty Grable."

their units for possible shipment to the Pacific. The rest of us stayed on to finish the course."

His February letter describes the urgency of the situation and reveals his thoughts about policies of national defense. *We have as usual been busy as can be. We are on call, or Alert, 24 hours a day and we never know just where we will be tomorrow or, for that matter, the rest of the day. Last night a Jap sub shelled a refinery just a few miles below here. It didn't amount to anything, was just a gesture attempting to scorn the hour of the president's speech.*

We here are part of the western defense command and are always expected to be ready to move at instant notice. I have been moving around a good deal since coming here, the division is still in the process of break down, the division staff is being reduced about 50% under the new triangular set up [three regiments instead of four], and some of us will go to new assignments.

Please don't get to thinking back there that all this expenditure for defense is unnecessary. Whether you can believe it or not, we are right here in a combat zone. That is how close to your front door the war has come. It is too bad that all this re-armament has to be done in such a hurry, but for one, President Roosevelt was in favor of getting at this business of being prepared several years ago when it would have been easy, but no—the conservatists and isolationists would have none of it.

Now we are in a spot where we haven't sufficient time to protect ourselves from nations who have been arming themselves, and unless we do something about it in a hell of a hurry, we too may become surfs such as are many of the weaker nations of the eastern hemisphere. The way in which this job of preparing for defense is being handled can always be criticized, but as yet I haven't heard many better suggestions. They would be merely as well subject to criticism, and no doubt those critics of the present administration would make just as many and perhaps worse mistakes, in that they are not experienced in dealing with such strong arm men as Hitler and the Japanese warlords. Let's make the best we can of the situation and when we have finally fought our way out of this terrible mess, let's not let ourselves get in such a hole again.

While Alexander was stationed in California, "Mary and I corresponded and were in touch by telephone. We had decided to get married. She had gone into the service on a one-year contract, but with a war on, the separation request was refused. The only way for her to leave the service was for us to be hitched first. Nurses were not allowed to be married."

Well then, they would get married as soon as possible. Alexander, however, now the executive officer of a reconnaissance company, could not get any time off. Luckily, his time as athletic officer still proved to pay dividends: knowing the division personnel officer, Colonel Kaster, he explained his situation and received an emergency pass. He would have to travel to Columbus, Georgia, get married and return all within three days. Even if it all went perfectly, it wouldn't be much of a honeymoon.

"I talked to Mary and she agreed to meet me at the church. I flew in one of those old Constellations with four motors. We got into a storm real bad going over the Rockies. It was raining like hell all over the rest of the Midwest. So they grounded the plane in Memphis, Tennessee, and I had to get on a train.

"I arrived in Columbus, Georgia, at 10:30 a.m. The ceremony was at 1:00 in the afternoon that same day. I had time to go to a hotel, check in and take a bath. I went to the church and Mary had gotten the license. I had already taken a physical and blood test in California.

We got married in the Episcopal Church in Columbus. Mary and two of her girl friends had everything set up when I met them at the church. It was just the four of us and the minister there. We took Mary's girl friends, who also served as witnesses for us, to dinner at the hotel. Mary and I had one night together and I had to load on a plane and come back."

Mary put in for separation from the army. It took about a month and a half for the paperwork to go through. She briefly went home to Easton, Pennsylvania, before heading west to join her husband. En route, she stopped in Kansas for a few days and met her new in-laws. Other than the jaw-dropping news that Mary was a Democrat—it seems that everyone in Lawrence at the time was Republican—the visit went extremely well. She was immediately welcomed as one of the family.

Mary knew the army and she also knew that an officer's wife can greatly influence her husband's career. Upon reaching the West Coast and moving in with Alexander, Mary unpacked and pressed all of her clothes. He introduced her to Colonel Kaster, who told Alexander he had done well indeed.

No sooner had Mary arrived in San Louis Obispo, than Alexander received a telegram on April 1 from General Richardson's headquarters of the western defense command. As he reported to his family: *So, you can tell 'em all, Mark finally got that promotion. Have been awfully worried about it—thought I had been left out on a limb.* As pleased as he was, the promotion put Alexander in "a kind of untenable situation," for it arrived ten days before that of the CO of his company. "I was a captain and the commanding officer was still a lieutenant. I wasn't going to try to take over the company from him, and not wanting any trouble with my friend, I requested a transfer."

His request was granted almost immediately. Alexander shipped off to the Presidio in San Francisco to work for division intelligence, but had to leave Mary behind. She would not rejoin him for several weeks. A letter to his parents expresses regret at leaving his new wife, but otherwise shows him figuratively and almost literally "on top of the world."

I am now with the 137th Inf. [Regiment of the 35th Division] at the Presidio of San Francisco, an old fort established way back in 1776 or thereabout. There are many different forts and military establishments about the bay here, and indeed I find all this hustle of a port of embarkation very interesting.

My abode is at present in the bachelors' quarters on a cliff edge just below and east of the Golden Gate Bridge. From our front porch I can see all up and down the bay for miles. Just to the left and high above me is the great and beautiful Golden Gate Bridge; far to my right I can hazily see the Oakland Bridge. Far out there in the center of the bay, in all its solemn fastness, stands Alcatraz Prison. Along the shores are clustered great docks and ship after ship loading with war materials and supplies for ports unknown. Every day war ships escort great convoys in and out of the bay. Almost any time one can look out to the traffic lanes between buoys marking mines and submarine nets and see some sort of war craft plowing along or, looking into the sky, one sees all sorts of war planes.

I am assigned to the 137th as assistant S-2 and 3; 3 is plans training, 2 is military intelligence. I am the acting regimental intelligence officer, and if I do not get to go back to the reconnaissance troop, I hope I can remain in this capacity. I surprised some of my buddies of old a bit when I went back to the old regiment as a captaincy. I've had a few battles on my hands, but can take care of them in good shape.

Sorry to be so brief, but must go now—some of the men are taking me downtown to show me the sights. I had to leave Mary in Morrow Bay for a few days, as I am on the move. We are going down there next week and then I can again be with her. I hated to leave her, but had to.

Mary's about the best thing that ever happened to me. She's right in there pitching for me in anything I want to try, and every minute too.

When Mary rejoined Alexander at the Presidio, she unpacked and pressed all of her clothes again. Within a few days, the long-awaited orders came through for Alexander to report to jump school. "I had to go back to Fort Benning right away, and Mary joined me a little later. When you are assigned to a place you don't have a choice as to how much time you've got. Not in wartime anyway.

"Mary had been with me about a month and a half. She had gone out to San Luis Obispo and pressed her clothes. Then we get transferred to the Presidio, so she presses her clothes again. Then I get transferred back to the parachute school. She told me, "'I'm not going to press anything until I'm ready to wear it.'"

When Alexander arrived at Fort Benning, "there were 150,000 soldiers at the base. All housing was taken. Columbus was just north of there. It was a city of about 35,000, and there was no room there either. We needed a place to rent, but nothing was available. It was a real scramble.

"Finally I found that they had converted the ladies' restroom at the country club into a little apartment. But it was way out from town and very isolated in the evenings. I was gone many nights on training exercises and had to leave Mary alone. I'm sure she wondered how she had gotten into such a situation. I bought her a .22 pistol, and the golf course manager taught her how to shoot."

The 35th Division had not pushed Alexander's physical limits. He was in good shape before joining, and one of the fittest men in the division. The paratroopers, however, were another matter. "I remember reporting to the parachute school for duty with five other officers. A major stood us all to attention and did everything but cuss us out. He told us what a bunch of nimrods we were and how tough it was going to be.

"He was right about how tough it would be. Immediately we were put through some of the toughest physical training I have ever experienced. Five mile runs before breakfast, 25 push-ups for any mistake, and so forth. I was 31 years old, a lot older than most guys trying to be paratroopers, but I was in real good shape physically. I could run with any of them and wear most of them down."

Jump school was a very intensive four-week course. "The first weeks we spent half a day learning to pack parachutes, and the afternoon doing all kinds of exercises from rope climbing to tumbling on the hard clay ground. During the second week we made controlled, simulated jumps from a 34-foot tower and slid down a cable. The third week we dropped from 250-foot towers. During the fourth week we made parachute drops from C-47 aircraft." Throughout it all, the conditioning was severe. It

Above: Students at parachute school climb over an obstacle in the "Frying Pan."

Above right: Fort Benning, Georgia. In addition to hours of grueling physical conditioning each day, parachute school taught the fundamentals of jumping from an aircraft. Here students practice landing after a jump.

The 250-foot jump tower dropped a man suspended from a parachute. The top of the chute was connected to the tower at all times by a cable.

The third stage of training required students to jump from a 250-foot tower. *U.S. Army photograph courtesy of Bob Murphy*

didn't help that the weather was exceedingly hot—so hot, in fact, that the training area was aptly nicknamed "the Frying Pan."

Alexander took well to the training, but suffered a setback when he received an injury. "One exercise we did called for four guys to carry a telephone pole. It takes coordination and cooperation. I had the tale end. The guy up front stumbled and fell down, and the pole dropped off of each man's shoulder. I tried to hold it and get it out of the way, but I didn't get it off of my shoulder in time and it hit me on the neck. I got a big bruise out of it, and damned if I didn't develop a bad infection in the gland running down the right back side of my neck.

"I tried to stick it out with the training, but found I was going downhill. Poor Mary worried and worked with me for three or four days, continually keeping hot packs on my neck after I got home from school until I fell asleep each night, but it got worse all the time. So I finally went to the hospital. They gave me ether, made a crucifix-shaped incision on my neck and took out a lot of bad tissue."

When Alexander reported back to parachute school, his class had graduated and he had to start over with the next group. Roughly one-third of each class washed out. Failure to keep up on one of the many runs meant you were out of the paratroopers and back to your old unit. Others refused to jump from the towers or C-47s. There were no second chances.

"Some people can control themselves under stress and others can't. Most of them didn't want to jump, even though they all volunteered for it. I think most everybody is pretty scared on their first C-47 jump. When you initially get up there in an airplane and you're about to jump, you're looking down at the ground, thinking, 'What the hell am I doing up here about to jump out of a perfectly good airplane, when I could be down there on the ground with the rest of those guys?'

"I enjoyed going through school with those men. Some of them wanted to make it in the worst way and were scared shitless. After we got off at 5:00 p.m., we'd all go try to lie down and rest for a little bit. Even after all the running and exercise, some were so keyed up they had trouble getting any sleep." Jokes and pranks were also abundant. Alexander laughingly recalled "a guy who was always playing tricks." His buddy, a nervous type, "was lying on his belly asleep, probably dreaming about jumping. The jokester slapped him on the back and shouted 'Go!' The shocked GI jumped up yelling. I said, 'Don't ever do that to that poor guy again! He can hardly get out the door as it is!'"

He also remembered the anguish of men desperate to qualify, but desperately afraid of jumping. "There was a lieutenant who had just graduated from The Citadel named Roundtree, a real southern gentleman. I noticed the first time we jumped together, he had a hell of a time getting out the door. So I talked to him. He said, 'I'm having a hard time jumping. Would you stand behind me in the door, and if I don't jump, kick me out? I'm determined I'm going to qualify.'

"So I jumped behind him after that. I gave him a little shove once, but I never had to kick him out the door. He told me before he got the fifth jump in, 'as soon as I qualify, I'm going to request reassignment. This jumping out of airplanes is killing me.' I could see it was."

Roundtree completed his fifth C-47 jump and received his parachute wings. The paratroopers were very reluctant to release qualified soldiers, "but somehow he maneuvered to get out and went to a line outfit." Alexander did not fault him for it. "He was a hell of a nice guy. Different people, different ways. Jumping just wasn't for him."

The static line breaks free and the canopy opens. On flights into combat, Mark Alexander would stand in the open doorway and wait for the green "go" light to flash, then lead his stick of men out into the sky." *U.S. Army photograph courtesy of Phil Nordyke*

CHAPTER THREE

EARLY DAYS IN THE 505 PARACHUTE INFANTRY REGIMENT

O N GRADUATION FROM PARACHUTE SCHOOL, Alexander reported to the 504th Parachute Infantry Regiment with the understanding that he would be sent to the 505th PIR as soon as it was activated. This occurred a few weeks later on July 6, 1942, when Alexander and others were pulled out of the 504 to form the backbone of the new unit. The rest of the regiment would be built around them.

Lieutenant Colonel Orin D. Haugen commanded the regiment for several weeks until the commanding officer, Colonel James M. Gavin, arrived from Washington, where he was finishing up work at army headquarters. Haugen then put together the cadre for the newly formed 511 PIR by taking officers and men from the 505. "He requested that I be transferred to the 511 along with him," Alexander stated, "but Gavin called me in. He said, 'Mark, I have to give up a certain number of officers and noncoms, but you don't have to go if you don't want to. I have a right to hold a limited number of them back.' Haugen was a good, hard-nosed commander, but I said, 'I'd rather stay right here with the 505.' Otherwise, I would have eventually gone to the Pacific with the 511th." [1]

Gavin was an excellent commander from both a tactical and a leadership perspective. He was also the kind of leader who could allow his men to retain a rough edge and yet garner their complete loyalty. He commanded great respect while rarely ever raising his voice.

"Not long after Colonel Gavin took command, he called me into his office. He said, 'F Company has nine AWOLs. I want you to get it straightened out.' He also said, 'You've got a lot of leeway as to how you take care of it.'"

Early Days in the 505 Parachute Infantry Regiment

James M. Gavin took command of the 505 Parachute Infantry Regiment shortly after being promoted to the rank of colonel. This photo was taken later in the war when he wore the stars of a major general. *Photograph courtesy of Bob Murphy*

Alexander used that leeway as soon as he took command, putting his men to work to build a stockade of barbed wire and steel posts in the middle of the company street. "Then I sent out messages to all the towns where the AWOL soldiers came from, notifying the sheriff and city police. They picked them all up fast and brought them back in manacles. One of them was picked up as he was going into church to get married. They let him get married and then took him to jail.

"I put them all in this stockade and each got two blankets and a half a bale of straw. There were two men to a tent and a guard on them with a rifle, but no bullets. They got a week in the stockade. The guard would take them to the john and back, and we'd pass them food through the wire.

"Then I told them, 'If any of you go AWOL from now on, I'm going to request that you be transferred out of the paratroopers.' That shook 'em down pretty well and I didn't have any more AWOLs. Gavin let me do it. He didn't say anything. After the war he laughed and said, 'I didn't want to know what you were doing down there.'"

The Colonel knew that a paratrooper landing behind enemy lines might have to fight on his own for days or weeks before linking up with other friendly soldiers. He worked to craft men who would take orders, but also had a strong independent streak. The last thing he wanted was a regiment of automatons who did not act until told to do so. This applied from the top all the way down to the lowest private. He realized that combat could not be far off, and his newly formed regiment had a long way to go before it would be ready.

Captain Alexander's leadership techniques, although not found in any United States military manuals, were ideal for their time. Gavin saw Alexander's leadership qualities first-hand, and F Company was cleaned up in quick fashion. Gavin was impressed enough to call Alexander into his office after he had commanded Company F for a month and a half, and offer him enrollment in Command and General Staff College (CGSC). This was a huge break: although Alexander had attended infantry school, many airborne officers were graduates of West Point with four years of military schooling compared to his four months. His quick cleanup of F Company was almost certainly the primary reason he was selected, but the fact that he had a college degree, no matter that the subject was art, also likely influenced the decision.

CGSC "was staff work and I needed it because I didn't know the organization of the military worth a damn. I took what they called the G-1 course. If you came out of there and passed, you stood a good chance of being the G-1 (personnel officer) of a division."

In a stroke of further good luck, the school was in Leavenworth, Kansas, 28 miles from Alexander's parents' home. He and Mary packed up and drove their trusty Ford "Betsy" to Lawrence, where Mary stayed with Alexander's parents.

"I had to stay at Leavenworth most of the time because we had to study night and day. There were big assembly halls and lectures attended by every rank from captains to full colonels. Most students were majors and lieutenant colonels. Many were National Guard guys and reservists who had been in a long time, but not necessarily in the regular army. There were about a hundred of us.

"They were making a drive to enlarge the army quickly. On the first day they told us, 'This course is normally a year long, but we're going to give it to you in four months.' I believed them, because the first day they lectured all morning, and gave a two-hour shotgun quiz afterwards. Seventy percent of the class flunked it. They made believers out of us immediately. Everybody settled down and really went to work. They hit us with the quiz on purpose to get us zeroed in.

"I was there a little more than four months. I'd see Mary almost every weekend, but I mean, it was tough. They gave us so much so fast. I remember Mary was disgusted with me because I studied every weekend, trying to keep on top of things. During the four months, guys would disappear. No one would tell you where they were, but they washed out.

"There was another captain from the 505 who was absent from the class one day. "I said, 'What happened to him? I've noticed some other guys have been disappearing as well.' 'Yeah,' I was told, 'We don't say anything. We just call them in and give them a ticket back to their base.' If someone was failing, they would just ship him out, that's all.

"I never told anybody about that captain flunking out because he didn't come back to the 505. If you flunked the course, Gavin was not going to take you back. No way. And if you ever requested a transfer, he never would take you back. He wanted your loyalty all the way or he didn't want you. He was a get-it-done guy."

Doing a poor job in class wasn't the only way to get kicked out. Fighting would also do it. "In my class there was a guy named Foster, kind of a big guy. He and I got in a fight in the quarters one night on the weekend. He got smart about something and I called him on it. Then he thought he could put a pounding on me because he outweighed me by about 40 pounds.

"I told him, 'We don't want to fight in here. If they catch us, they'll kick us both out of school!' But he kept coming and kept coming, and there were a bunch of guys standing around watching us. It was drawing attention. Finally I pinned his head between the mattress and the coiled springs, and I wouldn't let him up until he said he'd had enough. All I wanted to do was quit before we got caught. I was afraid somebody was going to come in and catch us fighting. And I might have gotten kicked out. Probably would have.

"They brought in instructors from the other services to supply classes on co-ordination with their branches of the military. It was very interesting to a guy like me who never had significant exposure to them. Before we got through CGSC, 35 percent of the class flunked out. I was luckier than hell to get through, because I had had so little military experience. I was sweating it, because I knew what would happen if I flunked out.

After graduating, Alexander and Mary loaded up Betsy yet again and drove back to Fort Benning, where Gavin assigned Alexander as the executive officer of the 2nd Battalion under Major Jim Gray. Because the Alexanders had given up their apartment to move to Kansas, they now had nowhere to live. "We again had great difficulty finding living quarters. Mary was pregnant and we were looking at garages and everything. So finally I said, 'Mary, let's go back to the hotel and have lunch.'

"Over lunch I said, 'I think we're going about this all wrong. Let's pick the best-looking house we can find up there on the hill and try there.' So we picked this two-and-a-half story white colonial mansion with big pillars in front and a couple of gardeners working in the yard." The lady of the house, Mrs. Butler, answered the door. "I introduced myself and explained our situation. She said, 'Well, bring her up here. I want to meet her.' She met Mary and said, 'Now you both come back tonight about 7:00 when my husband is home, and we'll see what we can work out.'

"So we went back and they gave us a big bedroom with a private bath, laundry service, and a white carpet on the floor. Actually, it was for Mary more than anything else. She could have breakfast in bed or any place she wanted it, and there were people to wait on her." Mary was practically accepted as the Butler's adopted daughter. Mrs. Butler was from one of the oldest families of the community, and truly exemplified what southern hospitality was all about.

"Of course I could only get back there about three times a week. When I was there, I had to get up at 5:00 a.m. because it was 15 miles to our training area. We were doing a lot of night training, but how I loved my nights with Mary and the luxury of the room and bath."

The 505 was soon involved in very intense weapons, tactical and physical training in addition to daily four- or five-mile runs and a weekly march of 20 or 30 miles. If a trooper didn't keep up, he was transferred out. Colonel Gavin was determined to have the best regiment in the U.S. Army.

Training also included multiple practice jumps. "We sometimes landed in the middle of a peanut field during training jumps. A lot of the guys would grab a few peanuts for a snack. The

Max, a large boxer belonging to 2nd Battalion commander Jim Gray, became a national celebrity when he became the mascot of the regiment and jumped with a special parachute and harness.

Early Days in the 505 Parachute Infantry Regiment

government paid the farmers for using their fields, so it was all covered."

Practice jumps at night were particularly dangerous. On one, several men were killed when they mistook the glistening asphalt of a roadway for a nearby river in the dark of night. Not wanting to land in the water and be weighed down with gear or entangled in their parachutes, they released from their chutes early and crashed onto the unforgiving pavement.

During another jump, a thirty-mile-an-hour wind kicked up after the formation of aircraft was already airborne. Usually drops were cancelled when the wind hit 10 or 15 miles an hour, because jumpers would often break legs or ankles. Strong wind blew paratroopers along the ground, making it harder to land well and more likely to hit trees or buildings. After hitting the ground, men could also be dragged over rocks or into fences.

This time, however, it was too late to cancel the exercise. "We all jumped and there were several injuries. I landed hard, injuring my hip. It healed and I continued jumping, but every now and then it would be re-aggravated throughout the war and later in civilian life. Sometimes it didn't take much. I might just stub my toe the wrong way." The injury usually did not bother Alexander, but when it did, it could be extremely painful.

Jumps were only one of the many hazards of training. "Once during artillery training one of the guys dropped a round in the barnyard that was way away from the range. He put three increments on the artillery piece when he was only supposed to do one." Instead of going high but not very far, it traveled a very long distance. Nobody got hurt and no cattle were hit, but the army had to pay for the barn, which took a direct hit.

The rambunctious nature Gavin fostered in his men made them ready for anything. They not only aggressively attacked training problems, they unfortunately also got in frequent fistfights at the many town bars. These were often brawls with a nearby tank division, whose members also considered themselves top dogs in the military, but fights broke out against local townsfolk or soldiers from other units as well.

On one occasion, a melee ensued between a group of paratroopers and the local police. Officers tolerated fighting among the men, but battling it out with the town police was going too far. Gavin personally picked the guilty troopers up from jail and promised the police it would never happen again. He then took the entire regiment on a full gear, 24-hour forced march of 54 miles. All 109 men who could not keep up were flushed out of the regiment the following morning. The punishment had the desired effect. [2]

On February 12, 1943, the 505 moved to Fort Bragg, North Carolina, and became part of the 82nd Airborne Division. The 82nd initially fought in World War I and was then decommissioned. It had recently been brought out of retirement and newly designated as airborne. It consisted of two parachute regiments, the 505 and 504 PIRs; one glider regiment, the 325 GIR; and supporting artillery, engineer, medical, anti-aircraft and other units. General Matthew B. Ridgway served as the commanding general.

The men of the 505 were proud of their regiment and did not much care for being called 82nd Airborne. The first time General Ridgway addressed them as such, a chorus of "No, no. Five-oh-five, five-oh-five!" went through the crowd. Ridgway handled it well and said the day would come when they would be proud to be a part of the 82nd. That day quickly came. [3]

Training continued to be rigorous and it even intensified. During down time, the men found ways to relax or blow off steam. One was famously in the form of practical jokes. Alexander recalled one instance with amusement: "One afternoon, Capt. William Hagan came in. While we were talking, he started playing with a pair of handcuffs that were sitting on my desk. He locked them around his wrists and pulled a little bit.

"He said, 'Give me the key, will ya?'

"I said, 'I'm sorry, I lost the key to that pair.'

"'You son of a bitch. You sat there and let me put these on.' So he had to go down the road to the smithy and have them cut off. He brought them back and threw them on my desk and said, 'There you are. They aren't much good now.'

"I said, 'I know. I'm going to have to charge you for a pair of handcuffs. You destroyed government property.'

"He said, 'God damn you, Alexander,' picked up the handcuffs and stomped out the door. He came back a little while later and they were welded back together. We both had a good laugh over it."

Alexander recalled another stunt with far less amusement. This time, he had been the brunt, and the joke was not so harmless. "I was checking some of the training out at the riflery. I came back and Major Gray, the 2nd Battalion commander, and four of the staff were in our headquarters building. I sat down at my desk while talking to somebody and reached in a drawer that had been booby-trapped. Someone had rigged up gun propellants with a delay. The damn thing went off after I got my hand in it. It burned my fingernails white and really scorched

Early Days in the 505 Parachute Infantry Regiment

my fingers. And man, it hurt like hell.

"I was so dammed mad I said, 'I don't know who did that, but if you'll meet me out behind the mess hall, you better bring the others because I'm going to beat the shit out of you.' If there were going to be any fights among the men, they were supposed to occur behind the mess hall. I don't know why. Guys just did it that way.

"Nobody would admit to setting the trap, and to this day I never found out who did it. I was lucky I didn't lose my fingers. I was a pretty good-natured guy most of the time, but that one was too much." The culprit, later uncovered through Ed Ruggero's research, turned out to be the battalion training and operations officer (S-3), Captain Paul Woolslayer. He had been an All-American football player in college, and was a tough-minded officer who drove men hard during training exercises.

"One advantage we had as airborne is that we were all volunteers. And only the best were selected from the volunteers. Most of the problems were weeded out early," Alexander reflected. "There were, however, some arrogant bastards. When I was sent to Command and General Staff School, for example, I recommended Pinky (Charles) Sammon, my XO, to replace me as the F Company commander. But there was a guy named Pointeck, who had been a noncom for ten years and was a lieutenant commanding one of the platoons. He was senior and somebody moved to appoint him as captain and gave him command of the company. I wouldn't have done that because I knew he was a mean son-of-a-bitch. I'm saying he was just mean.

"One of the lieutenants came up to me after I returned from school and said, 'Major, you've got to move me to another company or I'm going to kill Pointeck.' Pointeck had stood the lieutenant up in front of his men, cussed him out and completely berated him, making it difficult for him to maintain the respect of his men.

"I had the lieutenant transferred to another company. You don't embarrass any lesser rank officers if you don't have to, or any superior officers as far as that goes. I tried very hard never to embarrass a lesser rank officer or noncom in front of his men. No deal! Luckily, we didn't have many people like that. Usually we got rid of them."

Two terribly tragic events took place while the regiment was stationed at Fort Bragg, the first occurring on "the first regimental training jump into Camden, South Carolina. During the jump, one of the C-47s got caught in the prop blast of a leading plane, causing it to lose altitude. It went through a whole stick of paratroopers, killing three of them.

"One of our medics, Kelly Byers, had his chute risers cut off two feet above his hands by the propellers. He opened his reserve, landed on the roof of a farm cottage, slid off onto the ground, rolled up his parachute and walked over to Colonel Gavin and me. He tossed the parachute on the ground in front of Gavin and said, 'You can stick this chute up your ass. I'm through with parachute jumping.'

"Gavin replied, 'Okay, Kelly,' and Byers walked away."

Buyers' comments were so out of line that most commanders would have come down on the man immediately. But Gavin, who had as much respect and loyalty as a leader can muster, let it ride. He knew what kind of soldier and medic he was. The comment was clearly brought on by coming so very close to a brutal death.

Ten days later, Buyers checked out a chute and began jumping again.

As one of Gavin's officers said years later, "We would have stormed the gates of hell for that man." Another, who rose to the rank of lieutenant general, said, "He set us on fire." [4]

The worst incident that occurred while the 505 was still in the States took place in a company that was having trouble with men going AWOL. The new commander took a page from Alexander's book and built a containment area to house them. The critical difference was that the company commander "was stupid enough to put a guard on them with a loaded rifle and told him to shoot anyone who left his tent. Sure enough, two soldiers sharing a tent got out and this guard shot both of them. Killed them dead. The lieutenant never did live that down." (He remained a 1st lieutenant for the rest of the war.)

"We were scheduled to go overseas in less than two months and nobody wanted to fool around with courts-martial and all that stuff. So they just took the guard out and sent him to some line outfit. I don't know where he went. They transferred him that night. The chief inspector general from Washington was down there right away. He knew that we were scheduled to ship out, so there was no open investigation.

"I remember when I heard about it, I was told by a senior officer, 'We're going to try to just let this die. Don't talk about it. If you hear people talk about it, tell them not to.'" The affair was handled internally, and did not affect the deployment of the division. This began on April 17, 1943, when the 82nd "began to move by train from Fort Bragg to Camp Edwards, Massachusetts, as the first step on its journey overseas." [5]

Chapter Four

North Africa

Orders came down for the entire 82nd Airborne Division to move to Camp Edwards, Massachusetts. Alexander was allowed time to load up Betsy and drive Mary, now seven months pregnant, to her parents' home in Easton, Pennsylvania. He said his final goodbye, left the car with her and returned to Fort Bragg.

"In addition to my regular duties, I was designated packing officer for overseas shipment of all regimented equipment. We still didn't know where we were going, but we were to ship out of New York Harbor on the Matson Liner, *Monterey*. As I remember, we packed 2,125 boxes measuring four feet wide, four feet long, and four feet deep, plus equipment of other dimensions."

His commander, Major Gray, enjoyed his liquor, especially Old Taylor, and he brought Alexander a case of it to pack with the rest of the equipment in spite of the rules against it. Alexander told him he didn't like the idea, "but Gray said, 'You'd do it for me, wouldn't you?' And the way he said it, I knew I was in trouble." Alexander did as his CO asked and packed the Old Taylor in box number 2,001.

The division boarded trains and traveled north. The war department wanted the whereabouts of such an elite unit to be kept secret, so the men were ordered to remove the 82nd Airborne insignia and pull their pant legs out of their jump boots in order to look like any other straight leg division.

A week later the division was transferred again to New York. They boarded the USS *Monterey*, a passenger ship converted to a troop transport, and sailed out of New York Harbor on April 29, 1943. Now that there was no danger of word leaking out, the madly circulating rumors were put to rest when they learned their destination was Casablanca, Morocco. On November 8, 1942, the Allies under command of General Dwight D. Eisenhower had invaded North Africa, and the fighting was still hot and heavy.

While at sea, there isn't much for a packing officer to do, so Alexander was made the mess officer for the ship. All of the chairs and tables had been removed from the dining room and replaced by long narrow tables to allow as many men as possible to eat at the same time. "There were 2,300 men in the regiment and we also had 700 of the 307th Engineering Battalion and a few miscellaneous troops on board that were attached to the 82nd. I had to break the men down into groups and give them assigned times to eat." Even though the men ate standing up, there were so many on board that each was only allowed through the mess line twice a day. Initially it was quite a task to organize, but once the pattern was established, Alexander's duties were much less demanding.

It also had its perks. "The chief steward, James Gold, who had control of the food supplies on board, was a pretty senior guy. He and I got to know each other, and about every other day he asked me down to his suite. It was on the lower deck where he had a nice living room, bedroom and toilet and all that. They took care of their crew accommodations. I'd go down and have dinner with him and I didn't have to get in that chow line. We ate steak, frozen strawberries, et cetera." This was really first-class treatment compared to the food and conditions in the cafeteria.

"One day I was standing there talking to him, and Lieutenant Colonel Gorham, the commanding officer of the 1st Battalion, walked up and said, 'Say, Gold, how come you invite Alexander down to have dinner with you, but never invite me or anybody else?' Gold replied, 'Because Alexander is a gentleman,' and turned around and walked off. That really got Gorham. He talked to a couple of other officers about that and they laughed the same as I did. He walked right into that one."

The 82nd was at sea for ten days. "We played poker every night on the ship. I played with mostly field grade and one general officer. Since we all got paid more than most of the men, and there wasn't a whole lot to do on the boat, the pots could get pretty big. I lost a $700 pot on the very last hand of the last game. I had a full house and thought I had it won, but was beaten by four deuces. Later that night, one of the guys was playing around with that deck and discovered it contained five deuces! But it was too late to call foul.

Alexander had nothing to complain about. Over the course of the trip he won $3,700, a small fortune for the time. He sent most of it home to a very surprised Mary, who wisely put it all in the bank with the $800 she acquired when she sold Betsy, the little black Ford.

The USS *Monterey* arrived in Casablanca on May 10, 1943, making the 505 the first American parachute regiment to deploy overseas. [1] Although the movements of the 82nd were supposed to be kept under wraps, a band was on the dock playing "Johnny the Jumper the Parachute Man" for all to hear. The land campaign in North Africa had ended just three days earlier, and a portion of a destroyed French warship poked above the waterline, reminding all that the war was no longer a far-off mystery.

The division disembarked and carried their gear five miles in the sweltering heat to a bivouac area outside of town. The equipment and boxes were piled nearby. Major Gray approached Alexander, who had resumed his duties as packing officer, and asked for his case of booze. "I searched for box 2,001 containing Major Gray's Old Taylor whiskey, but it was gone! He had me turn the pile over twice. I didn't want to pack it in the first place and I didn't want to do this either. But it didn't matter." Box 2,001 was not there: somebody had short-stopped it. [2]

Training taught the troopers to set up camp in a quick and orderly fashion. Tents were pitched, straddle trenches dug, and guards posted. On May 12, Alexander described conditions in a letter to his family. *Right now it is 9 PM. I am sitting in my very dirty and cold tent attempting to do something about this letter. We have been here two days now and are learning rapidly about Arabs, French-Portuguese and some few German aliens. Yes, also the sun is very bright, the wind blows up clouds of red dust all day long, the days are warm, and the nights very cold. (My writing is not so good—this candle is very poor and keeps blowing out.)*

We are encamped in tents about 5 miles outside the city and will move on within two or three days. The city of Casablanca is of about 300,000 people. It is a rather beautiful old place in its picturesque setting on the sea coast. Casablanca is a great contrast of very old buildings and, right along beside them, extremely modern buildings of French and American architecture. Some of them run up to 20 stories in height.

[…] I hope you are keeping in touch with Mary. She will be having our child in about a month now and I am wishing again and again that I might be there with her. Perhaps she will come to see you when she is fully fit again—I do hope so. She's a wonderful little wife and deserves

more than she is getting from me.

I hope Don, Ed, and Harold are still in the U.S. and I must know if ever they are sent across, and if possible, where to.

Mother, Dad and Virginia, take the best care of yourselves. I love you all very dearly and will soon come back to be with you.

The beauty and intrigue of Casablanca strongly contrasted against its widespread poverty. Many of the Arabs were so poor that they hungrily dug through garbage or anything else the soldiers discarded. The fighting by this time was hundreds of miles away in Tunisia, where Gen. Erwin Rommel's men were making their stand. After a short time outside of Casablanca, the 505 moved east, closer to the front.

Most of the 82nd boarded 40 & 8 train cars, so-named because they held either 40 men or eight horses. The rickety railroad had been established in French colonial days, and was now run by the Free French. Luckier troopers traveled on one of the available trucks.

"I was left behind to make sure everything was cleaned up in the 505th's bivouac area," Alexander stated. "The last thing I saw on our way out was one Arab holding another by the ankles while that one was down in a straddle trench with a stick, stirring the shit around to see if anything had been dropped in there. They were scrounges, but had to be to survive.

"It took us two days, almost three, to go across Morocco to Oujda near the Algerian border. Where we bivouacked, there was nothing but

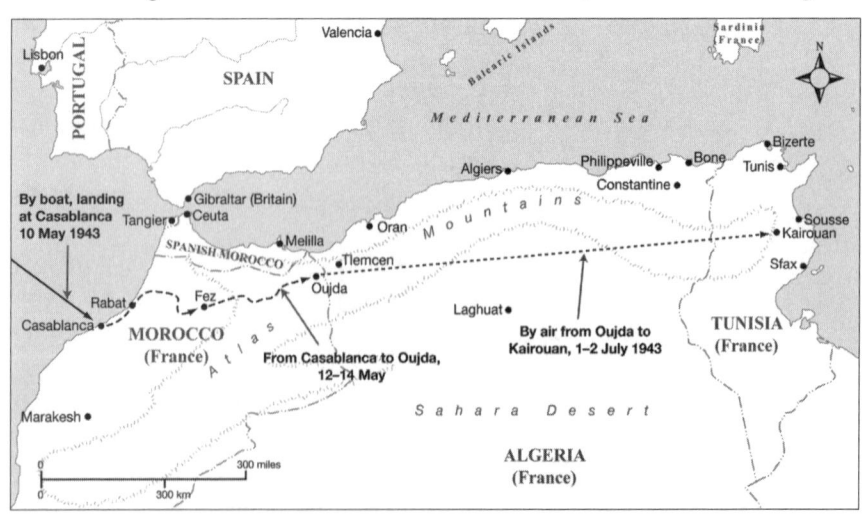

Route taken by the 505 through North Africa in preparation for the invasion of the island of Sicily

dust and rock." The small Arab town of Oujda sat just west of the Algerian border, still inside Morocco and about 30 miles south of the Mediterranean Sea. The ground, hard, rocky and dry, offered little cover. The site was selected because of its proximity to a large French airfield. [3]

Len Lebenson, a corporal on General Ridgway's staff, described conditions thus:

> Africa was hot and dusty, full of tiny scorpions that stung, persistent flies that appeared in clouds whenever food was exposed, and generally miserable conditions. We pitched our camp in an area that was north of the Sahara but nonetheless a desert, with the principal foliage being scraggly cactus. The ground was hard, whitish and grainy, almost impossible to dig into. Latrines for the men had to be blasted out of the earth with dynamite [...].
>
> We set up rows of pup tents, each joining with another man and his shelter half to make a tent which became home for a couple of months. [...] We heard about the Sirocco. Then found out what it was. The days would start off cool, then relentlessly begin to heat up about 9 AM. By noon, the heat and sun were brutal and by two in the afternoon the temperature would be hovering about 110 degrees. At 3 PM, almost without fail, came the Sirocco, a fierce wind blowing clouds of blinding sand from the desert toward the Mediterranean in the north. The sand got into everything, including one's mouth, nose, eyes and ears. It was impossible to do anything except go for cover when the wind was blowing. After about an hour it would die down and taper off until dusk when the chill of evening started. [4]

The hard, rocky ground made for numerous injuries on training jumps. Drinking water, stored in Lister bags and tank trailers, sat out in the sun, making it hot, and so much chlorination was required that it burned the throat. [5] Showers were just a memory. The dust was Alexander's most vivid memory. "All that damn dust was blowing in everything we ate." When the Sirocco did not blow them away, the flies were worse than the scorpions, ants, yellow jackets and hornets combined. It was generally necessary to shoo them with one hand while eating with the other. As Alexander succinctly summed it up: "This was the worst-picked bivouac area I ever saw."

"Practically 100 percent of the men got dysentery. There were so many diseases that we had a regulation that nobody ate fresh eggs or chicken. We only ate issued rations because so many guys got sick. Terribly sick. For breakfast we ate powdered eggs, powdered lemonade, powdered milk, hash in a can and beans in a can. At one point the supply chain wasn't moving very well, and for a week we had almost nothing to eat but powdered eggs and powdered lemonade. Some of the guys nearly got into fights over who was going to get to eat beans." Allergic to eggs, Alexander would not eat them, powdered or not. "That was a lean week for me, but I was able to scrounge up a few things.

"Of course there were no toilets, so we had straddle trenches instead. I had a little tent for my men, a working tent for the battalion headquarters in the training area. It so happened that part of the traffic to and from the trenches would go past my tent. I finally moved it because there were so many guys going down there. I remember hearing one of our captains run by. Pretty soon he came back and he was cussing. He got right even with the tent and said, 'Oh, god! Not again!' And he turned and ran back to the trenches." Out in the field, men would break ranks right in the middle of an exercise and run for a trench, or as close as they could get. It happened so often that it almost went unnoticed.

As in Casablanca, there were plenty of poor Arabs in and around Oujda. "They would get closer and closer to your tents. If they got near enough, they'd run and grab something and take off. In camp we had to tie everything down. They would steal anything they could get their hands on. The 2nd Battalion adjutant was Capt. Clyde Russell. When they drew near our camp I would say, 'Russell, they're in close again. Get them out of there.' He would grab a couple of concussion grenades and jump in a jeep. When they'd see him coming, they'd take off running in all directions. And he'd throw a couple of these concussion grenades at them. He loved to do that.

"If you didn't do anything and they got in close enough, they'd take the tent pegs or the tent or anything. There were probably 50 of them around the edges, waiting for a break to get in there. They'd just keep walking up a little closer, a little closer. And there were enough of them that you'd have a hell of a time grabbing one. Then at night we posted guards who had to watch them all the time."

Alexander and everyone else railed against the local population for stealing, but he himself was not above theft when the occasion required it. "The wind was again blowing like hell there in the desert. As always, it was getting in our food and everywhere else. Gavin had a tent set up for his headquarters, but it was on this dirty sand floor. And I heard him say 'I sure would like to have a floor in this tent.'

"Well, I knew where a lumber train came down out of the mountains. It was French and came from deeper in Morocco. They stopped at about 10:00 in the morning every day at the same spot to water up and put some more coal in the tender. The engineer and the brakeman always went and smoked a cigarette, so I figured I would engage them for a while.

"I had a couple of two-and-a-half-ton trucks and ten men, lots of labor. I said, 'You guys pull up on the other side of the train and load lumber just as fast as you can get it. One of you watch me. And if I take my cap off and then light a cigarette, get your ass out of there as fast as you can.'

"To keep the Frenchmen occupied, I'd give them cigarettes. They were hard to get in those days. I think there were three on the train crew. Anyway, I moved so their back was to the train." Alexander's men quickly piled the lumber onto their trucks and made their escape before anyone was the wiser.

"I took that lumber back to camp. Gavin asked, 'Where did you get all that, Alexander?'

"I said, 'Sir, you don't want to know.'

"He grinned and said, 'Well, okay,' and turned around and walked off. I dumped about half of it there. The rest of it was used to make floors for other tents and tables for the mess hall. It was one of the things you do that you're not supposed to."

By this time, the generals and full colonels in the 82nd knew that the division was preparing to invade the island of Sicily, code-named Operation HUSKEY. Landings would take place "on the southeastern extremity of the island, with British and Canadian forces on the east coast and Americans on the south. The American forces would consist of the 3rd, 1st, and 45th Infantry Divisions (with attached units) landing on beaches in the vicinities of Licata, Gela, and Scoglitti, respectively, and with parachute troops from the 82nd Airborne Division dropping inland from Gela to pave the way for the 1st Infantry Division as it was considered the area most vulnerable to immediate attack." [6]

Sicily was a rugged, mountainous island with few roads, and the Allies foresaw difficulty moving cannons and supplies over such unforgiving terrain. General Ridgway told General Gavin that someone "high in command" thought mules would be very helpful during the invasion. It was left to Gavin to figure out if and how they could be parachuted in with the troops. He, in turn, gave that assignment to Alexander.

"Being an executive officer is kind of an oddball job. You pick up a lot of loose ends, but sometimes you get a bang out of it. I was charged with dropping mules out of a plane. Corp. Robert Bales, Corp. Fred Freeland and Sgt. Jack Gavin (no relation to Colonel Gavin) were assigned to help me." [7]

They went into town and after some haggling purchased two mules. Now all they needed was a plane and pilot to take them up. Alexander drove out to the airfield and met with Tommy Thompson, the executive officer of the 64th Troop Carrier Group, which consisted of about 100 C-47 transport planes. Major Gray, and to a lesser extent Alexander, had developed a relationship with the command of the group, since they would carry the 505 into the upcoming Sicily invasion.

"Thompson was a fighter pilot who had busted his eardrum. He had problems at times on account of that, so they put him in transport command. We were having a hard time finding a pilot to take us and a mule up for a jump. Finally, Thompson agreed to do it for us crazy paratroopers." Thompson was just the man for the job. He could have ordered another pilot to carry out the mission, but it would have been out of character to do so. His eardrum made him unfit for fighter aircraft, but his heart hadn't changed. If there was fun to be had or a challenge to be met in the air, Thompson wanted in on it, regardless of the type of plane.

"We strapped a 48-foot cargo chute to the animal and tried to get him in the C-47, but he wouldn't go up the ramp no matter what we did. Someone had the bright idea to put a blindfold over his eyes and then we were able to lead him into the plane.

"Thompson took off and climbed to 600 feet. Just before we reached the drop area, the mule got smart and lay down on the floor of the plane. All together, we pushed and slid it out the door. I was pushing so hard that I fell out on top of the mule. I watched it falling below me until my parachute opened."

The poor animal extended its legs and broke three of them in the landing. He had to be put out of his misery. There was no reason to drop the other mule: parachuting the animals into Sicily was not feasible. When they invaded, the Allies discovered the island already possessed an ample supply of mules. There was no need to supply them from the outside.

The dead mule did not go entirely to waste, however. Captain Paul Woolslayer had it strung up over one of the straddle trenches. He then led a training drill with most of the men in the battalion bayoneting the carcass, so they would experience their weapon thrusting into actual flesh. It was designed to prepare them for the carnage of real combat. The unfortunate animal was soon mutilated. The smell of the carcass covered with flies in the heat, combined with the stench of the latrine, was enough to make some men in the training vomit. [8]

Another supply challenge Alexander faced for Sicily "was figuring out how to drop blood plasma. We were dropping plasma containers in canvas and felt-padded bundles, and breaking about half of them. I heard that the British had some aluminum bundles, which were about 18 inches in diameter and about six feet long. So, instead of requisitioning them, which would have taken too long, I had a couple of guys go and steal two at night. We called it 'night-time requisition.'"

Going through regular army channels would have taken at least a week, but Alexander knew his superiors would not be pleased with the delay. "Some things you could not requisition, at least not in a timely manner. Your men would have to appropriate them for you. Luckily, the British were camped right close to us.

"We filled the aluminum bundles with bottles of water and I talked Tommy Thompson into flying us again. There was a big door that you could drive a jeep through, and then there was a small door in the middle of the big door. We had the small aircraft door off and open. We thought the aluminum bundle could easily fit through it.

"When we were airborne and approaching the drop zone, one of my men and I, in preparation, slid a bundle part way out the door." The slipstream hit the end of the bundle and blew it sideways, wedging it against the big door and causing its hinges to turn loose. The door popped off, flew back and wrapped around the tail of the C-47. The whole plane started vibrating badly.

"Thompson came running from the cockpit screaming, 'What are you bastards doing to my airplane now?'

"I said, 'Tommy, don't worry about it. We just accidentally knocked your door off and it's stuck on the tail of your plane.' Then I said, 'We'll see you later,' and we jumped out!"

Unlike the mule drop, this experiment was very successful. The bottles in the aluminum bundle drops experienced almost no breakage. The plane, however, was a little beat-up. "Later Thompson told me he had a terrible time landing that airplane."

Combat was weeks, or even days away. Everyone knew it, but no one knew the exact date. Training seemed to go on almost around the clock. During one exercise, Captain Pointeck, who had taken over F Company from Alexander, finally went too far. His evil ways were about to catch up with him.

"One night we were on night maneuvers. Major Gray and I had a tarp pulled over our heads, looking at a map with a flashlight. There must have been a spot of light showing through somewhere, because a voice out of the darkness shouted, 'Turn that god damn light off!' and a big rock hit Gray on his helmet."

It was Pointeck. "I said, 'Gray, have that son-of-a-bitch reclassified. When we get into combat he'll get some good men killed.' Gray relieved him, but it took a rock on his helmet to do it."

Although training jumps continued, they were largely curtailed when it became apparent the hard ground made them counter-productive. "We jumped a battalion in one of our training exercises, but we had quite a few injuries on the rocky soil. So we decided we'd have one with only two jumpers in each plane, the jumpmaster and one assistant, to reduce the chance of injuries. This was training for the troop transport pilots more than anything else. They had to have the right formations and right controls and be able to navigate to the drop zone."

Alexander was the jumpmaster for one of the aircraft and needed one more man to go along. "So like a damn fool I said, 'Who wants to jump with me?'

"This little guy volunteered, but I had treated him so rough, I wasn't sure I wanted to take him. I had him sleeping on the ground back in the States because he was AWOL. When I took command of his company, I disciplined the hell out of him because he was fighting all the time, and I transferred his buddy out of the paratroopers. His buddy I didn't trust at all. He was so god damn mean that some of guys were scared of him. That's no good, so I got rid of him."

The soldier who volunteered to jump with Alexander was a car thief out of New York City. Alexander had his record and learned he had gotten out of jail by joining the paratroopers. "I thought for a minute to figure out what I was going to do. He really pleaded to go on the jump, so I decided to take him.

"That night we took off, and all the time I was in the plane I was thinking, 'What if he cuts my static line? At least I've still got my reserve.' I was looking over my shoulder when I went out the door.

"He didn't cause any trouble. For some reason he took a liking to me. After that, he was my runner part of the time. I had treated him rough, but he wasn't mad about it. I don't know. I guess he respected me for cracking the whip on him. So he was around on special jobs and did good work."

The men were given occasional breaks during their stay near Oujda, although they were few and far between. Alexander took half the 2nd Battalion on a daylong trip to the seaside. "We had a little recreation time and I wanted to take part of the unit to the beach to get them relaxed a little bit. I took 25 two-and-a-half-ton trucks full of men for a day's excursion on the Mediterranean. And I of course had 25 drivers and their assistants.

"We went to the coast and stayed there all day and then loaded up to come back. Some of them had been drinking wine that you could buy at a couple of the shops there. So I checked every driver down the line, to be sure he was sober enough to drive back. And yet on the way back, one of the guys got tired of driving, and traded with someone who was half drunk. He then crashed the truck, getting a lot of guys bruised up bad.

"The next morning the inspector general came down and said, 'I've got a bill for you for a two-and-a-half-ton truck.' I had to prove that I had inspected every driver, or I would have to pay for it."

Otis Sampson, one of the outstanding sergeants who had been on the trip, stepped forward and spoke up for Alexander. "We were all at the beach having a nice day. I decided to come back a little early and got in back of one of the trucks. Major Alexander was checking to make sure each driver was in good enough condition for the trip back. Our driver was drunk, I guess. The major asked, 'Is there a relief driver?' Somebody said, 'Yes, I am.' And he took the wheel.

"We got going and the road climbed along the side of a cliff. It was just a cliff running straight down two or three hundred feet to the sea. We stopped and our damn truck started rolling backward. I was in the front left corner in the back of the open truck. I could see through the little window into the cab that the driver and passenger were switching seats. I was a sergeant and didn't want to panic in front of the other guys, so I just sat there. They got situated up front and we started going again.

"We went along for a while. Then our driver tried to go around a turn and didn't make it. The truck went off the side of the road and rolled, dumping us all in a creek. There was no water, just rocks. One of the guys in the back, D.L. Gorman, had two dozen eggs with him. He didn't after that. He and a lot of other guys were thrown over my head. It reminded me of a bunch of potatoes getting dumped out of a bushel basket. Guys were banged up pretty good and I think there may have been a broken leg or two.

"The next day I heard that the major was being charged to replace the wrecked truck. I vouched for him because he did try to help us out to see that the drunken driver was relieved." [9]

On June 14, Alexander's wife Mary gave birth to a blonde baby girl while she was staying with her parents. Alexander received the news on June 25, when a telegram finally arrived. Both mother and daughter were doing very well. "I had bet $100 that it would be a boy. After the war I won the $100 back when my first son, Mark Junior, was born, and wisely quit betting."

"On June 21, Gavin gave the key personnel the big picture orientation of Operation HUSKEY. The next day, Gavin relieved Gray as battalion commander and replaced him with [...] Alexander." [10] Gray had not attended the orientation: he had simply vanished. "We looked for him for four and a half days," Alexander remembered. "Gavin called me in everyday and asked where Major Gray was. I didn't know and I was his exec. I said, 'Sir, I really, honestly don't know.'

"On the fourth day in the evening, Gavin called me in and said, 'Alexander, as of now you are commanding the 2nd Battalion.'

"I said, 'Sir, don't you want to wait until Major Gray gets back and explains himself?'

"He said, 'No, I've waited long enough. He could have gotten back here no matter where he was or at least gotten word in.'

"Gray had flown to Cairo with some of the flyers from the 64th group. He didn't get back until the fifth day. So when Gray came back, Gavin called him in and said, 'You are no longer commander of the 2nd Battalion. Alexander is.'" Gray said he went to observe a night drop by the troop transport group that would later be carrying them into combat, followed by a flight to Tunisia to see the airfield they would use for the assault on Sicily. It didn't matter. Gavin had made up his mind. [11]

Alexander was now in the unenviable position of taking over for a relieved commander less than two weeks before the unit's first combat mission. He was not aware of the exact date of the jump, only that they would be in action in the very near future. Although he was not young for a battalion commander, he had only two years and eight months of military experience, considerably less than others of equal position.

There was a lot of ground to cover, and quickly. Alexander had been with the battalion almost as long as anyone else, but Gray was the primary contact point when dealing with Colonel Gavin, division headquarters, the air force and others. These relationships had to be solidified. He needed to figure out who were possible weak links in combat and had to be ready to control over 500 men in battle. It was also crucial to make sure everyone accepted him as commander, regardless of personal feelings regarding Gray's dismissal.

He called his troops together and made a simple speech. The gist of it he captured in two sentences: "I'm the new commander. I'll do my best, and I expect you to do yours." [12]

"That was only 12 days before we invaded Sicily. It really put pressure on me as I had a lot to do to get on top of things. There were a lot of good men in the battalion. But some of them were still Gray's men, and I had to fight that issue because they didn't understand why he was being relieved.

"Of course the first move was, I needed an exec. Gavin said, 'Who do you want?'"

"I said, 'Colonel, why don't you pick him for me? I prefer you pick an Academy man, because I'm weak on army background and a bit weak on administration, and that's what I need.' So he picked Jack Norton."

Gavin had instructed Capt. John "Jack" Norton at West Point and knew he brought a lot to the table. When Gavin delivered the news that he had been promoted to executive officer of the 2nd Battalion, Norton was not happy. He was a company commander in the 3rd Battalion and very badly wanted to lead his men into combat. [13] Gavin listened, but did not budge. The 2nd Battalion needed him and that was the end of the discussion.

Although not pleased with his transfer, Norton accepted his new position completely and backed the new battalion commander 100 percent. This was crucial, since Alexander "had quite a little problem getting Gray's hand-picked staff zeroed in as my staff." Gavin couldn't have picked a better man. Not only was he an excellent officer, he and Alexander made quite a team.

"A few days later I was walking by a tent, and Norton was inside with the guys from the battalion staff. A couple of them were giving some lip about why didn't I do this or that. And I heard Norton say,

Captain Jack Norton, executive officer of the 2nd Battalion, played a crucial role in the battalion's success during the Sicily invasion. *Photo courtesy of Bob Murphy*

'Look, you guys, you've got a new commander. Make the best of it and give him your loyalty. If you don't, you're going to have to deal with me.' Words to that effect. He never said anything to me, of course. And I never let on that I knew about it. We got them straightened out all right, although I did remove one or two."

A few days after Alexander assumed command, the troops moved to Kairouan, Tunisia, the 82nd's jump-off point for the invasion of Sicily. Kairouan is a holy Muslim city partly surrounded by high walls and not open to outsiders. Luckily, the men were able to pitch their tents in an olive orchard, a good change from their last camp. "On the coast of North Africa there're quite a few olive, lemon and orange orchards. Then you get inland three or four miles and it's desert. Rocky as a bastard."

The most inviting characteristic of Kairouan was the ocean breeze that kicked up in the afternoon. Nevertheless, it was even hotter there than in Oujda, routinely hitting 120 to 130 degrees. In a letter to his daughter on July 7, Colonel Gavin noted, "Yesterday in Maj. Mark Alexander's [Second Battalion] area it was 142 degrees. [...] Things like pencils, ammunition, weapons, get too hot to pick up and water exposed to its effects is far too hot to drink. Yesterday, I put my hand in a can of water I had in the shade of an olive tree where I was sleeping and I had to take it out because of the heat." [14]

The move to Kairouan reinforced the idea in the minds of the rank and file that a combat jump could not be far off. The most obvious clue was the change in diet. "We were still eating the same old army rations. One morning, they drove a small herd of cattle into camp and over to the butcher. This tipped the men off that we would be going into battle soon. That was why they were being fed so well. We all ate beef for about a week before jumping into Sicily."

Alexander finally learned that July 9 was the date of the jump. There were not enough C-47s and other aircraft to carry the entire 82nd on the first night of the invasion: only the 505 and part of the 504 would go. "The 64th Troop Carrier Group, led by Col. John Cerny, with Tommy Thompson as executive officer, would take the 2nd Battalion."

Practice jumps had not gone well. Paratroopers were often badly scattered, and Alexander wanted to be sure he had a sizable fighting force when he met the enemy. Cerny, Thompson and Alexander "made an agreement, that no matter where they dropped us, they would make every effort to drop us all together, so we would have the opportunity to organize and fight as a battalion."

On the evening of Friday, July 9, 1943, the soldiers gathered up their gear and trucked out to the airfield, found their planes, secured equipment bundles and adjusted their harnesses. In the time remaining before takeoff, slips of paper were passed out among the men, containing the historic message below, addressed to "Soldiers of the 505th Combat Team":

Tonight you embark upon a combat mission for which our people and the free people of the world have been waiting for two years. You will spearhead the landing of American force upon the island of Sicily. Every preparation has been made to eliminate the element of chance. You have been given the means to do the job and you are backed by the largest assemblage of air power in the world's history.

The eyes of the world are upon you. The hopes and prayers of every American will go with you.

Since it is our first fight at night you must use the countersign and avoid firing on each other. They bayonet is the night fighter's best weapon. Conserve your water and ammunition.

The term American Parachutist has become synonymous with courage of a high order. Let us carry the fight to the enemy and make the American Parachutist feared and respected through all his ranks. Attack violently. Destroy him wherever found.

Good landing, good fight, and good luck.
(signed) James Gavin
Colonel, Commanding [15]

Sicily was defended by Italian soldiers, some German troops and a few tiny Italian tanks. At least, that's what the paratroopers thought. In reality, Allied intelligence had learned that several highly trained German divisions consisting of 30,000 men and 120 tanks were on the island awaiting a potential invasion. To prevent the Axis from realizing some of their codes had been cracked, this information was not passed down to General Ridgway, Colonel Gavin or any other invading commander. [16] Tanks, especially German tanks, presented the greatest threat to lightly armed paratroopers. Their main weapon against the metal monsters was the bazooka, and Gavin's boys were about to learn the hard way how relatively ineffective bazookas were against the thick metal skin of a panzer.

The Allied plan called for the 505 and one battalion of the 504 to drop hours before the sea landings by American and British forces, to prevent the enemy from reaching the invasion beaches. The primary objective was to take and hold the high ground northeast of the Sicilian city of Gela. The following evening, the remaining 504 men were to parachute in and join the fight.

"Finally the time came to 'chute up' and board the planes, and at 2110 hours the first planes began to take off and by 2116 hours the complete Combat Team was airborne." The first mass regimental combat jump in United States history was about to take place. "As the five serials in the long sky train straightened out in the gathering dusk on the nearly due east course that led to the island of Malta, everything had gone exactly as planned. Thereafter, very little did." [17]

Chapter Five

Sicily: From the Jump to Biazzo Ridge

"Tommy Thompson piloted the plane I was in for the Sicily mission. I stood in the door most of the way watching the Mediterranean. Finally, we seemed to be getting close to the Sicilian coastline, but the red light came on while we were still way out to sea. We hooked up and prepared to jump.

"When the green light came on, the signal to jump, I could see we were still out over the ocean. I blocked the door and of course the men tried to push me out, they were so eager to get out and get the jump over with. If someone stops, they think he's frozen from fear, so they just push all the harder.

"I yelled, 'Get back, dammit! We're still over the water! Get back!' I was holding on and talking to them as fast as I could, trying to hold them up. My orderly, Sanders, was the next guy in line. He could see the ocean too and he helped me fight them off. They almost pushed Sanders and me out the door.

After they stopped pushing, I went up to the cockpit and cussed out Thompson. He said that the co-pilot was nervous and had gotten in too much of a hurry.

"I said, 'He sure as hell did!' and moved back to the door.

"We probably would have all ended up drowning. We were all loaded down with equipment. If you jumped in that Mediterranean, you'd have a hell of a time getting all that equipment off before you ran out of air. Plus, we were still way out to sea.

"I could tell we were actually coming to the coast when the anti-aircraft fire started coming up. We flew in right over an artillery installa-

Paratroopers carried such a heavy load into battle that it was hard to climb into the aircraft. If they jumped and landed in the water, it would be a race against time to cut their chutes, equipment and weaponry loose before drowning. *Photograph courtesy of Bob Murphy*

tion on the shore. The plan was to drop on ground about 350 feet above sea level, but instead we were dropped on an area about 600 to 700 feet high. The aircraft came in at a certain altitude and stayed at it during the jump, so they had not changed altitude to account for higher ground.

"When the green light came on again, I figured we jumped at less than 400 feet because everybody had a quick slam to the earth. I think we had 25 men with injuries, mostly sprained ankles or a bonk on the head. You tried to judge where you were going to hit the ground, so you could pull up on the risers of your chute instead of hitting so hard. But at night it's harder than hell to judge. You really can't do it effectively."

Alexander's chute pulled him backward upon landing, slamming his head into a stone wall, making him see stars. When his head cleared, he was on his back with his head up against the wall. "The tracers were going right over the top of it. I sat up gingerly and stayed there for a little bit, shaking my head. When I got up, I walked up to the top of a little knoll. It was a little foggy. In the dark of night I saw someone standing with his bayonet on his rifle and pointing it at me. Of course I had my gun on him, too."

"George!" The shadowy figure called out the sign. "Marshall!" Alexander called back the counter-sign. The man with the gun pointed at Alexander turned out to be his orderly, Sanders.

The next person they came across was LeRoy Leslie, the F Company radio operator. He was just pushing a dead man off his chest as they approached. An Italian soldier had wounded him with a grenade before he was able to cut his chute off, and Leslie had killed him in hand-to-hand combat. Alexander pointed his .45 and said, "Les, is that you?"

"It's me," he said, still struggling to catch his breath. He managed to get up and gather his equipment, and the three moved on. [1]

Captain Norton was almost killed by the first person he came across. He approached what appeared to be a house and heard low voices. "George!" he called out. An Italian voice called back, "George, hell!" and nearly shot his head off with a machine gun. Norton later learned that he had used the call sign on an enemy pillbox.

The sounds of battle could be heard in every direction. Alexander didn't know it yet, but they had dropped on top of a network of Italian pillbox fortifications. The men from his stick landed in and around a big pillbox and a farm. "We gathered some men and drifted up the hill toward the farmhouse. I wanted to get higher, so I could see more of the surrounding area." There was a rock wall around the farmhouse, and a handful of soldiers were already on the scene.

On arrival, Alexander discovered that a bad event had just taken place. "One of our sergeants had landed ahead of me. He went up to the farmhouse and knocked. An old man with a white beard came to the door and the sergeant shot and killed him. I was heart broken about that, so as soon as I could I went and apologized to the family. But of course that didn't help them any.

"The sergeant was almost crying about it himself. But he was all scared when he first landed and he shot the old man. When men first go into combat, they're not very steady. But they steady down real fast, particularly the volunteers that we had in the paratroopers.

"The sergeant was really a pretty good man. I talked to him about it and told him, 'Don't be jumpy like that. Take your time when it comes to shooting somebody. Especially someone with a long white beard.' I could have brought charges against him, but it wouldn't have been a good idea. Everybody was all keyed up because it was their first time in combat. Things happen and you wish they hadn't. I couldn't think of what else to do besides apologize."

Sixty years later, Wilton Johnson, one of the battalion machine gunners, could still remember the sound of the old man's wife wailing over her dead husband. It was the first civilian casualty that Alexander encountered, but it would not be the last.

"Normally, you locate your CP (command post) in the middle of your planned drop zone. But we were not in our planned drop zone and I didn't have any idea where we were. Fifteen or 20 of us had already assembled at the farm, so I made the house my CP. Norton came in about that time and started setting it up. We were above the large pillbox that was nearby, so the elevation helped protect us from being fired upon."

It soon became clear that the battalion had jumped on and around a concentration of five pillboxes guarding a road intersection. The pillboxes, surrounded by barbed wire, were mutually supportive: if one was attacked, others were positioned to fire on the attackers.

Some in Headquarters Company dropped right on top of the pillboxes and barbed wire. Lieutenant Clee, one of only two battalion surgeons, landed in the wire near one of the larger pillboxes. "Doc Clee was a nice young doctor who had been out of med school about a year," Alexander recalled. Within a minute of entering combat, he was dead, killed by machine gun fire as he struggled to free himself from the barbed wire. Corporal Fred Freeland, who had helped with the mule parachuting experiment in North Africa, also got hung up in the wire near Clee. He played dead and survived.

Patrols were sent out to find other paratroopers who had landed scattered about, and coordinated attacks formed against the Italian positions. One 505er, Sgt. Otis Sampson, single-handedly took out a small pillbox with a grenade. [2]

With Norton running the CP, Alexander went down to help direct fire on a nearby pillbox. "It was a big round one with slits to fire through all around it. It was to the right of the CP, next to the road that led inland from the sea. I don't know why they put it there. It was a stupid place for it. It should have been up on the hill. When it's down below, they can fire back at you, but they take big chances standing behind one of the gun ports.

"I was with the machine gunner and directing him to fire into the fire ports. The assistant machine gunner, Corporal Eider, said, 'I'm hit.' He got one through the neck. I can't figure to this day how it didn't kill him.

And he just bled a little bit. I looked at him and said, 'Eider you're bleeding in the back of your neck.' And then I looked and he was bleeding in the front, too. There was more blood in the back where the bullet went out, but not a lot.

"That bullet the Italians used was about a .25 caliber. Not as big as our .30 caliber. It had evidentially gone right straight through without rotating. That's where it starts to tumble. It would have cut his head off if it had been rotating. And it didn't hit a main artery or his spinal cord.

"I wrapped a bandage around his neck and he continued to fire his machine gun. I always marveled at that. I later left him there still firing at that gun port. His neck started getting sore later in the day, and I turned him over to the doc.

"I went over to directing some mortar fire with Lieutenant Connell on mortar ops. We dropped some mortar around the pillbox and another place not in a pillbox, where we knew there were some Italians. Knocking out a pillbox generally requires a coordinated effort by machine gunners and riflemen. Lieutenant [William] Wilson had the machine gun section. He had his light machine guns pouring fire into the apertures while a guy crawled up along side of it. When we saw that he was ready, we ceased firing with the machine gun and he threw a grenade in. It takes a lot of guts to crawl up to a pillbox. It's not a good job to have. But we were trained to do that. We worked in teams."

After a few grenades detonated inside, a white flag waved out from one of the orifices, and the surviving Italian soldiers surrendered. Corporal Freeland, still stuck in the barbed wire, immediately came back to life and wiggled his way out.

Alexander returned to the command post to find that Jack Norton had things well in hand. Alexander's S-2 was extremely busy gathering and organizing information on the status and supplies of all the companies of the 2nd Battalion. He had also sent out further patrols, which were now bringing in more and more men. "When you drop into an area where you're not supposed to be at night," Alexander commented, "you're wondering where the hell you are." The jump occurred at 1:30 in the morning, and by shortly after daylight, 400 men had made their way to the CP. For anyone unfamiliar with parachute operations, this might seem like a long time to form up. Considering it was a night jump and the battalion was dropped off target, it was, in fact, very fast.

The efficacy of the battalion S-3, Capt. Paul Woolslayer, however, was another matter. Woolslayer had the job of establishing the operations center and planning possible next moves, but Alexander discovered that the only thing he had done was dig himself a large foxhole to hunker down in. Norton had been too busy doing both of their jobs to try to coax him into action.

Alexander was very annoyed. "Woolslayer was kind of the bull of the woods. He had been an All-American football player in college and was real tough back in training." It was he, for example, who had strung the donkey up for bayonet practice in North Africa and (unknown to Alexander) set the booby trap in Alexander's desk drawer that burned his fingers back in the States.

Since his S-3 was clearly not performing his assigned duties, Alexander gave him another task. A two-story pillbox in a better, higher spot was still in action and he sent Woolslayer out to get it. "This one gave us the most trouble. If I looked over the rock wall from my CP, I could see it. They were spraying bullets around the area and directing most of them our way, firing at us from first- and second-story apertures.

"I told him, 'Paul, I want you to take a platoon and circle around and get that pillbox that's giving us so much trouble.'

"He said, 'I'm your S-3.'

"I said, 'I know damn well you are. But that's what I want you to do, and don't come back until you get it.'

"After I said that, he looked at me so damn funny. But I gave him a platoon of men under a good lieutenant named Sprinkle and they went out. They did get that pillbox and one other. Sprinkle and two other men got killed. I'm not sure how much Woolslayer did.

"I learned later that Sprinkle and the other two crawled around in back of the pillbox to get to its door and throw some grenades inside. They were all three shot and killed from the side. I saw them afterward. I knew where the shots had come from by the way they had fallen and where the rounds hit. There was a small, two-man pillbox about 60 yards away, but it was somewhat obscured in the trees. Some sharpshooter there shot Sprinkle and another man through the head and the third man was shot through the body.

"It makes you feel bad. I have often wondered if I should have sent Woolslayer on that job. You ask yourself a lot of questions like that. I don't know if it would have been any different if I had not placed him in charge."

The casualty rate of the officers in the 505 PIR during World War II was as high as that of the enlisted men. This is because they led from the front. Lieutenant Sprinkle, a good aggressive leader, was killed leading an attack that he probably designed himself. The attack was successful, despite the tragic loss; only if he had known about the smaller pillbox nearby is it possible that no one would have died. Woolslayer returned to the CP after the pillboxes had been taken, but he was still on thin ice with Alexander.

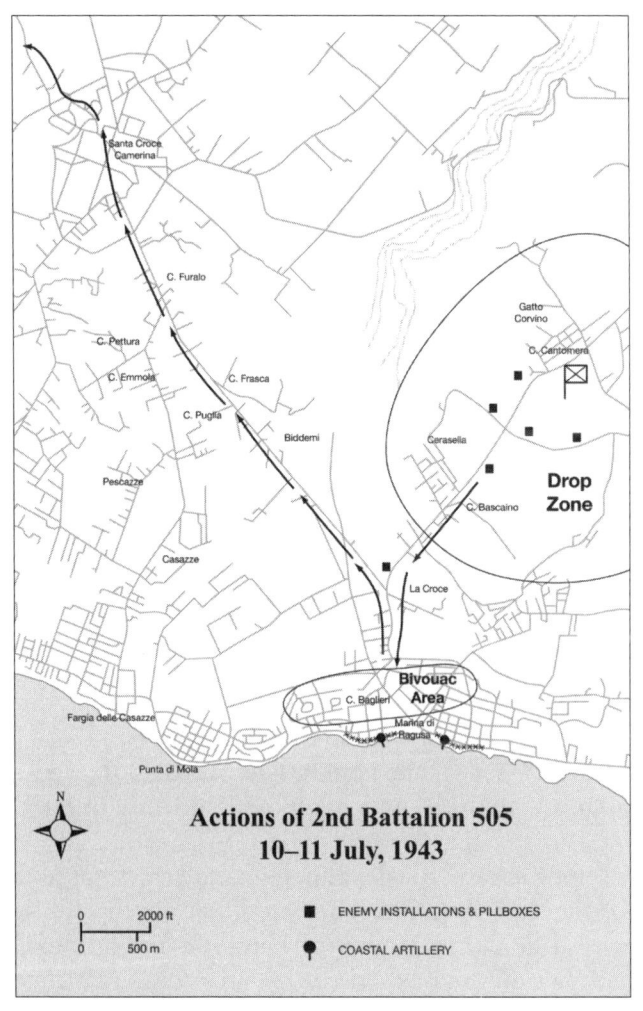

Shows pillboxes and route taken to coast. The 2nd Battalion, 505, landed on and around a group of pillboxes during the morning of July 10 and later marched to the sea, attacking and taking over coastal artillery fortifications. The next morning, they marched northwest on an indirect route toward Gela.

Alexander's men cleared up the pillboxes and other nearby enemy troops by about 10:00 a.m. By that time his fighting force was close to 475 strong. Even better, they had figured out their exact location. The 2nd Battalion had dropped 32 miles southeast of their designated drop zone. They were almost closer to the British than to the American beaches. [3]

After dropping the 2nd Battalion in Sicily, the 64th Troop Carrier Group returned to Oujda. "Colonel Cerny caught hell at Wing Command because he was the only group commander who admitted he had not made the drop on the targeted drop zone." In fact, in large part due to the 30- to 35-mile-an-hour directional wind, only one company and part of another out of the entire 505, and one battalion of the 504, actually landed near the right place. This is less than ten percent of the roughly 3,000 troops that jumped that night.

The 2nd Battalion was further away than most, but Colonel Cerny had kept his promise and dropped almost the entire battalion in one place. "Because of that, I was the only guy that had a full battalion on the first day," Alexander stated. His group was by far the largest, the next being Maj. Ed Krause's group. About half of the 3rd Battalion had found its way together under his command.

"We lost some good men that morning, three officers and six enlisted men. Since Doc Clee was killed, Doc Stein took care of all the wounded. He said that we had 25 or 26 guys with leg injuries of some kind or head injuries," most of which occurred during the jump. There were also a few paratroopers who had been wounded in the fight.

"By 11:00 we had assembled almost the entire battalion, plus 21 men from the 456th Field Artillery, the artillery battalion that supported the 505. One artillery battery jumped with each battalion. Lieutenant Colonel Harrison Harden, the commander of the 456, and one 75mm howitzer cannon with 30 rounds of ammo, landed with ours."

Hardin was senior in rank to Alexander and had the right to take overall command of the 2nd Battalion. "But he didn't attempt to do it. And I was relieved that he didn't. It was my battalion and he shouldn't try to supplant me." Hardin had experience commanding parachute artillery, but not parachute infantry. The men had all been cross-trained on the various weapons: the infantry could all work and fire the 75mm howitzer, just as the artillerymen could all fire a rifle or mortar, but they specialized in different tactics. Hardin also had no previous working

Paratroopers learn to operate and fire a 75mm howitzer on a range at Fort Benning, Georgia. This is the same model that Lieutenant Colonel Harden used to support Alexander's battalion in Sicily. It was parachuted in pieces and assembled on the ground.

relationship with the 2nd Battalion. He did not know their personnel, their individual strengths and weaknesses.

Alexander was pleased to have Hardin and his cannon with them, especially after learning that German tanks were nearby. "My adjutant, Russell, gave me a strength report at noon on D-Day. Our total strength was 536 men, inclusive of the 21 from the 456th. Then I had to decide if we should move to our original objective or stay there and fight. Through my field glasses I could see German tanks up the road to the north. We had been told there weren't any German tanks in Sicily. Paratroopers are lightly armed and don't have much to fight tanks with. I knew if I stayed there, I was gonna have a hell of a fight. I don't know why they hadn't attacked us already. I think it was because they figured either we were too strong for them or they were told not to attack while their main focus was fighting the landings near Gela.

"I decided to move toward our objective over 25 miles away. We couldn't go straight to it, because there was no road and very mountainous terrain that way. There was an extensive Italian coastal artillery fortification at the village of Marina di Ragusa, on the coast to the south of us. The map showed it was on a point of land sticking a little ways into the sea, and I had seen it from the airplane the night before.

"The road went straight down the hill to it. We got the march order out, got the companies in single file lines strung out on either side of the road and started off. That's generally the way you progress. You try to keep at least 20 feet between men because they are less apt to be hit that way. They crowd up a lot of times, talking. But you don't want them to get too close together because if one shell comes in, it's going to get a lot of guys.

"One thing that few people realize is that a good commander covers about twice the distance his men do because he's working his way back and forth, up and down the advancing column. So you've got to be in pretty good shape. That's why it's required that battalion and company commanders be relatively young. You *need* to cover a lot of ground. If not, you're not as likely to know what's going on. And you need to know to make the decisions."

Alexander put the lead company in a spread position to make sure they were not caught off-guard by enemy forces. [4] The fighting that morning had certainly let any and all German and Italian troops in the area know his men were there. They crossed a road junction previously controlled by another pillbox, but the Italians stationed there had wisely abandoned it before the paratroopers arrived.

As Alexander's force approached the coastal artillery installation, the Italians manning it opened up with rifle fire. Their big guns were pointed toward the sea, so they couldn't bring any cannon fire on the paratroopers. Alexander asked Colonel Hardin to use his 75mm howitzer to "throw a few rounds in there and see what happens." Hardin put his gun into action. After two rounds, the Italian commander put up the white flag.

They had several reasons to surrender. "First, knowing that we had some howitzer fire. They didn't like that. Second, we had more men than they did. Third, there was also a British cruiser off the coast, and I think the Italians were afraid we would signal it and really do some damage. I think they kept very quiet in the day, because they didn't want that cruiser to lay a salvo in there. The fortification only had six guns and the British could have really put it to them. Their surrender tickled me to death."

Alexander had one of his men who spoke Italian call them outside. They captured about 60 Italian soldiers under the command of a captain and two lieutenants. In addition to their guns, the fortification had several .50 caliber machine guns facing the sea. The paratroopers disabled the guns, throwing the breach blocks and other weapons into the ocean.

It was now late in the day, and Alexander decided to stay for the night. He moved his entire force along with more than 100 prisoners, some taken in fighting earlier that morning, to high ground north of the village and established a perimeter defense.[5] The guards and the battalion command worked in shifts so that everyone would get some sleep. Alexander and Norton were on for the first shift, and Woolslayer and another staff officer were to take the second for the rest of the night.

"Norton and I took one shift until 4:00 a.m., but before my shift ended we started getting fire from the hillside. Snipers. Two machine guns and several rifles on the hillside above us started spraying our area. They were blind-firing more than anything else."

The ineffective firing had not hit anyone yet, and it was possible Alexander's luck would hold until morning. Alexander seemed to have two options: send men out to drive off or kill the snipers, or ignore them. Instead, he did something else. "That British cruiser was still floating off the coast. Rather than get our men dispersed, because I knew we were going to go out the next morning, I decided to ask them for a hand.

"Well, we couldn't reach them by radio. We couldn't find the right frequency, so I had Lt. Frank Scymkowicz request fire support with a flashlight using Morse code. I always called him Sym. I couldn't pronounce that damn name of his.

"One of the guys asked me how I was going to call for it when I didn't have a map of the area showing coordinates to target. I said, 'Sym, tell them to use the flashlight as a marker and put it in 100 feet over our head.'

"He identified who we were, 2nd Battalion, 505, and made the request. The cruiser immediately laid in two salvos with its four big guns. Then I realized what a salvo from a cruiser could do. It sounded like a freight train going overhead, and the whole slope above us went up in flames. Nobody fired at us for the rest of the night. Nobody.

"I had Scymcowicz thank them before he closed. The British said they would be standing by if we needed anything else. Boy, was I awake then. Later, when we changed shifts, I went and slept for a little bit." These were the largest guns that Alexander ever had support him. Everyone on the hillside was certainly dead. It would be hours before anyone else got into position to snipe again.

While Alexander and Norton slept, Woolslayer was the ranking officer in charge. Alexander awoke several hours later when sniper fire started up again. It was harassment more than anything else, but regardless, he was now awake. "I went down to the basement where I knew Woolslayer and the other officer were, and they were both sound asleep. That really teed me off. I woke them up and gave them hell. I was really mad at them, but particularly at Woolslayer, who was the senior officer." The junior officer was almost relieved, and it definitely was the last nail in the coffin for the S-3.

"That put the clincher on Woolslayer, as far as I was concerned. They were supposed to stay alert until I relieved them. Somebody's got to be on top of the situation all the time. I reclassified him a few days later. Got rid of him. I didn't want him to get anybody killed." Jack Norton was more philosophical about Woolslayer's meltdown, remembering years later that Gavin had commented that every man has his breaking point. [6]

Later that morning (D + 1), the battalion prepared to move toward the invasion beaches and their objective. "The men had assembled the damnedest collection of transports you have ever seen: donkeys, donkey carts, wheelbarrows and even a few Italian porters. One of the men from Headquarters Company came out with a saddle horse that belonged to the Italian captain. It was a beautiful animal, shiny black with white stockings. He brought it to me all saddled up and ready to go. He said, 'You won't have to walk, Major. You can ride this horse.'"

Alexander thanked him but declined. "I wasn't about to get on that horse and ride him up and down the line. I'd be a prime target. Those snipers would pick me out for sure." The trooper who brought it out was a little disappointed, but the horse still went to good use. They tied a machine gun and four boxes of ammo on its saddle. "That sharp-dressed Italian captain had it made there before we arrived. He was the commander and chief of that whole area. He would probably get on his horse and ride out to visit with the signorinas."

Because Doc Clee was killed the first morning, the battalion's only surgeon, Doc Stein, was caring for 32 crippled or otherwise wounded paratroopers. Alexander decided to leave Stein behind with the casualties. There were benefits to this decision, for they had a long way to go and needed to move quickly. Alexander had an objective to get to as rapidly as possible, and taking the wounded would slow the entire battalion. Moving the wounded also often aggravated their injuries, so they themselves were better off staying in one place.

There were, of course, several risks as well. If the battalion got involved in a major fight, they would have only medics to take care of the wounded. Stein and the wounded could also be easily captured or killed by enemy troops. Even if this did not occur, depending on how the invasion progressed, it could be days, weeks, or longer before help could reach them.

Going to war without a doctor is always risky, but Alexander knew that every step closer to the beaches also brought them closer to field hospitals and other doctors. He further thought that no German or Italian soldiers would want anything to do with his wounded. Taking them as prisoners would simply be a burden.

In fact, Alexander had already decided to release most of his own prisoners. "The Italian soldiers decided that they didn't want to fight, especially against our superior numbers." There is no doubt that the Italians fought like hell defending the pillboxes and other strongholds on the initial morning. However, the fanaticism fuelling the German and Japanese war machines was largely missing from the Italian army. This was partly because the Italian officers lived far better than the enlisted men, and looked down on them. Average soldiers viewed themselves in many regards as fighting the officers' war, not their own. Once they learned a new sheriff was in town—that is, that the Allies were there to stay—they generally had a change of heart. With the threat of German reprisal for retreat or surrender no longer looming in their minds, most of them just wanted to return home.

"I didn't want to bother with them anyway. I was supposed to get over to near Gela. It would have been a lot of trouble to take our prisoners with us, and it would have tied up a lot of our men. There wasn't any sense in it. We had one of our Italian-speaking men tell them, 'We're going to let you go, but we are going to trust that you won't get involved in any more fighting.' I could see smiles on some of their faces. They were not very dangerous anyway, because we threw all their equipment in the ocean. We turned loose all but the captain and two lieutenants, who became porters for some of our equipment. [7]

"The men made a hospital tent out of an equipment parachute. We put the wounded in there. I asked two Italian medical noncoms to stay and help Doc Stein. Then we went off and left them, because I figured nobody would want to tackle them anyway."

The battalion organized and strung out on both sides of the road. Because of the shape of the Sicilian coast, there was no direct road between Marina di Ragusa and the American beaches. Deep, rocky defiles made such a path impossible as ridge after ridge dropped down into the sea. The battalion traveled far inland toward the northwest before the men were able to turn toward their goal.

"We marched all day with snipers taking shots at us in route, but they didn't want to tackle us because we were too big a force. We were trying to get to an objective, so all we did was counter-fire and keep moving. We didn't deploy. I wanted to move as fast as possible, not only to get to our original objective, but because there were few trees and very little cover. I had seen German tanks north of us before, and I was afraid that we might get caught in the open with tanks coming after us.

"About noon, we invaded the rather large city of Santa Croce Camerina. We ran some Italians out. They didn't want to stay and fight, and I was glad since my objective was over near Gela." Although Alexander spoke lightly of this battle, there was nevertheless plenty of shooting, but his men had enough firepower to drive the defenders out by mid-morning. His battalion next cleared out the town of Vittoria.

Later in the afternoon they met a patrol in a jeep from the 45th Division, which had successfully landed east of Gela and was moving inland. Alexander's force had cleared a significant portion of the area fronting the 45th Infantry Division's invasion beaches, and the 45th thus got ashore with many fewer casualties than expected, and was able to proceed inland much faster than anticipated. [8]

Alexander now had another decision to make. He could continue straight toward his battalion objective as planned, but that would mean crossing in front of the 45th Division, and passing in front of a unit on the move is a good way to get shot up by friendly fire. "We cut over to the coast road as soon as we could, to get in behind the 45th." Entering the beachhead from the side, the battalion passed through troops holding their ground, guarding the beachhead flank. This gave Alexander's men more time to identify themselves than they would have if they were passing through an advancing unit.

By altering his route, however, Alexander unwittingly caused his men to witness one of the most horrific incidents of friendly fire in the history of warfare. Due to the lack of aircraft and trained pilots, only one full regiment of the 82nd Airborne Division, the 505, and one battalion of the 504 had been able to jump on D-Day. Now, on the evening of D+1, the rest of the 504 was scheduled to parachute in and fortify the beachhead.

"After dark when we hit the coast again, we could see the invasion armada in the water off Gela. From our strung-out position along the coast road, we saw two German bombers fly in, bomb the fleet and fly off. I'd say about two minutes behind them came 48 C-47s carrying the rest of the 504th paratroopers. They came in at roughly the same altitude and from the same direction as the German bombers.

"The navy opened fire. From where I was, I could see the planes were our own, but the navy got excited and just kept shooting. Finally they stopped, but they had knocked down 23 planes. Some of them were able to make a hard landing on Sicily, but a whole bunch of men were killed. Even the 45th Division got in on the shooting. They thought the Germans were attacking." General Keerans, the 82nd Airborne Division's executive officer, on one of the planes that was shot down, was killed along with more than 300 other paratroopers.

The 505 possessed a kinship with their sister regiment that made the emotion of witnessing this tragedy all the more gut wrenching. Alexander's decision not to cross in front of the 45th, however, may well have saved them from taking casualties from friendly fire themselves.

As the 2nd Battalion approached the town of Scoglitti and the rear of the 45th, they came under friendly fire. "I crawled in a ditch toward their line," Alexander recalled, "and argued from a distance to one of their captains for about 15 minutes. I had a heck of a time convincing him that we were U.S. troopers coming through until I started cussing him out—in English, of course. Then he finally had me come forward and identify myself. He called for a ceasefire in our direction and let us pass through.

"The captain told me they thought we were German paratroopers.

"I said, 'What a load of bull you guys are thriving on.'

"As we got closer, I had been able to communicate with General Ridgway by radio. He sent a convoy of trucks that he borrowed from Patton, picked us up and brought us the rest of the way to his command post. I turned our prisoners, the Italian captain and two lieutenants, over to the military government.

"About dawn I met Ridgway at his headquarters. I told him I had a difficult decision to make, whether to stay where I was and fight, or come there for my original mission. The general said, 'Alexander, you made the right decision.' We must have made some of the right moves, as about ten days later I found myself promoted to lieutenant colonel."

Of the three battalion commanders in the 505, Alexander had by far the least experience, and he had only been a major for a short time. The senior commander, Lt. Col. Art Gorham of the 1st Battalion, was killed on the morning after the jump. Alexander was promoted to lieutenant colonel ahead of 3rd Battalion commander Ed Krause, who had more time in grade and in command of a battalion.

Despite Alexander's lack of experience, Gavin and Ridgway clearly liked what they saw of his instincts and leadership in the field. But

Alexander himself continued to feel doubts about his rapid rise in rank, although he was justly proud of battalion's accomplishments, as expressed in this letter to his father: *Just a little before we left Africa, Major Gray, my former battalion commander, was relieved and I was given command; quite a load to take on a battalion one week and jump it in combat the next. Well, we did an excellent job, and as a result I have received a battlefield promotion to lieutenant colonel. I am very proud of it, but it scares me when I think of my responsibility and that only two years and seven months ago I was a private in the National Guard of Kansas. Enlisted October 26, commissioned December 23, 1940.* [9]

Not until after the Sicily Campaign did Alexander learn the details of why, in Ridgway's eyes, he had made the right decision to pursue his original mission and carve a path toward Gela. Up to the point Alexander arrived at the Division CP, the General had just 375 men under his control, only a little better than ten percent of his troops in action. The rest were fighting or surviving as best they could, and he had been without contact with Gavin since the jump. When Alexander showed up with 536 more men, "Ridgway felt a lot better."[10]

At 9:30 a.m. on July 13, Colonel Gavin reached the Division CP, reporting he had gathered 1,200 men. On the morning of July 11, he and the small band of troopers he had been able to muster at that point had unexpectedly discovered and attacked a critically important hill, Biazzo Ridge (also called "Biazza Ridge"). Although this was not part of the original 505 objective, Gavin recognized it as a crucial piece of real estate, ideally situated for launching enemy attacks that would split the American beachheads. If the Axis forces were able to concentrate their firepower on one beachhead at a time, they were far more likely to push the Allies back into the sea.

Gavin's surprising and vicious push drove the Germans off. They soon returned, however, in greater numbers and backed by tanks. Other troopers streamed into the fight. At the end of a long, brutal day, the 505ers still hung on by their bloody fingernails.[11]

In other early fighting, A Company of the 1st Battalion, attached to the 116th Infantry Regiment, 1st Infantry Division, accomplished the objective of almost the entire 82nd Airborne in Sicily. Captain Ed Sayer and roughly 250 men captured and held three small hills, notably Hill 41, blocking German armor from taking another route to the landing beaches. Many men lost their lives in the fighting, and Sayer's exceptional bravery earned him the Distinguished Service Cross. It was here, too, that the 505's senior battalion commander, Lt. Col. Arthur Gorham, met a heroic death as he struck and disabled a Tiger tank with a bazooka.[12]

On July 13, Ridgway ordered Alexander's battalion to Biazzo Ridge, but by the time they arrived the fighting was over. "When I showed up on the ridge the next morning, a lot of our wounded were still lying on the ground. The day before, part of the regiment had a big fight there. I think they had 45 casualties, which means it was a pretty good show. They knocked out a couple of these big German tanks with bazookas.

"I went up to one of the knocked-out tanks. That was as far as I went in that particular area. We dug in on a hillside looking out over a valley with an orchard to our back. We were now behind the front lines in a blocking position in case the enemy made a major push toward the beach."

By afternoon, Alexander had his men dug in on Biazzo Ridge. "The Germans were starting to hit back at us, and several times they sent fighter aircraft in to try to mess us up a little. At one point after we were situated, Norton and I were standing on the edge of an orchard on the front slope of the ridge, watching these ME109s strafing as they flew down the valley. Then they turned and headed right at us. Everybody ran for cover. I stood there a little because I knew I had a foxhole that my new orderly, Cpl. Chick Eitelman, dug for me.

"It's spectacular to watch a plane come in like that, but you don't stand around too long. I turned around to run and take a dive, but when I got back there, my foxhole was full. It already had three guys in it. I jumped behind a tree stump." Alexander was in the crosshairs. Bullets chopped dirt in a B-line straight to the stump, splintering off wood. Then the fighter was gone.

"I always teased Norton about that, saying, 'I bet you were the one that was at the bottom of my fox hole!'" He wasn't. Norton had his own hole to jump into.

Two days later, ambulances picked up the wounded left near the artillery installation in Ragusa. "Doc Stein said that after we pulled out, a German patrol came, looked in the makeshift tent, saw what it was, and went off and left them. They didn't want to take care of anybody else's casualties."

The 505 and 504 stayed in the area for almost a week while stray paratroopers found their units and Patton's divisions solidified and moved past the beachhead. He took the bulk of the American force in Sicily and attacked toward Palermo in an indirect race to beat the British to Messina, a port close to the Italian mainland.

Chapter Six

On to Trapani

AFTER A SUCCESSFUL CAMPAIGN, many 505ers thought they would be going home for a little rest and relaxation. They had certainly earned it. But on July 18, the elements of the 82nd in Sicily—the 505 and 504 PIRs and their supporting units—received orders to relieve the 3rd Infantry Division at Palma di Montechiaro. They were to be prepared "to advance west as part of a Provisional Corps General Patton was forming to take Palermo and clean out all enemy troops in the western part of Sicily. So began the movement, better described as an almost non-stop, 150 miles in 6 days, attack." [1]

The 504 took the lead and attacked through the town of Sciacca. Then the attack turned north, with the 505 leading the way when the 2nd Battalion passed through the 504 on the morning of July 21. Later recalling the terrain through which they passed, Alexander was still impressed by the way the Sicilian peasants managed to farm the uneven and mountainous countryside, terracing with rock and planting on level strips of dirt along a mountain or hillside. "Over centuries, the families had worked at it until they had well-terraced planting areas. They grew tomatoes and squash and other vegetables. I don't remember seeing any corn. They particularly had a lot of tomatoes. They also had a few flat places where they could raise grain, but not many.

"One night we were in a swampy area. My orderly, Chick Eitelman, said, 'I don't know where I'm going to put your blankets tonight.' I told him not to worry about it, but he said he would fix it. There was a wooden shed a little ways off. He tore the whole side off it, carried it over on his back, threw it down and said, 'There, I'm going to put your bed on that. You'll be good and dry tonight.'"

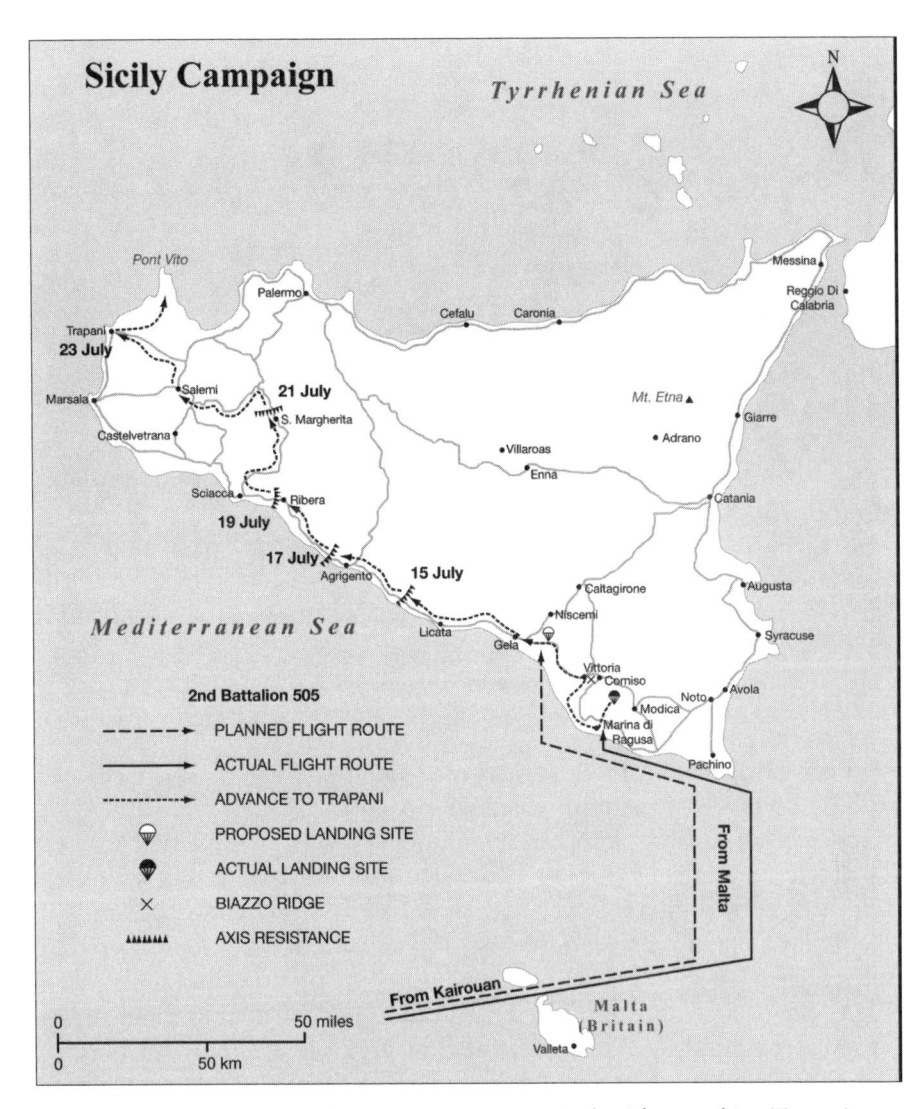

Route taken by the 82nd Airborne Division across Sicily. After reaching Trapani, Alexander led the 2nd Battalion, 505, northeast toward Point Vito. He here had dinner with a very poor, but proud Sicilian mayor, one of his most memorable experiences of the war.

Alexander leading the 2nd Battalion in Sicily, 1943. Following from left to right are company commanders Capt. Neal Lane McRoberts (F Co.), Capt. Talton W. Long (E. Co.), and Capt. Casey Rice (D Co.).

Ever resourceful, Eitelman served Alexander extremely well. He stood about six feet tall, weighed around 210 pounds, and was practically all muscle. Another strong quality was his loyalty. He liked his new boss and took his job as orderly and bodyguard very seriously. "He was a loyal guy if I ever saw one. I think he would have stuck a telephone pole up somebody's ass if I would have asked him to," Alexander mused.

As the 505 crossed Sicily, each battalion had its turn in the lead. At Italian strongholds, the defenders always fired a few shots "for honor" before waving the white flag. "After we had gone most of the way across Sicily, there was a rock escarpment a few hundred feet high—a geological freak. It was very flat on top and a village sat up there. They built it in the old crusader days, and it was a real defensible position. The Italians had a couple of artillery pieces set up there. As we came up, they fired on us, wounding one man and killing another one. I said, 'Wait till we get up here a little further and we'll take care of them.'

"Captain McRoberts, the F Company commander, and I were about ten feet apart. I was explaining that I wanted him to go around quickly

ON TO TRAPANI

Chick Eitelman with his trusty shovel in Sicily.

Chick Eitelman served as Major Alexander's orderly and bodyguard in Sicily, Italy and Normandy.

and come in from the backside. Just then, the Italians fired a cannon and dropped one right between us. I heard a thud and looked down and saw a hole in the ground.

"I said, 'That must have been a dud.' When McRoberts didn't say anything, I looked up and he was as white as a sheet, staring at that hole.

"Then he said, 'Yeah, I think it was.'"

The artillery pieces were firing from a castle fortification called Noreechi. The plan of attack was to move forward so fast that the

Italians would not be able to depress their cannons in time and the Americans would be upon them.

Colonel Gavin arrived and was not very keen on Alexander's plan. He was considering bringing up Allied cannons and launching a larger-scale attack. Captain Norton, knowing a delay and cannon battle could be costly in terms of both time and men, but not wanting to get in the middle of two senior officers, chose his words carefully. "Sir, if we don't go now, we could lose a lot of men." Gavin thought for a moment and then agreed. Alexander launched the attack. [2]

"The second F Company moved, the Italians put up the damn white flag. It made our men madder than hell. They did that to us about three or four times on the march across. It was frustrating because they killed one of our men and we were not given a chance to retaliate. I sent a platoon up on the mountain to be sure everything was okay. There was no resistance. We continued on and walked all the way across Sicily in columns on either side of the road. There were still a few Germans around, but they kept pulling out before we got to them."

They continued the march to the west coast, outside the city of Trapani. The 3rd Battalion, 505, took the city's surrender and the long march was over. During the six days across the country, the 82nd captured 23,191 prisoners. A handful were German and the rest were Italian.

Initially, the 2nd Battalion made camp next to Trapani, one of the few places in Sicily with flat land around it. The 2nd Battalion bivouacked in an orchard adjacent to a small stream. Alexander here wrote to his brother Don back in the United States, describing the accomplishments of his men: *We jumped the morning of July 10 at 0028, thru tracer and flack, right on top of pillboxes and wire. It was rough going for a while, but we had relatively few casualties. My battalion did a wonderful job and I am very proud of them and their accomplishments on the island here. The only trouble with our troops is that they sometimes have more guts than sense. One has to hold them back instead of urging them on. They will walk right into a buzz saw if you tell them to. [...] My regiment alone has captured some 21,000 prisoners. I have had four colonels and five majors surrender to me personally.*

Before jumping into Sicily, Alexander had been given a handful of gold coins to help take care of his battalion, since it was not known how long they would be on their own before linking up with seaborne forces. How he used them was up to his discretion. He now decided to break

Sicily, 1943. Left to right: Famous war correspondent Jack "Beaver" Thompson, Emmitt C. "Sure Shot" Shirley (back to camera), Maj. Mark Alexander, Col. James M. Gavin, Maj. Ed Krause.

into his funds at Trapani. "We were hungry and tired from the fighting and our march across Sicily. I asked our supply officer to get us blankets, vegetables and beef, if available. I supplied him with some gold coins I had been given prior to leaving North Africa, and he found a Sicilian man who spoke passable English. The Sicilian was about 45 or 50 years old and wanted to see the commandant, so they brought him over to me. He said his name was George and he could get anything we needed.

"I said, 'What we need most of all is blankets and vegetables.'"

He said he would have them for us the next morning if the Americans would supply the trucks to make the pickup. The next morning, 16 trucks accompanied George to his warehouse. They came back full of blankets, vegetables and a few other requested goods.

"I placed another order the next day. I said, 'Now we need some meat, if you can get it.' He got it." The trucks again ran out to his warehouse and made the pickup.

"And then, about the third day, the Headquarters Company commander, Capt. Hubert Bass, came to me wearing a big, two-karat diamond ring. He said, 'See that? I bought that for two hundred bucks.'

"I said, 'Wow, Bass, where'd you get it?'

"He said, 'George got it for me.'

"And I thought, 'What the hell is going on here?'" George seemed to have everything the army wanted and a whole lot more. Sicily was not a rich island, and the war was ongoing. Not even in the U.S. were goods so readily available.

"I inquired around about George and found out he had a robber gang. Trapani had been partially vacated because of the war, and they would go out and steal everything I ordered, and have it in the warehouse by morning. He stole the blankets, the vegetables, everything. I also discovered that he had been deported from the United States because he had been a rumrunner on the Great Lakes during prohibition, hauling booze back and fourth from Canada to the U.S.

"I put out the word: 'We'll do no more business with that guy. There are plenty of legitimate Sicilian merchants here to do business with. No more George.'"

Alexander wasn't the only one jumping into Sicily with gold. Undoubtedly the other battalion commanders were provided similar amounts. The man with the most was the regimental supply officer, who climbed aboard a C-47 with a bag of gold worth $25,000. When he jumped, the opening shock tore it loose and it was lost. Some lucky Sicilian hit the lottery that day. But the supply officer was on the hook for all of it, lost or not. After the war it took an act of congress to prevent him from having to pay back the $25,000.

Of the many thousand prisoners captured on the Allied march across the island, the 2nd Battalion had charge of 4,000 men, held in barbed wire containment areas. The vast majority were Italian: the Germans had slowly pulled back in a fighting retreat to the northeastern end of Sicily in preparation for their evacuation through the Port of Messina and across the narrow straight between Sicily and Italy. Because the paratroopers were on the west end of the island, they saw and captured very few of Hitler's "supermen." [3]

All the prisoners had been searched and their weaponry had been removed, as had other items. "My adjutant, Clyde Russell, was supposed to be handling the prisoners. He came in one day walking like his arm was real heavy. He pulled up his sleeve and had wristwatches all up his arm. I said, 'Russell, we're not going to take watches or any other personal property from them. Give them all back.' He thought I was foolish to return the watches, since they were from our enemies. But we wanted Italy to capitulate. We didn't want to fight them or give them a reason to want to fight us." Although the Italians really didn't want to mix it up with the Allies, Alexander knew that could change if word leaked out that their countrymen were being mistreated.

On the other hand, any weaponry stripped off the prisoners was for the taking. Most of the 505ers likely picked up a souvenir of some kind before the prisoners were turned over to the Allied Military Government of Occupied Territories (AMGOT). This was certainly Alexander's case, as Mary here reports in a letter to his parents dated August 13, 1943. *I feel like a millionaire today, for I had a letter from Mark yesterday and today written on the 27th and 29th of July. He said that he's collecting souvenirs like Italian rifles and pistols and flags and that he had a pistol for you, Dad, if he can get the stuff back to the States. He said they jumped with one toothbrush, one razor and one bar of soap and that he lost his in the first day of fighting and has been without toilet articles since. [...] Poor Mark, all that rank and he doesn't even have a toothbrush.*

Now in a bivouac area, Alexander and his men finally had the luxury of taking a bath. The men discovered hot springs and pools upstream from a little creek near the battalion encampment. "The springs were coming out of the limestone on the side of the hill and ran into the stream, forming seven or eight pools of hot water. We hadn't been able to wash ourselves or our clothes in ten days or so, which made this quite a treat.

"I had gotten fleas from sleeping in barnyards along our journey, and was standing out in the middle of a pool with my clothes off, picking the nits from the seams of my jump suit, since I had no change of clothes. I looked up and General Ridgway was sitting on a rock, watching me. I said, 'General, give me a chance to get these wet clothes on, and I'll be with you.'

"He said, 'No, it looks like the job you're doing is more important than the one I have for you. I'll see you later.'"

The fleas were almost as rough on Alexander as the Germans. They would bite anyone, but really seemed to gravitate toward him. They were not the worst of the pests the Americans faced in Sicily, however. Malaria became an increasingly dangerous threat, and a major cause of attrition. Mosquitoes thrived around the stream and hot springs.

"After we had been there [at the encampment] two days, Doc Stein came walking into my CP with his elbow out at an angle. 'I want you to look at this,' he said. There was a mosquito on his arm. He said, 'See, that's an anopheles mosquito. We've got to get out of here or we'll all have malaria soon.' I put in the request immediately, but didn't get authorization to move for another two days. We had already been there three."

Alexander moved camp, setting up a second bivouac area in an olive orchard. The damage, however, was done, and before too long, the men began to come down with malaria. As the side effect of jaundice set in, their skins turned yellow and many were evacuated back to North Africa.

Disciplinary problems also arose in the new encampment. Two of the battalion's demolition men approached Alexander's tent and asked if they could speak to the Colonel privately. "I said OK and invited them in. One of them had a finished wooden box under his arm. Their story was that they had gotten drunk on native wine the night before and blown a small bank vault at a nearby village.

"They took a box of jewelry and Italian money and set it on my desk. They said they were awfully sorry and asked if I would give it back and not let anyone know where I had got it. I said I would try to smooth it out, but fined each one a month's pay and restricted them to hard labor for a week, to be provided by their company commander. I didn't want the details of a court martial any more than they did. I told the company commander of the incident and he agreed to my decision to keep it quiet since we had a war on and didn't want to waste time."

Within two hours, two U.S. Army police officers came into camp. They told Alexander that a small bank had been robbed the night before. Following their leads, they had determined that the perpetrators were from the 2nd Battalion.

"I said, 'If I can get the stolen goods back for you, will you drop the case?'"

They looked at each other and then agreed since there was a good chance they would never find out who robbed the bank. Alexander's desk was an improvised affair, made from a couple of boxes and some boards. He reached into one of the boxes, pulled out the coffer of jewelry and money and set it in front of them. Their eyes popped wide. The Colonel had pulled one over on them. "I could tell they were kicking themselves, because had they pursued it, they would have had the stolen goods and the men who had done it as well." But the police officers kept their word, took the box and left. "After that, I had two very loyal demolition men."

Alexander kept an eye on his bank robbers. They behaved. Meanwhile, word got around in the battalion that he had kept the men out of serious trouble and jail time, which increased his reputation with the troops.

Men were still coming down with malaria, and Alexander and Norton soon had it too. Malaria generally takes ten days to four weeks for symptoms to develop. The best and most used treatment for the disease was quinine. Unfortunately, it came from trees in the South Pacific, and the Japanese had cut the supply as soon as the war broke out.

The only other known treatment was Atabrine, a bitter yellow pill that imparted its own sickly hue to the skin. Some of its side effects were headaches, nausea and vomiting, and in a few cases it produced a temporary psychosis. It was so unpopular with the troops that medics or NCOs stood at the head of mess lines to ensure that the men took and actually swallowed their little yellow tablets. "I hated that damn Atabrine that we took," Alexander recalled. "The Japanese controlled most of the quinine, but the Germans had a supply of it too. And we captured some in Sicily and gave it to the doctors.

Being a battalion commander had its privileges; there wasn't enough quinine to go around to all the sick men, but Alexander was able to receive treatment. "They loaded me up on quinine and knocked the fever down. My head went fuzzy once in a while, but I didn't have bad attacks." [4]

Despite his malaria, Alexander remained in command of his battalion. "Gavin got word that there were still some Germans up at Point Vito, a point of land jutting out into the sea on the northwest tip of Sicily. He called me up on a field telephone and said, 'Get ready to move out right away.' By this time I was feeling lousy. I had both a fever and dysentery. I got off the phone, ran out to the straddle trench and went at both ends. I walked back to my CP and there stands Gavin. His CP was not far away. He must have hung up the phone, immediately got in his jeep and driven down.

"He said, 'Why haven't you moved out yet?'

"I got mad. I said, "Dammit, Colonel, I just called for my company commanders. See there? They're just arriving. I'm going to give them the order and move out right away."

Norton, also in the CP, quickly realized Alexander was likely to land his butt in hot water, so he stepped between his two superiors to try and calm things down. It didn't do much good. "Norton, don't step between us. Get the hell out of the way!" Alexander barked. He was mad and feeling terrible.

This was the only time Alexander was ever angry at Gavin. And Gavin, knowing full well he could come down hard on the junior officer for letting his temper get away from him, smartly chose another route. "Well, OK, Colonel," he said, and left. Gavin had his regiment's unquestioned respect and loyalty and Alexander was no exception.

Gavin, much like Gen. Omar Bradley, didn't do much, if any, yelling. He didn't need to. In this case, he knew there was no need to flex his power, so he didn't. Alexander was no fool, and knew he had pushed the boundaries. If anything, Gavin's reaction made him all the more loyal. Sixty years later, he continued to speak of Gavin's outstanding leadership and how lucky he had been to serve under him.

The 2nd Battalion organized and moved out on foot. After a long forced march, they arrived to find the Germans had already evacuated by boat. The day was wearing thin and the battalion prepared to camp for the night. There was no immediate need to move anywhere. Generals Patton and Montgomery were beating the Axis soldiers back to the northeastern corner of the island, so Alexander's battalion would remain in place. This was fortunate, as it allowed him to see a small slice of Sicilian life that turned out to be one of his most unforgettable experiences of the war.

Soon a visitor approached from a very small village nearby. "He wanted to speak to the commandant. They brought him over to me and he spoke just a little bit of English. He called me 'General.' I said, 'No, I'm a colonel.'"

Alexander asked what he could do for the man. The response was, "Carabinieri no good. You shoot!"

A young paratrooper who knew Italian translated. It turned out that this man was the mayor of the tiny village. The Americans had gotten along well with the Sicilians and the mainland Italians once the initial fighting had ended, but it was becoming apparent that the Sicilians and Italians didn't get along with each other. Apparently, the military police, or carabinieri, were mainly Italian and had taken considerable advantage of the Sicilians. Now the mayor wanted the paratroopers to round up the military police and kill them.

Alexander explained he couldn't very well go around doing that, but he would help the mayor make a formal complaint to the Allied military government that had been set up in Sicily. The mayor was somewhat disappointed but probably not surprised. He continued on to another topic.

"'Do you know my brother Mario?'" he asked through the translator

"No, I'm afraid I don't," Alexander replied.

"'Well, you should know him. He lives in the United States and works for Henry Ford.'"

Bemusedly recalling the incident many years later, Alexander commented, "I tried to explain to him that there were 145 million people living in the United States, and I probably had never met his brother Mario.

"The next day the mayor came back and wanted some 'little sticks.' I couldn't figure out what he meant. Then it dawned on me. He wanted dynamite. He was going to go fishing. I didn't have any dynamite, but I had some concussion grenades and gave him five of them." This method of fishing meant throwing the explosive into the water. After it went off, fish killed by the concussion floated to the surface. There wasn't much sport involved, but it was very effective.

"He was happy and went home and brought me some fish the next day. And the next day, he wanted me to come to his house for dinner." Luckily, Alexander was feeling better, allowing him to accept the invitation.

"He and his family had lived there generation after generation. They didn't move around much. If a family had 10 acres, generally they'd give their sons, and maybe a daughter, a site to build a house on. Consequentially, these little villages would develop. They were very self- and mutually supportive.

"Most of the Sicilians were very poor people. The mayor had a rock house about three car lengths long up on the side of a hill. Half of it was for living quarters. A pig and a cow and five or six chickens had access to the other half. A wooden ladder went up to the loft where they slept. We sat down at a little table, and in one corner of the room there was a hearth about chest high. They were burning bundles of twigs. That's all they had for fuel.

"The mayor's wife cooked the meal and their little ten-year-old girl, waiving a branch with leaves on it, fanned the flies off while we ate. It was spaghetti with some little black pieces of meat. I was afraid to ask him what it was. I was afraid it was going to be dog or cat, or who knows what. They were really starved for food and it could have been anything. Yet it was very good. The spaghetti had little dark specs in it, which means they ground their own meal. There was delicious tomato sauce from the tomatoes growing in terraced areas along the side of the mountain.

"We could talk a bit, because he'd learned a little English from his brother in the States. At the last, he pulled out a bottle of orange wine in a green bottle. He said in very broken English, 'My father made this wine before I was born. I keep a few bottles and want you to have one.' So we drank a bottle of wine together and he gave me another one. It was quite an experience to have dinner with that guy. He was nice and personable and showed me the royal treatment."

After a few days, the battalion marched south again and bivouacked near some small Sicilian airfields. Free time became available. Everyone who wasn't ill was able to venture out on his own or with friends. Alexander posed at a photographic studio near Trapani, and swam in the Mediterranean with Norton and a few others, where he received a scare when a dolphin darted by. On August 20, 1943, the conquest of Sicily was complete. Two days later, C-47s began airlifting the 505 back to Kairouan, Tunisia.

Alexander poses for a photograph in a studio near Trapani, Sicily.

Studio portrait of Alexander, August 1943, at the end of the Sicily Campaign.

CHAPTER SEVEN

RETURN TO NORTH AFRICA AND PREPARATIONS FOR ITALY

"ON THE WAY BACK TO North Africa, Tommy Thompson was my pilot again. I had 20 men in the ship [plane] and another pile of guns, ammunition and equipment waiting to be loaded. It weighed a ton. I said, 'Tommy, I've got a hell of a load on there already. You better look at this before we pile in the rest of it.'

"He looked at it and said, 'Aw hell, throw it in.' We damn near didn't get off the ground! And when we got back to North Africa, we pancaked from about 20 feet, tore up the suspension, and the plane ended up against the fence at the far end of the field before we were able to stop."

The Sicilian campaign had been a success, but many in the upper echelons wanted to cancel all further airborne operations. The paratroopers had been very, very badly scattered and jumped up to 40 miles from their intended drop zone. Eisenhower was furious when he learned about all the 504th men killed by friendly fire, and questioned the wisdom of trying it a second time. (A very similar, but less deadly, fiasco in the British sector had occurred a few days after the 504 tragedy.)

Nevertheless, a single company of roughly 125 paratroopers had managed to accomplish almost the entire objective of the division, which numbered more than 5,300 men in Sicily. [1] Patton, who led the American landings and troops, came to the rescue, saying he would have been held up on the beaches for an extra 48 hours without the parachute landings. He very likely saved the day. Ike decided to give them another chance, but changes were necessary. Gavin set in motion a program to find new technologies and techniques to avoid repeating the many miscues of the first jump.

In other fallout from the Sicily campaign, Lieutenant Colonel Hardin, whose 75mm cannon had come in so handy to Alexander on D-Day, lost his rank and assignment once the shooting ended. "In my military career I saw only two officers get demoted—not just transferred, but demoted," Alexander noted. "One was in Sicily. The division had a regiment of artillery, which served under Colonel Taylor, the artillery commander for the 82nd Airborne Division. Taylor had ordered the 456th Artillery Battalion, attached to our 505, to take all mortars into combat. No 75mm howitzers.

"Lieutenant Colonel Hardin, commander of the 456th, who landed with us near the pillboxes and fired his cannon into the Marina di Ragusa Italian fortification, was in trouble. He took his big gun with him to Sicily. When Taylor found out about it, he busted him from lieutenant colonel down to major and sent him back to the States. I thought that was a lousy way to handle it."

A second factor also likely contributed to Hardin's demotion. As the 82nd was fighting to take Trapani, Ridgway ordered Hardin's cannons to move forward and take on Italian artillery. When the Italians opened fire, Hardin's men scattered. General Ridgway calmly walked out to the abandoned guns, putting himself at risk. This act buoyed the spirits of the gun crews, bringing them back into action. Apparently Ridgway believed there was a lack of leadership on Hardin's part and ordered Taylor to relieve him. [2]

On August 24, 1943, Alexander wrote home to his parents, noting that Norton had returned from Sicily, where he had been hospitalized for malaria, and that replacements had arrived. *Today we received many new officers and men fresh from the States. They are a good, clean-looking bunch and are eager to get at this business of whipping hell out of the Axis. I have known all along that we have a wonderful group of officers and men in parachute works, but the most outstanding characteristic about them is their fearlessness and guts. Honestly, if you told them to, they would walk right into a buzz saw. In Sicily they earned the admiration of fighting units all along the line for their aggressive spirit and desire to get at the enemy. A great deal of what you read in the papers is true. Some of it, of course, is just poppycock.* [3]

Alexander had Norton back, but not for long. Colonel Gavin promoted him into the regimental staff and put him to work improving C-47 navigation and identification aids. No one, all the way up to the president of the United States, wanted a repeat of the Sicily drop, especially the horrible friendly fire incident.

Once again Gavin asked Alexander to choose his battalion exec, and once again Alexander asked Gavin to pick an Academy man for him. Gavin picked Capt. James McGinity, a West Point graduate, class of 1936, who had served in Panama before the war with the 503rd Parachute Battalion, one of the earliest formed at Fort Benning. He had a clear understanding of the inner workings of the army, which was something Alexander still believed to be his weak spot. Alexander liked the choice. McGinity was a friend from Fort Benning and Fort Bragg, before the 82nd shipped out for Africa. He had bought a dress in North Africa for Mary Jo right after she was born and sent it to Mary back in the States.

The 505 immediately went into intensive training in North Africa to incorporate the new soldiers and prepare for the next combat mission. This included several night jumps, weapons practice and unit maneuvers. Alexander soon was incensed to learn that "every one of those air force guys who had flown us into Sicily had been decorated. Every one of them. And they dropped us all over the place. Very few landed on the button, where we were supposed to be." He went to the camp that housed the air personnel, and inquired as to where he could find Tommy Thompson. He was directed to a tent with a pair of feet sticking out the front. They were indeed Thompson's, and he was, for the moment, enjoying a nap.

"On the way down there, I'd picked up a tent peg, and I hit him on the bottoms of his feet. He let out a yell. I said, 'You son-of-a-bitch, come on out fighting. I'm going to whip the shit out of you for dropping us over 25 miles from where we were supposed to be.'

"He sat up and said, 'Jesus, Alexander, I'm staying right where I am while we talk this over.'

"I laughed and wasn't really mad at him. But I was kind of annoyed they all got decorated for the misdrop. Particularly, everyone in my plane could have ended up drowning. We were loaded down with equipment. If we had jumped in that Mediterranean, we would have had a hell of a time getting all that equipment off before we ran out of air."

Alexander was just giving his friend a bad time. A few days later he and Thompson, who still had a lot of daredevil in him, had a closer look at Kairouan. "Kairouan was a holy city with big 80-foot walls clear around it. And no infidel was supposed to go in there. They would chop you up into little pieces if you did.

"We had a wire connection to the airfield. One day Tommy Thompson called me up and said, 'Alexander, I have a cub [a small two-seat plane] for us. Do you want to take a flight with me to look around?'" Alexander agreed and went out to the airfield.

"We climbed in and he said, 'Let's go look at that holy city.' We fly over there and he put the plane into a dive down to about 50 feet, inside the city walls. These old religious guys ran off in all directions. They were having a fit. If they could have done it, they would have knocked us out of the sky. I know that.

"On the second pass, they were down on their knees praying and moving their arms up and down. I said, 'Tommy, let's get the hell out of here before they drop us!' Anyway, I had a look inside the courtyard," which was a rare view indeed for a Christian.

"We flew from there to the only lake around that area. We flew over it and thousands of birds were down on the water. Tommy said, 'Let's go down and have a closer look.'

"I said, 'No, no, Tommy! Don't do that!' but he was already diving. The birds got scared and came up from everyplace. We hit three of them, but luckily none hit the prop or caused serious damage to the plane." As Thompson proved, you can take the pilot out of his fighter, but can't take the fighter out of the pilot. He flew like a fighter pilot, regardless of aircraft.

On September 3, 1943, Alexander again wrote to his parents from Kairouan to let them know as much as he could about the likely near future for his unit. *We have been back here in Africa a week and a half now and it is only a temporary stop. Today the English and Canadians opened up on the boot of Italy. There'll be no stopping now. Will try and let you know as soon as possible where I end up. [...] Yes, the British are everywhere over here and they have some damned fine soldiers. Right now the British Eighth Army has beaten us to the punch with the Italians.*

He also expressed his views on the dismal conditions in North Africa and the longing for any- and everything American felt by all the men. *It is now 5:45 p.m. I have just 15 minutes before chow. It will be a rather gritty one as we are having a rather mild sand storm. [...] Believe me, my appreciation of the American way of living has improved with lack of contact with those very same things. I haven't seen a Coke or beer since I landed in Africa. G.I. stew has become abominable; picture shows—well, I saw two in Oujda, but the sound and projection were* *almost a blur. These boys of ours will pay $25.00 for a Coke anytime, or anything just for the sight of an American woman. I might even walk a few blocks just to see a pert American lassie.* [4]

As Alexander foresaw, the 505 was soon embroiled in the fighting on the mainland. Gen. Bernard Montgomery (British Eighth Army) invaded the southern tip of Italy on September 3, followed on September 9 by Gen. Mark Clark (U.S. Fifth Army, attached to the British), whose forces made a major assault at Salerno on the western coast, code-named Operation AVALANCH. The 82nd Airborne Division, now refitted and ready to deploy, did not take part in the initial assaults, but stood at the disposition of General Clark while numerous plans for supporting airborne missions were proposed then quickly abandoned.

Alexander vividly described the frustration and uncertainty of the planning period. "We battalion and regimental commanders were informed that our next mission would be a night jump on the Volturno River in Italy, north of Naples. My battalion had the mission of jumping on Arnone and Cancello [also called Conchello]," two villages straddling the river about seven miles inland from the sea." The rest of the 505 would also be at the Volturno, controlling different crossings, while the Fifth Army fought its way on shore approximately 40 miles away at Salerno Bay; if all went well, the infantry would tie in with the 505 within 48 hours.

The airfield near Comiso, Sicily. The 2nd Battalion, 505, camped nearby in preparation for an invasion jump onto the Italian mainland.

"In studying and preparing for the mission, none of us were even slightly enthusiastic about the plan, as we had little confidence that the seaborne attack would reach us in two days. If they were late, we would be in a lot of trouble because our lightly armed men would be fighting against German Marshal Kesselring's armored divisions." But that was the plan, and they would make the best of it. Because the jump would be over Italy, the paratroopers were moved back to Sicily, much closer to the target, where they settled in near airfields outside of Comiso and trained, trained, trained.

One exercise pitted the 2nd Battalion against the 3rd Battalion. The 3rd was normally commanded by Maj. Ed Krause, but in this instance Maj. Ben Vandervoort took his place. The 3rd went one way around a small mountain range and the 2nd was sent another. The object was to gain a superior position to defeat the opposing battalion when they met on the far side of the range. Similar to actual war, there really were no rules.

"They had a shorter, more direct route. We had to go further around, but we fooled them," Alexander recalled. "Instead of going around the mountain, I spotted a path heading up the side of the range. I then found a little Sicilian guy and gave him one of the gold pieces I originally jumped with to guide us over that mountain at night."

The range had escarpments climbing to around 3,000 feet. The route taken over the range probably peaked at 1,100. The hip Alexander had injured on a jump back in the States became aggravated. "I would stub my toe or something and it would kick that off so that I could hardly go. My hip was hurting me that night and I remember I was groaning all the way across that mountain. It was about a twenty-mile march and I mean, it hurt. But I made it all right. I used my carbine as a crutch part of the way. That was a *long* night."

It took nearly the entire night to go up and over, coming down into a canyon on the far side. Alexander determined the route the 3rd Battalion would follow. They would come up a path about five feet wide near the base of the canyon. "I got there first and split my forces. I had everybody stay quiet down behind the rocks on both sides. I said, 'Nobody moves or shows his face until I fire a round.' They were then allowed to fire one round apiece into the air, so it would really startle Vandervoort's men.

"The other battalion had no idea where we were going. Even the controller was trying to figure out where the hell we were. He thought we would meet on the other side of the mountain. When it got light, he kept saying over the radio, 'Where are you, 2nd Battalion? Where are you, 2nd Battalion?' Well, I didn't answer. I told nobody else to answer. If I would have, the 3rd Battalion could have picked it up too.

"The 3rd Battalion marched up the road, and we let a whole company and half of the next get into the middle of us before we cut loose on them. The guys stood up and cheered and some of them got exuberant and fired rounds in the air. They really got a kick out of ambushing the 3rd Battalion. That was fun."

Meanwhile the planners for the jump at the Volturno River in Italy had a change of heart and decided that it was too risky to assume the landing force would reach the paratroopers within two days. "Finally good sense prevailed and the mission was cancelled." It was, however, replaced by an even riskier plan, which called for the 82nd Airborne Division to jump on or near three airfields east and north of Rome. The 2nd Battalion had the mission of jumping on the main Rome airfield and holding it for air landings that would bring in reinforcements. The Italians had secretly agreed to turn on the Germans and help take Rome.

"None of us thought that was a good deal in Rome because we had heard there were a lot of German troops there." This proved out when it was discovered there were three, possibly four, German divisions within 20 miles of Rome. "They would have chewed us to pieces because two of them were armored and we didn't have much in the way of protection. We had bazookas and mines and that's about all." It also became evident at the last minute that the Italian Army would be of little help and would probably be unable to control the enemy anti-aircraft batteries over which the 82nd would fly.

Because the 505 RCT jumped first into Sicily, the 504 RCT would lead the attack on Rome. One 504 PIR battalion was loaded in C-47s and ready for take off when this mission was scraped. "The cancellation of the Rome operation was a great relief, as several of us, knowing the background by this time, had no confidence in the airborne planners at Fifth Army. I'd often thought afterwards, if we had gone in there, they would have wiped us out. We would have been cut to pieces before Allied reinforcements could get to us. I breathed a sigh of relief when they canceled that jump. It would have been a suicide operation."

The Allied Fifth Army would attack. That much was certain: it was simply a matter of where. Their planners reverted back to the original scheme. Although the paratroop jump on the Volturno River was cancelled, the seaborne assault would proceed. Clark's Fifth Army made an amphibious landing at Salerno Bay and heavy fighting ensued.

Italy capitulated on July 8, and Mussolini was overthrown. King Victor Emmanuel III resumed full constitutional powers on July 24. The new Italian government entered into secret talks with the Allied high command, and about the time Clark began his attack, the king announced over the radio that the country was switching over to the Allies. The Germans immediately swooped into Italian positions and made sure there was no uprising against them. The Italian Army would not help the Allies; but more significantly, it would not hurt them either. It was a large chink in the Axis war machine.

German Marshal Kesselring, who commanded all German forces in Italy, rushed tanks and men against Clark's Fifth Army. Soon the Americans lost most of the ground they had gained and were in danger of being thrown back into the sea. General Clark sent an urgent message to Ridgway on September 13 asking for "an immediate drop."

"Can do," was the General's answer.

It was still the 504 RCT's turn to spearhead an airborne operation. The regiment and Company C of the 307th Airborne Engineers loaded up that very night and jumped onto General Mark Clark's shrinking beachhead near Paestum. The 505 RCT would shortly follow.

Since the Sicily drop had been so badly scattered, measures had been taken to help the pilots stay on target. Navigational aids created and tested by Jack Norton and his team went into action. The most successful was probably the Eureka radar devices, which helped guide the C-47s. [5] Ridgway had also ordered the formation of a group called the pathfinders, who would fly into enemy territory with the best pilots and jump onto the drop zone before the rest of the troop transports arrived. They would set up the Eurekas and radio beacons, then raise two long poles (reminiscent of fishing rods), with two bright battery lights at the tip of each to draw oncoming pilots.

The 505 RCT had 24 hours to prepare for the jump on Italy. The next night, September 14, the 505 PIR and Company B of the 307th Airborne Engineers boarded C-47s and flew toward the beachhead.

Chapter Eight

From Salerno to Naples

"Tommy Thompson was my pilot again when we jumped into Italy. Ahead of us they already had a beachhead under General Clark, but they were getting the hell kicked out of them. We went in at night as reinforcement and landed behind our lines right next to the beaches at Salerno Bay. It was a much better deal than juamping into Rome."

The drop zone was an area about 1,200 yards long and 800 yards wide, located next to the sea in the southern section of the beachhead. General Ridgway said that control of anti-aircraft fire was absolutely essential after the disaster in Sicily. All such guns on land and with the fleet were silenced from 9:00 p.m. until further notice from Ridgway. Even if German bombers attacked the fleet, no one could return fire. No anti-aircraft balloons were to be flown.

This was the first time that pathfinders were used for an operation. "In addition to the Eurekas, or radar sets, they had flare pots for us to guide in by, which were cans full of sand and gasoline, lit on fire and aligned to form a giant T. The pilots had a much easier time finding the drop zone. Nearly all of us landed in the right place.

"Right after landing, I looked up and I saw a big British Somali soldier standing there in the firelight grinning at me. They had helped set up the pots. I was tickled to see him. It's nice to see a friendly face right after a combat jump. The Somalis had a very good regiment there. They were good fighters."

The 505ers who made the jump remember it as the easiest of the regiment's four combat jumps. The men landed together and formed up quickly. Their drop zone at Salerno had already been the scene of action the night before, September 13, when the 1st and 2nd Battalions of the

504 PIR had jumped into Italy, their 3rd Battalion arriving on LCIs. The 504 had fought like hell and turned the tide of the battle in favor of the Fifth Army. The beachhead was saved and the Americans were not thrown back into the sea.

There was still plenty of work to do, however. First they needed to push the Germans back and break out of the beachhead. "We organized right away and they marched us up into the mountains to relieve the 504 at Castel San Lorenzo, a little village on the mountainside east of the bay. It looked like they had a hell of a fight. There were dead Germans lying all over the place.

"I remember the contrast in the way people lived in that village. There was one three-story castle-like building. Everything else was

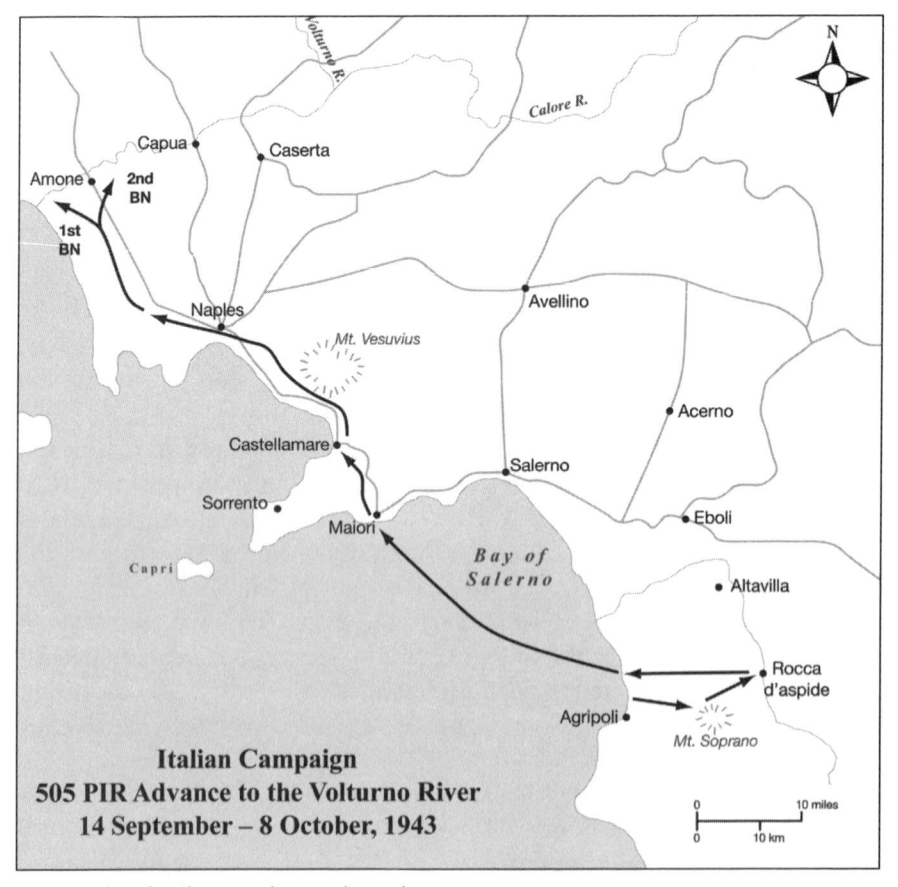

Italian Campaign
505 PIR Advance to the Volturno River
14 September – 8 October, 1943

Route taken by the 505 during the Italian campaign

single-story rock houses, except possibly the church. The castle-like place was the home of the mayor of this village. I didn't use it as my command post. I used a smaller house, but I went inside the mayor's place to see what was there. The ground floor held chickens and pigs and a cow. On the second story lived his relatives, who worked for him as servants. The mayor was up on the third floor and had mahogany and chrome furniture and all kinds of fancy stuff. That was the social strata. The mayor was the richest man in town."

Alexander and his men remained at Castel San Lorenzo while the beachhead was expanded and fortified. Then the Allies got back onto the offensive. The initial goal was to capture the large city of Naples some 50 to 60 miles to the north along the coast.

When the 2nd Battalion moved out, they left their barracks bags in a pile close to a dairy building. Private Turk Seeley was ill that day, so a lieutenant ordered him and three others to take care of the bags while everyone else continued on. Alexander and his men moved off, thinking their clothing and personal items were in good hands.

"We fought our way up along the coast toward Naples," Alexander recalled. "The 3rd Battalion advanced on the main road and I was given the inland area going over the foothills." The actual fighting was sporadic. Luckily, the Germans were using delaying tactics and not making a serious defensive stand anywhere. "There were a couple of German mortar-firing guns that gave us a bad time—20mm and 40mm guns, which fired either anti-tank or explosive shells. They used explosive ordnance here, which was rough on infantry. They accounted for some of our men being hit.

"Initially I had my battalion in a spread formation, but there wasn't too much resistance, so I only had the lead company advance that way. When we got real close to Naples, the Germans pulled out ahead of us and left the city open."

The Italians were told that there would be a big reception for Gen. Mark Clark. Most of the troops were held back and Clark and Ridgway rode into Garibaldi Square as conquering heroes. The only problem was that the square was completely empty! The cheering citizens of Naples were missing. Quick investigating found that the Italians were all in the other big square across town, awaiting their liberators. The Generals were rerouted and made their high-profile entrance in front of the cheering crowd.

Most of the city's inhabitants were happy the Allies had arrived. Like

2nd Battalion men in the middle of a busy Italian square. The 82nd Airborne policed the devastated and starving city of Naples.

everyone else, the Neapolitans were tired of war. But a far more important reason was that the populace was incredibly hungry. The Germans had disrupted and destroyed much of the city before withdrawing. There was no electricity, the port was in ruins, and the water supply from north of the city would soon be cut off.

That night, as the Allies began to get situated in the big city, German soldiers were found occupying a small airfield on a nearby plateau. Gavin sent Alexander's battalion to take care of them. As recounted by Ed Ruggero, trooper Frank Spence gave a colorful account of the events:

> On a moonless night, the GI's crept forward, trying to stay on line, even though they couldn't see one another. Every once in a while, Spence could make out Alexander's silhouette against the starry sky. The men were twenty feet apart, moving slowly, listening over the pounding of their own heartbeats for the enemy. Spence could barely see his weapon in his hands; he was

afraid he'd fall into a German position and be killed before he could get off a shot. He was afraid he might get lost or make some noise that would endanger his buddies.

"Suddenly we heard a tank engine—real loud and real close. There may have been more than one. We couldn't see them, but we could hear them, and they were headed right for us."

The paratroopers went to ground. They had seen how a moving tank can crush a man flat.

Then the tanks stopped. They weren't fifty feet away, idling

Someone had to figure out if they were enemy tanks, in which case the troopers would withdraw. If the tanks were friendly, they would move forward and continue the mission.

But the man who spoke up would give away his position and—if the tanks were German—most likely be gunned down. There was a long moment as every paratrooper waited to see what would happen next.

"Mark Alexander called out, 'Who's there?'

"A guy yelled back, 'It's us, the Brits.' Bravest thing I ever saw." [1]

As the 2nd Battalion continued on its mission, the Germans became aware of the approaching Americans and put their mortars into action. "They were dropping shells around us," Alexander recounts, "and during one barrage, everyone dove for cover on the side of the road. One guy thought he was diving into a ditch, but he really dove into a German straddle trench. I heard him cussing and said, 'Why don't you get out of there?'

"He said, 'I'm already in here. I'm going to stay until they stop shelling.'

"When we got to the tiny airport, there was a little shooting, but it was just a small group of Germans, and they had mostly pulled out ahead of us. We didn't have any casualties. Neither did the Germans, as far as I could tell. I really don't even know how many were there. It was blacker than hell that night."

While other forces moved north to pursue the slowly retreating enemy, the 82nd Airborne stayed in the Naples area and policed the city.

Initially, the 2nd Battalion's duties included policing the nearby hillsides as well. "We set up our tents and camped northeast of the big city on the side of one of those mountains. The first morning, a report came to me that one of our men had broken into the home of the mayor of a nearby village. The soldier had followed the mayor's daughter home the afternoon before."

Alexander took the young woman to identify the perpetrator. He then "took care of him." It's unknown whether that meant punishment or handing him off to be handled by Division Headquarters. What is certain is that the girl's father was pleased with the result.

"That afternoon the mayor himself came down on a donkey and he had a box for me that held five green handmade glass bottles full of wine. He spoke a little English and I had an interpreter there. We visited for a while, and before he left he said, 'You please bring green bottles back. Green bottle make better wine than clear bottle. Very old bottles. Hand-blown bottles.'

"I couldn't argue with him on that. If he said green bottles made better wine, well, then I guess they did.

"I was sure to get the wine around to the company commanders and we kept a couple of bottles for my battalion staff. I invited my staff to my tent for a drink. It was a small tent, maybe 6' x 10' that you could stand up in. Then after a while I said, 'That's enough, fellas. Let's break it up and get some sleep.'

"My adjutant Russell had gotten a little drunk. He hung around and started to get kind of nasty because I had taken over from his favorite, Major Gray. He started getting kind of smart-assed, letting me know that Gray would have done things differently. And I said, 'Russell, either get the hell out of here or I'm going to throw you out on your ass.' He left. I never had much trouble with him that way, but he was a favorite of Gray's and he kind of resented the fact that I had taken over the battalion. But he squared away and I never had any trouble from him after that."

As requested, Alexander made sure to return the green wine bottles.

After two days in the hills, the unit returned to Naples. The crescent-shaped city, built almost entirely of white and pastel-colored stone and cement, started at the water's edge and rose back and away onto an ever-steeper slope. [2] Each of the 82nd's regiments, the 505 and 504 PIRs and the 325 GIR, patrolled a third of the city. This was not a small feat, since it was home to more than a million people. Before retreating, the Germans had done a thorough job of destroying the city's infrastructure. During their occupation, riots broke out twice when the Allies tried supplying food and water to the desperate people. [3]

One of Alexander's men, Pvt. Spencer Wurst of F Company, describes the plight of the people:

The civilian population of the city was starving. The going price for prostitutes was one K ration or a C ration. Later, as the rear-echelon military personnel increased, the market price doubled to two C rations. Even at this low price, parents were actually selling their daughters into prostitution in order to provide for the rest of the family.

One of our many duties was to enforce discipline along the breadlines at the military government-established ration distribution points. Without strict control over the distribution of food, the situation quickly got out of hand. Life-support facilities were virtually non-existent. Safe drinking water, sanitary sewers, electricity, gas, food, supplies, transportation, medical services, refuse collection—in short, everything that makes a metropolitan area function—had been destroyed.

The black marketers were making a lot of money, but people on the poor end of the scale had a hell of a time staying alive. At the distribution points, we had to fix bayonets and actually prod the people into lines to keep them from going into mob action as we handed out food. Yet, after duty hours, any soldier who had the money—and most of us did—could walk a block or two, be seated in a black market restaurant complete with linen table cloths and candles, and be served a nice steak dinner with all the trimmings. Returning from the restaurant to our billets, we witnessed adults and children picking through garbage cans outside our mess areas. [4]

Alexander and his staff "set up Regimental Headquarters in a six-story building just off Garibaldi Square. After we had been there two or three days and water had been restored, my orderly, Chick Eitelman, asked to speak to me privately. He said, 'You go up to the sixth floor. In an apartment on the right, I've got electricity hooked up to the water tank and you can have a hot shower. You better not tell anyone for a while. They're all going to want to go up there.'

"I went up and took a bath, because it was hard to get a bath in those days. It was the first one I had in eleven or twelve days. I told two or three guys who followed me up there, and pretty soon everybody knew about it. Chick was quite a guy."

That is an understatement. Eitelman, in addition to being resourceful and loyal, had a heavy streak of ingenuity in overcoming obstacles,

The very resourceful Chick Eitelman.

including the lack of much-needed vehicles. The Nazis left Naples with very little motorized transportation. The lightly armed paratroopers did not have dedicated jeeps or trucks, other than a few for the brass. All Allied military transportation was used to move or supply the units chasing the Germans north. As Alexander put it, "we were short on jeeps about that time. Really, really short on them."

The ever-resourceful Eitelman found a broken, abandoned German motorcycle with a sidecar. He loved motorcycles and got it running, but

Mark Alexander in front of his Fiat. Chick Eitelman found the car in a barn in Naples after the Germans abandoned the city. He replaced the swastika with the American star.

Alexander sits on the passenger side of his "liberated" Italian Fiat on the outskirts of Naples in a photograph taken by his driver and bodyguard, Chick Eitelman.

it wasn't quite as good as new. Many years later, the memory was still vivid in Alexander's mind. "There were two holes in the gas tank where a bullet had entered and exited. When he drove me around, he would chew gum all the time and stick it over the holes. When it would start leaking, he'd put a new chew on it. It did catch on fire a couple of times from gas leaking out.

"Later Chick found a Fiat that the Germans hid away in a barn somewhere. He just took it without looking for the owner since it was marked with the swastika. Some German had moved out in a hurry and left it. Chick painted over the fascist markings on the side and put on our identification. He drove it in and said, 'I got you some better transportation.'"

It sure beat walking.

CHAPTER NINE

TO THE VOLTURNO: THE BATTLE OF ARNONE

"WE HAD BEEN POLICING NAPLES for a few days when I was called to headquarters and given a new assignment. My 2nd Battalion was officially attached to the British 22nd Armored Brigade, a regiment reinforced with tanks and artillery commanded by Brig. Gen. H.R. Arkwright. I reported to him for my orders."

The 2nd Battalion trucked to a position about halfway between Naples and the Volturno River to the north, just short of the area held by the Germans. Their mission was to seize five canal bridges en route to capture the town of Arnone, which sat on the Volturno River. One main road crossed all five bridges, and a railroad track off to the left also converged on Arnone. The bridges were essential to the movement of General Arkwright's armored brigade and to crossing the Volturno.

Alexander described the area as good land. "Much of Italy is mountainous and all they can do is build those shelves along the mountain sides with retaining walls made out of rock," but this was "a mostly flat area where they irrigated from the Volturno. The people who lived there were fairly well-to-do if they owned enough land with productive soil."

By strange coincidence, the area around Arnone and Cancello, directly across the river, was the originally assigned drop zone for the 2nd Battalion in Italy. Before the operation was cancelled, the 2nd Battalion's mission was to jump on and occupy these villages. This importantly involved seizing the rail and highway bridge, which both crossed the Volturno, and the bridges over the canals. Alexander had carefully studied aerial photos of the area and knew the locations of pillboxes, buildings, and other important features, which helped to

TO THE VOLTURNO: THE BATTLE OF ARNONE

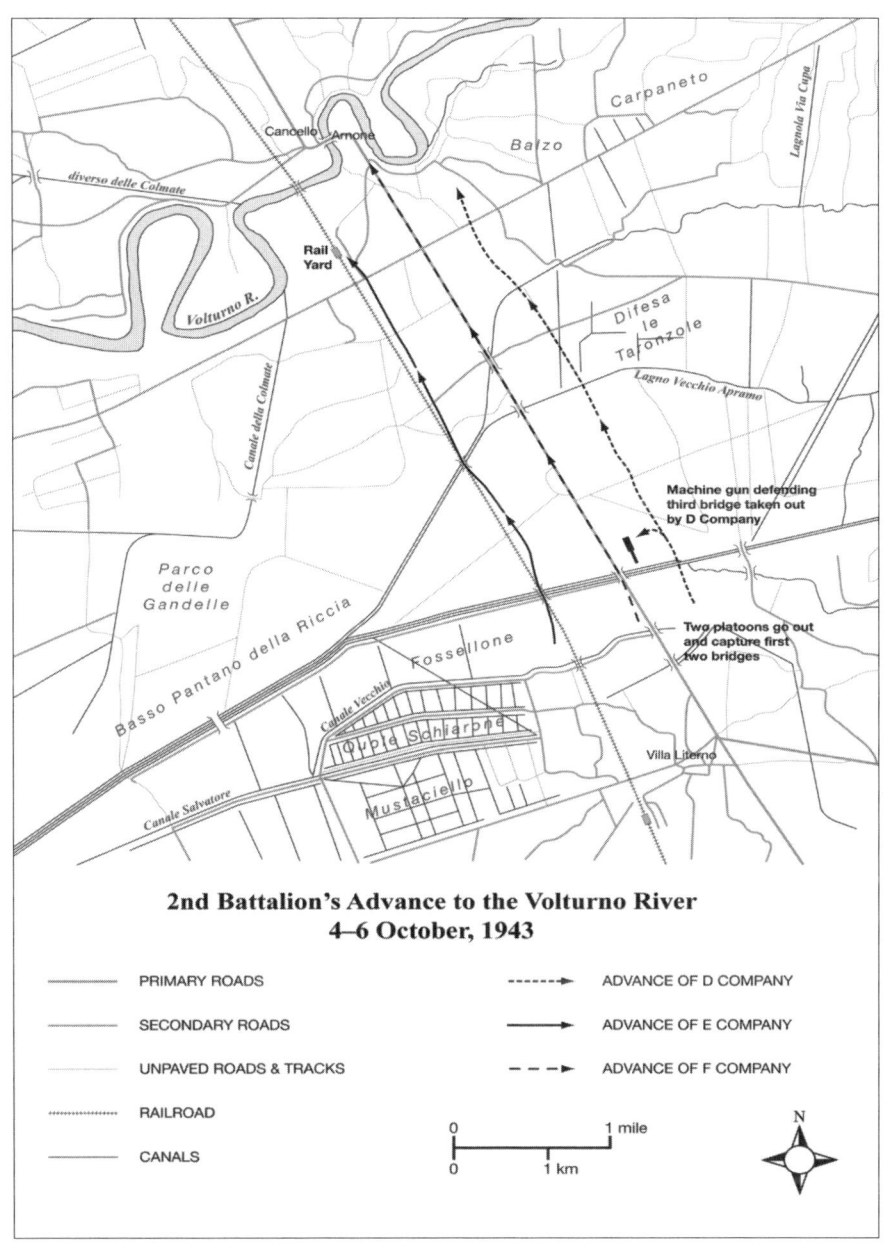

2nd Battalion's Advance to the Volturno River
4–6 October, 1943

The path of the 2nd Battalion, which captured five canal bridges on the attack toward the Volturno River. E Company had quite a shootout taking the train station and F Company faced an abundance of tripwires and mortar and cannon fire while capturing the village of Arnone.

reduce the German advantage of better knowing the contested ground.

Had the jump occurred as originally planned, another 505 battalion would have been down river holding another crossing. "Frankly, in studying and preparing for the mission, none of us who knew about it were even slightly enthusiastic about the plan. The assumption was that the Allied invasion beachhead would reach us in three days. In fact, it took a week and a half for Clark's Fifth Army to break out of Salerno, and at one point they were nearly kicked back into the ocean. Kesselring, the German commander, had all kinds of troops in the area. We couldn't have held out against them for that amount of time."

Alexander liked to know the ground he was attacking and often performed his own reconnaissance before sending his men into battle. His prior knowledge of the Volturno area and information provided by the 22nd Armored Brigade were likely deciding factors in his decision to attack immediately.

Alexander moved fast, arriving in the evening. "Rather than wait until morning, we went on a night attack. I directed two platoons of about 24 men each to move out as fast as possible in the dark to take

Lieutenant Colonel Mark Alexander outlines the attack toward Arnone and the Volturno River, surrounded by his 2nd Battalion commanders and his battalion staff.

the first two bridges. Each platoon had a light machine gun and a bazooka team. Sometimes they also carried a mortar. It was flexible, depending on the assignment. And we had to be flexible because we never knew what we would have when we got on the ground after a jump.

"They surprised the Germans, and with a loss of two men killed and three wounded were able to take both bridges before they could be blown up, and held them until the battalion arrived. When we caught up with them, we continued toward the third canal. The battalion followed in column on both sides of the road. The leading platoons had alerted the Germans and we heard fire fighting ahead of us."

As they advanced on this very dark night, multiple German machine guns let loose, sending tracer fire skipping down the concrete road toward the advancing paratroopers. Both columns of men took a dive into ditches on the roadside. Those on the right were surprised to find themselves diving into a five-foot concrete drainage ditch instead of a shallow gutter. "First I heard thuds and banging as the men on the right side of the road hit the cement bottom, then curses and moans. When daylight came, I could see cut and bruised faces from the dive to the bottom of the ditch."

The German soldiers were well aware of the encroaching Americans. The element of surprise gone, Alexander ordered his battalion to go into a defensive position. They dug in and held there for the night.

The 2nd Battalion consisted of four companies: D, E, F and Headquarters Company. F Company, under the command of McRoberts, dug in perpendicular to and on both sides of the road, closest to the third canal bridge. There were a few stone houses scattered widely about. Ahead lay the main town of Arnone, which was still no larger than a village, nestled against the Volturno River.

"I set up a CP in a pretty good-size rock house," Alexander recounts. "Lt. Col. Herbert Batcheller, the 505 executive officer, came up to see how things were going. He had a badly infected finger. After dark he was soaking his hand in some hot water. And I could hear the machine gun chatter on the outside of the house as the bullets periodically struck the stone walls.

"Batcheller said, 'What is that?'

"I said, 'It's a German machine gun firing from down the road.'

"He said, 'I don't think so. Have somebody check it.'

"'Well, that's what it is.'

2nd Battalion soldiers in the area of Arnone use cover provided by sloping ground along a canal near the Volturno River.

"'Just have somebody check it out.'

"So I sent Freeland out. He came back right quick, diving through the door. He said, 'It's a machine gun all right.'" [1]

The attack got underway again the next morning. Alexander recalled: "Before going into battle, my executive officer, James McGinity, would kneel and pray. He was a strong Catholic. Then he would get up and say, 'I'm ready.' And he was. He had things taken care of."

F Company advanced directly toward the third canal bridge, with Capt. Casey Rice and D Company to the right and Capt. Talton Long and E Company to the left. A and B Companies from the 1st Battalion had also arrived and been attached to Alexander's command. Alexander kept them in reserve.

A Company, commanded by Captain Sayer, had achieved the objective of almost the entire 505 in the Sicily campaign. As his men got into position guarding Alexander's flank, Sayer stepped off the edge of the road to urinate and tripped a bouncing betty, so-named because it popped up in the air about waist high before exploding. Sayer was "a hell of a good fighting man," as Alexander put it, but it would be quite a while before he was in combat again. [2]

"In the morning we drove on ahead to the third bridge. The enemy had partially blown it up. There was still enough of it standing to allow infantry to cross, but not vehicles. The Germans were putting intermittent fire on it from a farmhouse across to the right. It was holding up the lead company. I was back down the line a ways, but moved up when things stalled. Headquarters Company commander, Hubert Bass, was there.

"I said, 'Bass, we've got to get across to the other side of this bridge.'

"He said, 'There's a machine gun firing on the other end of it.'

"I said, 'Well, I'm going across. Anybody coming with me?'

"Bass said, 'Don't do that, Colonel,' but I took off, ran like hell and dove in the ditch on the other side."

Of course, nobody wanted to let "the old man" show them up. Once he ran they all followed, taking advantage of the few moments between bursts of fire. "A lot of times you take a chance when you're a commander and you know you've got to get things moving," Alexander explained. "But very often the first and second guy don't get hit. It's the third, fourth and fifth ones that get hit, because the shooters are aware of what's going on by that time. Maybe I was kind of selfish about that, but I'd rather be the first one across than the fourth or fifth one."

As F Company madly dashed across the bridge, "almost simultaneously, D Company, which I had moving parallel to the road about a hundred yards to the right flank, took the farmhouse and knocked the machine gunners out. They had waded across the canal down a ways. Then we almost had a free passes across that bridge." Distant rifle fire was still coming in, but it wasn't very effective.

The battalion advanced: E Company on the left, F in the middle straddling the road, and D on the right. Headquarters Company was following. As they continued, more machine gun positions opened up. "The Germans were trying to stall us. They would get in a house, set up a machine gun position and fire. As soon as we got close to them they'd pull back to another house and do it again.

"With my field glasses I kept spotting Germans withdrawing towards Arnone. I wanted artillery support, but couldn't get any from the British just then. American infantry companies each had their own mortar men carrying 60mm mortars, and Headquarters Company had a mortar platoon with larger and deadlier 81mm mortars. So I decided to violate one of the combat principles and bring mortars up to the very front as we advanced.

"I had a good mortar crew. [Ivey K.] Connell and Sanders, who commanded the mortar platoon, and I used them like artillery support. I was up front all the time with a pair of field glasses and I'd spot the Germans and have our mortar men drop some shells in there. They had a good shoot. They could see their targets and very accurately attacked them. Then the Germans would pull back."

One advantage of the Allies, especially the Americans, during World War II was motorized transportation. This didn't apply as much to paratroopers, but there were often enough vehicles to move men and equipment wherever they needed to go. The Germans, by contrast, did not have this luxury and made use of anything and everything available, heavily relying on pack animals.

"A lot of the enemy's hauling was done with horses and mules. I spotted a horse-drawn buggy about a third of a mile ahead, going down the road with probably six Germans accompanying it. They apparently had an anti-tank gun on it. I had Connell drop three or four mortar shells in there and they took off running, abandoning it.

"We got up there and saw it was a small one, the kind they used in the mountains because it's lighter and easier to haul. I turned it around, test-fired it the other way, and saw it was a pretty good little gun. It wouldn't have handled heavier tanks unless you hit them on a certain vulnerable spot. Generally with a light gun like that you had to hit a tank from the side for sure, or possibly the rear. Or, if you get a tank tilted up, you can hit it underneath. A lot of times a tank's underside becomes exposed when it climbs over obstacles in the road. If you're lucky you get a shot at its belly."

The Germans had the best and toughest tanks in the world. Fortunately, Alexander's troops hadn't come across any enemy armor, for their newly captured cannon would have had great trouble piercing the thick skin. It would be useful against men and jeeps, however, and so they took it with them.

"Out on our right flank was a flat plains area. D Company cleared out a couple of German transports. For the last few miles of the advance, a railroad ran along parallel to and about 100 yards to the left of the road." A dirt elevation for the train track made it several feet higher than the rest of the ground. "On our left flank near the railroad tracks, Captain Long, commanding E company, went into an attack position where you spread your men all out. You go a ways and dive down, go a ways and dive down. Well, what he was doing was combing the booby traps out. This was the first time my battalion or I had run into a lot of trip wires—those bouncing betties. The Germans had them all over the place.

"I got him on the radio and said, 'Long, don't go into extended formation. Get over there next to the railroad track and put your men in two columns, single file, and go down that way.'" This could be dangerous if a strong enemy position predicted such an approach and lay in wait, but Alexander correctly figured that the odds were against it. E Company advanced without tripping any more mines.

"My exec, James McGinity, asked me, 'How do you make all these decisions without referring to the book?' McGinity was an Academy man and knew all the do's and don'ts in the military field manuals.

"I said, 'Mac, I don't know the book. That's what I've got you for—to keep me out of trouble.' He thought that was kind of funny but I was serious about it."

The 2nd Battalion's rapid advance kept the retreating enemy off balance, allowing the fourth and fifth canal bridges to be captured

Chick Eitelman poses in front of some Italian ruins. As Alexander's very resourceful sidekick, he constantly found or fixed things and locations to make life easier for his boss. Picture taken in Sicily, 1943.

undamaged. German mortar and artillery fire was coming in sporadically. The closer the battalion got to Arnone, the more intense the fire became. A spent fragment from a German mortar or 88 round hit Alexander in the shin, drawing a trickle of blood. The wound was so minor he completely ignored it. "We set down for the night with the plan to attack the village of Arnone and the rail yard the next morning."

"Chick Eitelman dug me a trench to sleep in because there was a lot of mortar fire coming down in the area. I got a blanket someplace and lay down in the bottom of this slit trench, when couple of shells landed real close to me. Chick came running out and said, 'I thought they'd dropped one right on you'. Some dirt had blown in, but they didn't get me.

"I moved into a house nearby. I'm subject to fleas and there were a couple of sawbucks (sawhorses) there. I tore a door off the wall and put it across the tops of them. Then I crawled up on top, figuring that would keep the bugs away from me. I woke up after about two hours of sleep, and I'll be god damned if I didn't have fleas. They had jumped or crawled up the sawbucks, and I had them all around my waistline. I don't know why I attracted fleas. There could be other guys in the room

Mark Alexander (left) and Neil McRoberts (right) in discussion at Fort Benning, 1945. The two men got lucky in Italy when an enemy shell landing a few feet away turned out to be a dud.

and they wouldn't get bothered at all. Just me."

As morning arrived, the not-too-rested Alexander got his men in motion. Captain Long led E Company into the railroad yard and Captain McRoberts led F Company in the attack on the village of Arnone. Rice's D Company was positioned on the right flank. A and B Companies served as a reserve and watched the left flank.

The town of Arnone was only a couple hundred yards wide. Most houses were made out of stone with either slate or thatch roofs. A villager with a roof other than thatch was wealthier than most. The church had a red metal roof and was the largest structure in the village.

Responding to the F Company attack, the Germans put up a brief, but vicious fight before quickly pulling out and crossing the river to Cancello, the small town facing Arnone. "The highway bridge had three spans and the Germans tried to blow the far span after pulling back. Only one end of it dropped, however. Men could still walk up it, but you wouldn't have been able to get a tank across until you reinforced it."

Strategically placed in medieval days, Arnone was on a hairpin bend in the river that stuck out to the north and protected its inhabitants against raiders. Guarded on three sides by the river, they had only to defend the open area to the south. In the twentieth century, however, the river offered very little protection, and in this case aided the Germans in ambushing F Company. "In a way, they mouse-trapped us, because we had to be sure that everybody was out of Arnone and, therefore, had to go all the way in. But when they pulled out they left a lot of booby traps behind. As I said, that was the first time we had run into a lot of trip wires and that sort of thing. They had them all over the place."

The paratroopers were also barraged from three sides by artillery and mortars strategically placed across the river to match the arc of the bend in the Volturno. Some of these were the dreaded German 88s, long-barreled anti-tank and anti-aircraft guns that were often at their most devastating using explosive fragmenting ammunition against infantry. Alexander put it bluntly: "They shelled the hell out of us."

F Company's 2nd Platoon was sent toward the river's edge. [3] After receiving heavy fire, McRoberts decided they should return to Arnone where there was better cover. Pvt. Darrell Whitfield was there. "On our way back to Arnone, we came out along the levy, started out and then a mortar shell hit the town. We dove down when we heard it. We got up, started again and the next round hit behind us. We got up, started again. The next one hit a guy about 25 feet away from me while he was lying down. Hit right in his back. There was a hole where his back had been. Just his shoulders and head up here and hips and legs down there.

"I got wounded at that time, with pieces of steel in both legs and up and down my back, and I had a big chunk in my neck. Sergeant Gregory, who was lying a little ahead of me, got wounded across his arm."[4] The second platoon made it back into the village and out of direct sight of the deadly 88s.

F Company had quite a few casualties, some when they first went in and routed the Germans out and more when the Germans started shelling. Four men were killed and about ten wounded. Lieutenants Connell and Sanders, who led the mortar platoon and had done such a good job the day before, stepped to the edge of the river, probably to get a look at where the enemy firepower was located, and were both killed by a single enemy mortar round.

Once the soldiers were no longer visible to the spotters across the river, the shelling vastly decreased. Alexander continues: "I went back up into Arnone to see what the situation was and if we had any casualties left behind. I took a runner with me (not Chick Eitelman). I carefully looked around and saw where there were a couple more trip wires. I was very close to the church, which had a pretty high belfry that made a good observation point. Captain Boyd, our regimental communications officer, showed up. He said he was going up in the belfry to see what he could across the river.

"I said, 'if you go up there, just peek out and don't show yourself. They're right across the river and you'll draw fire if they see you.'

"Two minutes later, I look up and he's walking around on the church roof. I yelled, 'Boyd, get your ass down off the roof!'

"When he stepped out of the church, I ran him off and told him not to come back. He no more than started down the street when the Jerries mortared the hell out of the area. They had seen him up there. I had to take cover in the thick stone walls of the church. Boyd stayed away from me for about a week after that.

"After a while the shelling slowed a little, but was still coming in pretty regularly, especially in and around the village square. A soldier came up with a message from my British commander. I squatted down with my back to the wall of a two-story stone house, took off my helmet because I was hot, and wrote a message to General Arkwright reporting our position and progress, and a few messages to D and F Companies.

"Something told me to get up. I grabbed my helmet, stood and looked up. A huge pot of geraniums was teetering on the second story window ledge right above where I had been writing. Each time a shell landed, it rocked. As I was watching, it fell off the ledge and smashed to the ground right where I had been. I thought, 'That would be a hell of a way to die in a war. Killed by a flower pot.'

"My orderly had been waiting for me around the corner of the house. He came back and showed me a shell fragment about the size of a fat fountain pen stuck in the small bones in his wrist.

"He said, 'Do you want to pull it out?'

"I felt it. It was solidly in there. I said, 'No, you'll have a lot of bleeding and I might do more damage pulling it out. Go back and let the doctor have a look at that.' I gave him a shot of morphine and the messages and sent him to the rear. He disappeared and I never saw him again." He probably spent some time in a hospital.

While F Company fought to take Arnone, E Company launched its attack on the rail yard back and to the left of F Company. Here the Germans had no intention of retreating. With things well in hand with Arnone and F Company, Alexander headed for E Company. "I followed a dirt path toward the rail yard, approaching the back side of the passenger depot, and saw one of our men lying on the path about 40 yards from it. I got down on my knees and he was dead. I looked up and saw the flash of a gray uniform in the window of the depot.

"I dropped down on my belly and put a couple of shots through the opening, then rolled over to one side. The Germans inside planned on surrendering, because right quick they had a white handkerchief on a stick, waving it. That was a close one there, because I could have easily been shot dead. I took two Germans prisoner. As E Company had moved forward, these guys were cut off. They couldn't get back across the railroad bridge that crossed the Volturno near the rail yard. They were happy to surrender and I was happy I didn't get shot.

"I took them with me the rest of the way over to E Company and checked positions. I sent Chick Eitelman back late that evening to check out the railroad station, and he picked up a German light machine gun that my two prisoners had manned. They abandoned it when they surrendered to me. I got lucky there."

The Germans had a strong team in the railroad yard and had given E Company a bad time. After very close and bloody fighting, the remaining enemy withdrew across the river over the railroad bridge. "We lost five enlisted men and Lieutenant Packard, and had several wounded in the fighting around the boxcars and the passenger station."

Lieutenant Packard had been killed early in the fighting, leaving Sgt. Otis Sampson in charge of the forward platoon that was being beaten down by well positioned Germans. To buy his men some time he ran forward, drawing fire and killing several enemy soldiers before taking cover in a very vulnerable position. As Sampson recounts:

> I checked my inserted clip to see if I had enough rounds in it for another possible shoot out; I counted eight and reached for another one. There wasn't any! Frantically, I searched with the thought, "I couldn't be out of them!" I scanned the area thinking I must have lost them in the commotion I had gone through, but I saw no full ones. A feeling of panic seized me, and [I remembered] …a movie I once saw of Edward G. Robinson in *Little Caesar*, when he was told, "You are no bigger than your gun." […] I was no bigger than the tommy gun I held in my hands; empty, I was nothing. I had gone through all my ammunition; I must have been fighting longer than I thought. Time had stood still. […]
>
> A Jerry crawled near the bank and tried to take me out with a concussion grenade. It landed a little to my right rear; I glanced its way when it hit and I saw a cloud of dirt in a funnel shaped form shoot upward from the explosion. I thought little of the incident; just glad it had not been a potato masher. […]
>
> A large German soldier, in a lumbering run, tried to escape to the rear of the five-foot bank to get away from the bursting shells. Carefully I took aim to be sure of preserving my precious last rounds. I let one off; as if hit in the head by a large sledgehammer, he went down. I put another one into him to be sure. Another tried his luck, but with the same results. A third started, but changed his mind, knowing the fate of the first two. [5]

E Company now held the railroad zone and F Company controlled Arnone. After checking things out, Alexander brought the two prisoners back to the command post and turned them over to the S-2, the intelligence officer, who sent them to the rear, where they were pumped for information. Alexander reports: "I set up a command post in a farmhouse back about 200 yards from our defensive positions, then reported to General Arkwright that we had taken our final objective. I asked him if he wanted me to go across the river and take a bridgehead. He said no, because he wouldn't be able to support us. And they were very slow to get into a position to give support with artillery or other big guns.

Although the enemy had lost ground and been pushed back across the river, they were not done fighting. After one of the heaviest artillery concentrations Alexander had ever seen, he got his field glasses out. "I spotted the Germans making a counter-attack across the highway bridge between Cancello and Arnone. I again asked for artillery support." The German force was roughly battalion-size, backed by very accurately fired German 88s. Jack Norton, who had been following the 2nd Battalion, later said they used the 88mm cannons like large-caliber sniper rifles. [6]

This was a large-scale attack. As men flooded across the highway bridge toward the heart of Arnone, another company of Germans crossed between the two bridges in an attempt to hit F Company's left flank. [7] Up to this point, F Company's 3rd Platoon had been held back in reserve, but McRoberts now brought it into the fight. [8] They were not only under attack from the battalion coming over the bridge, and in danger of being flanked by the Germans that crossed between the bridges, but were receiving extremely heavy fire from in and around buildings in Cancello.

Spencer Wurst, positioned on a roof in Arnone on F Company's left flank, engaged the enemy across the river. Italy was Wurst's first combat jump, and he remembers the hot and heavy firing as his first real test under fire in combat:

> Sergeant Gore broke down our location into individual areas. We were about to get some on-the-job training in how to fight in a built-up area. None of us, including our sergeant, had any training or practice at this; at most, I'd watched a training film on it. Even when a unit is committed as a full fighting force at the same time—and we had been committed piecemeal—fighting becomes insulated in a town.
>
> I took up a fighting position on the far left flank, on the south slope of the roof of a one-story house. […] The ridge [of the roof] ran parallel to the river [which was] fifty to seventy-five yards wide. […] I had good observation to the far bank. My position gave me some cover and concealment, but I was still partially silhouetted from across the river. I remember thinking, "I've

carried this rifle for two and a half years with no real opportunity to use it, and I sure as hell am going to use it now."

German bullets crackled all around me, showering the house and the roof. My head and shoulders stuck up across the ridge; I kept moving my position left and right, so as not to present a stationary target. I also was afraid my smoke would give me away; our rifle and small-arms munitions were supposed to be smokeless, but compared to the superior German munitions, ours were almost as bad as the old black powder from the Civil War. It was impossible for me to determine the Germans' positions by observing smoke from their small arms. Mine, however, hung over me, like a sign saying, "Here I am." [...]

I kept on firing for a good while, shooting where I thought the Germans would be if they were in position to give covering fire for the assault on the 1st and 2d platoons. I do not know how long this went on: it could have been about an hour. I had to watch myself so I did not run out of ammunition. I knew we would not be resupplied. [9]

Alexander led E Company against the Germans that crossed by boat as they approached Arnone, preventing them from flanking F Company. Artillery fire remained heavy all over Alexander's position. [10] "General Arkwright took a chance and sent a tank and a British captain, an artillery spotter, up to me, but the road hadn't been cleared of mines yet. The tank commander was smart. He came down the edge of the raised road, tilting the tank sideways, not hitting any landmines. I gave the captain the far end of the bridge as the target. As an aiming device, they had a smoke shell that makes a big arc that looks kind of like a vapor trail from an airplane. It helps the spotter figure out how to adjust the firing. It's beautiful to see that smoke shell come in. It really makes you happy."

"Here come these two shells parallel across the sky and land right where we wanted them to. Then they laid in a real barrage. This was the first artillery support I had experienced." Combined with F Company's heavy fire, the barrage had the desired effect. "They backed off and withdrew across the river bridge. Then I didn't call for any more support. We really didn't need it, as the Germans didn't make any other attempts."

E and F Companies successfully beat the Germans back to their side of the water. "The town was clear, so other than two observation posts,

TO THE VOLTURNO: THE BATTLE OF ARNONE

American Sherman tanks like this one, employed by XIII Corps, Eighth Army, in Sicily, were widely used by the British in World War II. *United Kingdom Government photograph*

I pulled F Company back [several hundred yards from] Arnone. I didn't want them in that direct fire from across the river, and they didn't need to be all the way up there at that point anyway. I pulled E Company back a ways, so they would not be in direct enemy fire. Then I put the little cannon we had captured the day before in position in case the Germans did make another attack.

"I learned something about the British. They were very good soldiers and they fought a different type of battle than the Americans. The British lost one million people in World War I and had two million wounded. Their government made a policy decision that they were not going to decimate their manpower like that in the Second World War." In contrast to his views of a year earlier, before he had seen the tough, lean Desert Rats in North Africa, Alexander had come to respect the British and the way they fought. Serving under General Arkwright only strengthened this view. He knew that the general was reluctant to send artillery forward because the road had not yet been cleared of mines; this reluctance had nothing to do with the fact that the artillery was being requested by American troops.

"The Americans were very offensive. We were organized to go at things like Patton did. He would marshal all his forces and do it in one big push. The British were good fighters, but they were more defensive when they attacked, rather than taking an all-out run at it. It was a different way of looking at it. I understood their thinking." [11]

After making sure his forces were in good positions and prepared for any further counter-attacks, Alexander checked on the wounded. "We had about 25 wounded men sheltered under a culvert, but no doctor. I got on a field telephone and told Dr. Stein that we needed him at the forward aid station. He insisted that I should take them back to him at the rear command post. The logical thing is to take the severely wounded back as soon as you can, but in that case, we hadn't cleared the road of mines and I had no way to transport them. So he needed to come up where the action was.

"He was a stubborn-headed little guy and he argued with me. I told him to come forward or I'd go back there and kick his ass all the way up here. He didn't arrive, so I headed back to the rear to get him. I looked down the road and he was walking towards me, medical bag across his shoulder, a big white bandage around his head, his helmet on top of his bandage, and limping.

"I said, 'Jesus, Stein! What happened to you?'

"He said, 'You go to hell!' and continued to walk towards the forward aid station and the wounded.

Alexander cooks up a meal during a respite in the fighting near the Volturno River while some of the 2nd Battalion HQ men look on.

"I said, 'Okay, Stein.' He was going in the right direction, so what more could I say?

"I went down the road a little further and met Dr. Robert Franco and asked him what had happened to Stein. 'I was watching the ambulance head toward the forward positions,' he said, 'when it hit a mine and blew up in the air, coming down in a pile of junk. I ran to the site and was looking at what was left of the ambulance when a voice called out from the wreckage, *Don't just stand there, you dummy! Get me out from under here!* Franco said he pulled Stein out, bandaged his head, and off he went, headed for the front. The ambulance driver was only slightly wounded. Stein gave me a little trouble, but even after the war, we always remained friends. We had good doctors and medics. Good men."

Every night during the fight up to the river, Alexander sent out patrols. "Each one consisted of five or six men, because they were mutually supportive. They would space apart as they moved. That way you didn't get them all knocked off. You might lose one man. I didn't like to send them out because it was a dangerous job, but you've got to find out what's going on.

"This night I think I had four of them all together. One patrol came back after they stayed out about four hours, and the lieutenant leading it reported in. They were supposed to have crossed the river at a nearby ford and collected information about the enemy.

"I said, 'What can you tell me?'

"He said they hadn't really seen any Germans at all. He added, 'We know there are Germans over there, but we don't know how many.' He didn't have much of a report.

"I shouldn't have accepted it, but I did."

Not until years later did Alexander find out exactly what happened on the patrol. "I was at a 505 reunion at Fort Bragg, talking to one of the guys that was on that patrol. He was a real young guy at the time and spoke Italian. He said, 'I've been wanting to tell you something all these years. We never did go across the river that night. We just went out to the north, patrolled up along the river a ways and then came back.'

"The lieutenant lied to me. I always cussed myself after that for accepting his report. And the worst of it was, when we departed from Italy, I left him behind in Naples to look after some cleanup and so forth, and gave him that Fiat so he would have a way to get around. I bet he sold it for quite a little bit of money. They were hard to get about that

137

time. As it happened, he never did come back to the division. I don't know where he ended up. That guy gave me a big lie in a report, and I gave him an automobile."

Spencer Wurst was also on that patrol: "Our lieutenant did make one heroic proposition that night that is legend in 505 lore. Our patrol included members from other platoons, and Richard Tedeschi was one of them. Because Teddy both spoke and looked like a native Italian, the lieutenant got the bright idea of sending him into Arnone. He told Teddy to find some civilian clothes, swim across the river, and check out the Germans. 'Lieutenant,' Teddy answered, 'I'll go across if you come with me.' All of us spent the better part of the night on the riverbank in ambush position, including Teddy." [12]

In contrast to this lieutenant, one of Alexander's men always asked to go on patrol. Alexander found out that he had gone out six times in a row, and he told the soldier's superiors not to send him any more.

"They said, 'But he volunteered.'

"I said, 'I don't give a damn. He's taken his chances, someone else will have to take one.' Often in combat situations, you lose some of your best men because they're leading." This one was a leader, but he was pushing his luck. Some patrols did cross the river, becoming the first troops on that side of the Volturno in the Allied push north.

It was late and Alexander needed sleep. The house serving as his command post was full of men. "Chick dug a slit trench for me and threw a blanket in it. I went out there to get some sleep. The Germans were throwing some mortar rounds in that area, trying to find out where we were. And they again put a couple real close to where I was. Chick checked to make sure they hadn't hit me and then I went back to sleep again." It wasn't the easiest way to sleep, but at least there were no fleas in the trench.

By the next morning, the Germans continued to shell the area, but had not tried coming across again. Alexander went to the rear to meet with his commander. "I had a jeep at that point, which I left way back because the road was still mined against vehicles. I got back to it, jumped in and sped off to see General Arkwright.

"The 22nd was an armored brigade and tanks sat lined up along the road as I approached his headquarters. A British soldier stepped out in front of me with his rifle, bringing me to a halt. "He said, 'I say, Sir, slow it down a bit. We're having a spot of tay (tea) and you're kicking up a frightful dust.'

To the Volturno: The Battle of Arnone

"I couldn't believe that. Here we've been fighting at the river, so I was thinking about nothing but combat. And these guys are worried about dust in their tea. That was something."

"That night I was relieved by a regiment of the British. I had a battalion of 523 men. They relieved us with a regiment of, I'd say, 2,500 men. And I was glad to see them come. I spoke with some of them for a few hours before we started back to Naples. It started raining like hell the last day and got rather cold. The British supply sergeant brought me the biggest raincoat he could find. I don't know where he got it, but he brought one that hung about an inch off the ground when I wore it.

"General Arkwright called and his men dropped off four big jugs of Jamaica Rum for me. I passed them out to the company commanders and said everybody gets a swallow. It was very welcome. Everybody was soaking wet. We walked back to the rear quite a ways, loaded up on trucks and went back to Naples. I think they appreciated what we did because they later gave me a decoration, the highest they could give a non-British soldier."

The 2nd Battalion was reattached to the 505 and was once again under the command of Colonel Gavin. Alexander's men had quickly and efficiently achieved all of their objectives, but 60 men died in the process and more were wounded.

Chapter Ten

Duty in Naples

The 505th returned to Naples on October 8. For the first time since they'd left the Salerno beachhead, they were reunited with their barracks bags, only to discover they were all soaking wet. Pvt. Turk Seeley, who had been ill and left behind to care for them, was in trouble.

"Colonel Alexander only chewed my ass out one time. The battalion went north to the city of Naples. I was sick. My lieutenant said, 'Turk, you stay behind with these three other guys and guard the barracks bags.' They were in a big pile.

"We were there for two weeks, me and three other guys. We missed out on the fighting at the Volturno River and everything. We stayed in a little town and two of the local ladies said they would cook for us. This was great. They were about 32 or 33 years old. We thought that was really old!

"Anyway, what the lieutenant meant by 'take care of the battalion bags' was to look after them. What we did was let it rain on them. Nobody told us to take them out of the rain. But of course we took our own bags inside. Two weeks later a truck came to pick us up. We loaded everything and went to Naples. Two or three days afterward, a private came and said, 'The battalion commander wants to see you.'

"I said, 'OK, buddy, I'll go see him,' but I was a little worried. I wasn't sure what it was about, but I had a suspicion. So I went in and saluted and said, 'Private Seeley reporting.'

"Colonel Alexander said, 'You were in charge of the battalion equipment for the last few weeks?'

"Yes, Sir. I was, Sir."

"He said, 'My barracks bag and the bags of all of the other officers and men are soaking wet. Why didn't you take them out of the rain?'

"There was a dairy there and it would have been easy to move them inside. I said, 'Nobody ordered me to do that. My lieutenant just said to look after them. We made sure nobody took them, Sir.'

"So that's the end of that story. He chewed my ass a little and said, 'Now get the hell out of here.'"[1]

Fighting on the Volturno River was a test for all involved. For the first time they directly fought well-trained and well-led German soldiers. The 505 encountered new enemy tactics and traps, and were exposed to the dreaded 88s. The experience, although deadly, was invaluable.

Alexander's mental arsenal, like those of his men, was increased. He also picked up lessons not directly related to combat. "When we pulled out from the Volturno River and returned to Naples, I made a mistake and tried hard never to let it happen again. I thought I had everybody. But we hadn't made a thorough search of the shoreline around Arnone where F Company initially moved in and then backed off. We left a wounded man there.

"He was in a foxhole in a forward-most position. When his company pulled out, they probably didn't see him or thought he was dead. He couldn't move and the British found him the next day and notified us. He had been hit bad through the shoulder and I think the top edge of his lung. I thought, 'I'm never going to let that happen again,' and went to the hospital to visit him. I said I was awful sorry we left him.

"He said, 'That's all right. I just couldn't move or let anyone know I was there.' He was a good GI. I think he was from the interior of the United States, but I can't even remember his name. He lived, but was sent back to the U.S. when he was well enough. I always felt bad about going off and leaving that guy there, but it can happen. You learned things like that might happen, so you looked for them."

The 2nd Battalion resumed their duties policing Naples along with the rest of the 505th. Alexander's men lived in an empty apartment building with no furniture and hard marble floors. "I learned there was a mattress factory in the industrial area of town," he recalled with amusement. "They had all kinds of shop tools in there, cotton fluff and rolls and rolls of sacking, which held the stuffing in the mattresses. We confiscated enough materials to make a light mattress for every man in the battalion. Then we started building cots out of lumber. When regiment learned of this, they moved in and took over my mattress supply operation. But by that time we had made bunks with light mattresses for every man in the battalion."

Alexander's working relationship with Capt. Clyde Russell, his adjutant, was developing well, despite its rough beginnings. Russell was usually a highly effective member of the battalion staff, as Alexander noted. "He was a good staff man. Paperwork was the main reason I had him. You don't find that everybody can handle a typewriter and bang out an order and so fourth, and he was good at that."

Russell had served as a company executive officer, and Alexander made him a company commander: "He wanted a company real bad, and I wanted to get him out of the battalion headquarters anyway, so when a company vacancy came up, I had him assigned as the company commander.

"Our regimental commander, Herbert Batcheller, came down to inspect our area. Well, this Russell was smarter than hell. He had his cook whip up something special for him. He came bragging about how he got the regimental commander up in his CP and fed him and all that. And it made the regimental commander very happy. No doubt. He was a pretty good guy, but he was real slick at buttering up to people. I didn't regret giving him command of a company until the Normandy campaign."

Each battalion had a Catholic priest and a Protestant minister: Father Connelly and George Wood, respectively, served in the 2nd Battalion. They were certified paratroopers and neither one played it safe. One day in Naples, Connelly disappeared, much to Alexander's consternation. "I lost him and couldn't figure out where the hell he was, so I had the guys searching all over. They found that he had gone up on the sixth floor to a bedroom," and stayed there by himself. "He was sicker than a dog, but he was the kind of guy that would never tell anybody. I sent the medic up to take care of him. He also had a big carbuncle on his neck. Doc had to lance it. He was a nice guy and I didn't like losing him," even for a short while.

Italy wasn't all work and no play. Alexander attended at least two parties. The first was a first-class affair hosted by the British. "General Arkwright, who was no longer my commander, invited me up to dinner with all the officers of his regiment one evening." Arkwright's new headquarters was up in the foothills of the nearby mountains and it was a very dark night. The driver sent to pick Alexander up proved to be a daredevil. "We got going and this driver would really wheel around those curves." When Alexander asked how he could see well enough to drive so fast, he replied that he worked the graveyard shift driving a cab in London for five years, and had good night vision.

They arrived in record time "to a very formal dinner in a large tent. It had folding chairs and tables, white linen, china and silver. They even had waiters, British enlisted men in fancy white coats. We were served a grand dinner. I thought to myself, 'These British know how to live!' We Americans were still eating K rations. We had not yet learned to serve in such fashion. They brought all this stuff along with them on a train as their army advanced. That was the first I'd seen anything like that and I was amazed. They treated me as a guest of honor. It was nice that they did that and I appreciated it."

A number of important changes in leadership took place while the 505 was in Naples. Colonel Gavin was promoted to brigadier general and moved up from 505 regimental commander to executive officer of the division, filling the position formerly occupied by General Keerans, who had been killed in Sicily. Lieutenant Colonel Batcheller became the regimental commander, and Alexander was surprised to be tapped to become the regimental executive officer. Major Ben Vandervoort took over command of the 2nd Battalion.

Alexander knew everyone on the regimental staff, and was once again working directly with the very capable Jack Norton, whom Gavin had wisely promoted weeks earlier to regimental operations officer (S-3). They occupied the building that had served as the Fascist headquarters under Axis rule, which Alexander described in a letter as *the most pleasant living quarters I have occupied since leaving America—some fancy place. My desk is of polished mahogany and 8 feet long.*

Another letter home at this time expresses Alexander's more serious thoughts about his former unit and his new duties.

Somewhere in Italy
October 14, 1943

Dearest Mother and Dad:

It is too long now since I have written. True we have been busy and just now we are sitting down for a bit of rest.

My Battalion has had a lot of hard fighting and general hardships since our jump in Sicily and are now some fewer in number and a bit war weary.

I say "My Battalion" but it is no longer so. My Battalion did such a *good job in Sicily and again here, that two days ago I was made Regimental Executive Officer. I am proud of it of course but certainly hate losing my boys. We have gone through a great deal together and the ties are strong and binding. However, as Regimental Exec. Officer, I haven't exactly lost them and I intend doing the best I can for them in the job I now have.*

I can't help but feel that I have gone up too fast. Particularly as there are two Battalion Commanders, Regular Army men, who have a better background for it than I. Anyway, someone has to do the job and I promise to do the best I can by it. At least I'm honest and persistent in my efforts.

I am coming as close to enjoying myself these days as is possible under the conditions. This city, one in which Caesar used to play, is a mass of ruins, but gradually the people are coming back and life is picking up rapidly. I am very grateful the war is being fought in this world, rather than yours back there—destruction, hate and lust are rampant.

As ever your loving son,
Mark

As Alexander's letter clearly conveys, he felt he was moving up too fast. He also believed that he was far better suited to command than to serve

Italian civilians walk past an aircraft that has crashed and burned. In the distance is the city of Naples.

505 PIR soldiers on the move.

Much of Naples was destroyed in the fighting.

as executive officer at any level. His instincts and understanding of what was and was not possible in battle aided him greatly as commander. But an XO must handle the bulk of the paperwork, pick up untold loose ends, and do everything else necessary to allow the commander to lead and train his men. Such things require knowledge of the structure and often convoluted inner workings of the army, gained through experience and schooling. Good instincts were not suitable substitutes. All the same, Alexander assumed his new duties with determination.

"We were in Naples the better part of three weeks. And the guys hadn't had any attention to their teeth for six months. So I told our two regimental dentists, 'I want you guys to run the whole regiment.' We had portable equipment where a guy sat on a stool and pedaled and that powered the instruments. And fortunately, they did have Novocain available in Naples."

The dentists, who also served as medics in combat, weren't very excited about spending the next several weeks staring into mouths when Naples was almost like being on vacation. Who could blame them? They claimed they didn't have the necessary equipment. Alexander said they would get some from the Italians. Seeing there was no way out, the dentists looked again and found they had what they needed.

"I said, 'Good. I want every man in the regiment checked out and fixed up.'

"They said, 'Oh, we'll never be able to cover them all.'

"You will,' I told them. 'You're going to work eight hours a day until you get them through.' I checked on them and they were working. They ran the whole regiment, which was a good thing, because we didn't get a chance at it again for quite a long time."[2]

For the 505, now seasoned by two campaigns, Naples was an oasis in a sea of blood, sweat and toil. The local population, however, was starving. The military effort to provide food and restore water and other services to the devastated city took time, and by comparison with the Neapolitans, even the lowest private was well off. To give only one example, the cigarettes in the meal kits of every American soldier were considered a luxury item. They fetched a high price on the black market, and were very desirable as barter.

This situation led to a high level of fraternization between the GIs and the young ladies of Naples. The fact that many Italian men had not yet returned home after Italy's capitulation made a city full of strong, young Americans all the more attractive to the female population. "We policed the city for about three weeks after our fighting," Alexander recalled. "Even the guys who didn't smoke would take their allocation of cigarettes because they could trade them for most anything. Anything. A piece of tail or whatever.

"Ed Krause, the 3rd Battalion commander, came in one night to see me, since I was now the regimental executive officer. He said, 'I don't know what to do. Some of these Italian gals are doing it on the back lawn for three cigarettes. I can't stop them.' I laughed because it was a funny problem to have.

"We wanted to give the men a break. In Naples, there was what they called the 'Orange Garden,' a night club on the side of the mountain. It was a big one, like they have over in Reno or someplace like that. We confiscated it for a couple of parties. One was for all the NCOs (non-commissioned officers) and the other one for all the officers.

I assigned a couple of guys to set it up. An Italian doctor named Demarco was in on it. He had been there before Italy capitulated and had done a lot of underground work for the Allies. We had been told to find him because he knew people, had contacts and could help us out."

Of course a party was nothing without girls. "Where are we going to get women?" Alexander asked. "Demarco said, 'I'll get them. Don't worry. You just take care of the food and drinks. I'll get the girls and the band.'

"I remember being out at the night club the night of the officers' party when six trucks came in full of beautiful women. They came in and the guys paired off. There were, I think, 126 officers in our regiment. They were all there. And each would go out and pick off one of these women. Well, we had a heck of a ball that night, and later I found out that they were all pros. Demarco had put out the word that they were going to entertain the American soldiers. Then he came and picked them up and at the end took them back.

"There were some really sharp-looking women in there. Captain Russell liked one of them, a slim, willowy, dark-complexioned girl. And he insisted on taking her. Well, later he had problems because she was the wife of the bandleader. Russell was about to take her home when the bandleader came out and said, 'Not this one,' and took her away from him. Ah, that Russell!"

Sixty years later, the veterans who were at that ball still remembered it clearly. As one asked a friend at a reunion in 2007, "How many kids do you think our regiment has in Naples?"

Although duty in Naples was a far cry from front line battle, it did have its dangers, as a letter Alexander wrote to his parents on October 21 reveals:

This room is so filled with smoke I can hardly take a decent breath. We just went through a bit of an air raid by the Boch. The first we have had since we occupied this city. It was a real show. I stood on the balcony of our quarters and watched a fascinating display of fire and smoke.

The Jerries came in low, dropped a load and then all hell seemed to break loose. Never have I seen a more tremendous concentration of tracer in the sky at once. We knocked down one plane but the rest got through. How, I couldn't see, for the barrage was terrific. They started a fire with their bombs, but the damage was small. The smoke I just spoke of came from our many anti-aircraft guns set right here in the city and on the docks.

I am now regimental Executive Officer. My luck still holds out and I'm right proud to be promoted again so soon. Most of my good luck I attribute to those wonderful men I had in the 2nd Battalion. They would do anything for me.

A later letter dated November 11 takes much the same theme, but attempts to make light of the bombings and assure his parents of his safety: *Well, here I sit calmly at my desk while some few Heinies try to*

A lingering haze hangs over Naples after a German bombing run. The smoke was almost entirely due to Allied anti-aircraft fire, as opposed to damage by attacking aircraft. Soldiers and citizens in Naples were more likely to be hit by falling anti-aircraft rounds than to be killed by enemy bombers.

help Hitler keep the promise he made in his speech of not long ago—to level the city off flat. There's a hell of a barrage being laid down by our boys and Jerry doesn't like it one little bit. He has dropped a few bombs, but they seem to have done no damage. An air raid and the tremendous fire works that accompany it is a fascinatingly fearful thing to watch. However, we have gotten so we don't mind at all and in their enthusiasm about the spectacle, we have to order our men in under cover to best keep them from being hit by falling fragments.

Throughout the bombing raids, the 505ers went about the business of policing the city, talking to pretty girls, and going to bars on their time off. They also famously got into fights. Alexander recalled one such incident involving Chick Eitelman, who remained with him at regimental headquarters.

"Eitelman was a pretty tough cookie. He was about six feet tall, weighed about 210, and was nearly all muscle. Nobody fooled with him, although I did see him get evened up one day. There was a big cook. I think he was 6' 2" and weighed about 250. He was one of those guys built kind of roundish, like a bear. Got some extra flesh on them, but underneath they're a lot of power. A lot of football players are like that. And I don't think they get hurt as easily, because they've got some extra padding on them. This cook didn't look so bad or so vicious, but god, he was strong. He ran the regimental headquarters mess. If anybody spoke disparagingly of his food, they were in trouble.

"Well, Chick must have said something. One of the guys came running up to where I was about three blocks away and said, 'Colonel, I hate to tell you this, but your orderly and the chief cook are in a fight down by the mess hall.'

"I said, 'How's Chick doing?'

"He said, 'He's got his hands full this time. That cook is really tough. They're knocking the shit out of each other.'

"Well, they were both tough, but Chick didn't walk over him. I know that. I sent another officer down there to break it up. I didn't want to go near it.

"He came back with a black eye and a cut on his head and his jaw. I never did say anything except, 'I heard you had a little bit of a fight, Chick.'

"He said, 'Yeah.' I just let it ride at that. He would fight all right. But that big cook was a match for him."

More serious fighting broke out when German bombers struck a ship that was carrying paratrooper boots, and blew them all over the docks and harbor. Soon many quartermaster troops from a black battalion had replaced their shoes with jump boots. At this point, not even glider troops were allowed to wear jump boots: anyone caught wearing them who was not jump qualified had a very nasty fight on his hands. When a couple of paratroopers held down one of the quartermasters and pulled his boots off, nearby soldiers from both units jumped in and a huge fight broke out. As a result, the entire 505 PIR and roughly 400 quartermaster troops were restricted to limited areas in Naples.

Luckily, Alexander was ranked high enough to avoid the restriction. One of the highlights of this duty in Naples was a visit to the isle of Capri. "There were Italians with all kinds of little boats around Naples. Several of us took the hour run out to the island. I saw places where Napoleon and the nobility used to vacation. There were a lot of old buildings and very beautiful country. I stayed two nights and then had to go back to work."

Alexander's letters from Naples are headed "Somewhere in Italy,"

Cpt. Bob Piper, 1st Battalion commander Maj. Walter F. Winton, and regimental executive officer Alexander enjoy a smoke and a drink on Capri. After a two-day pass, they rejoined their regiment and the 505 moved to Northern Ireland.

Duty in Naples

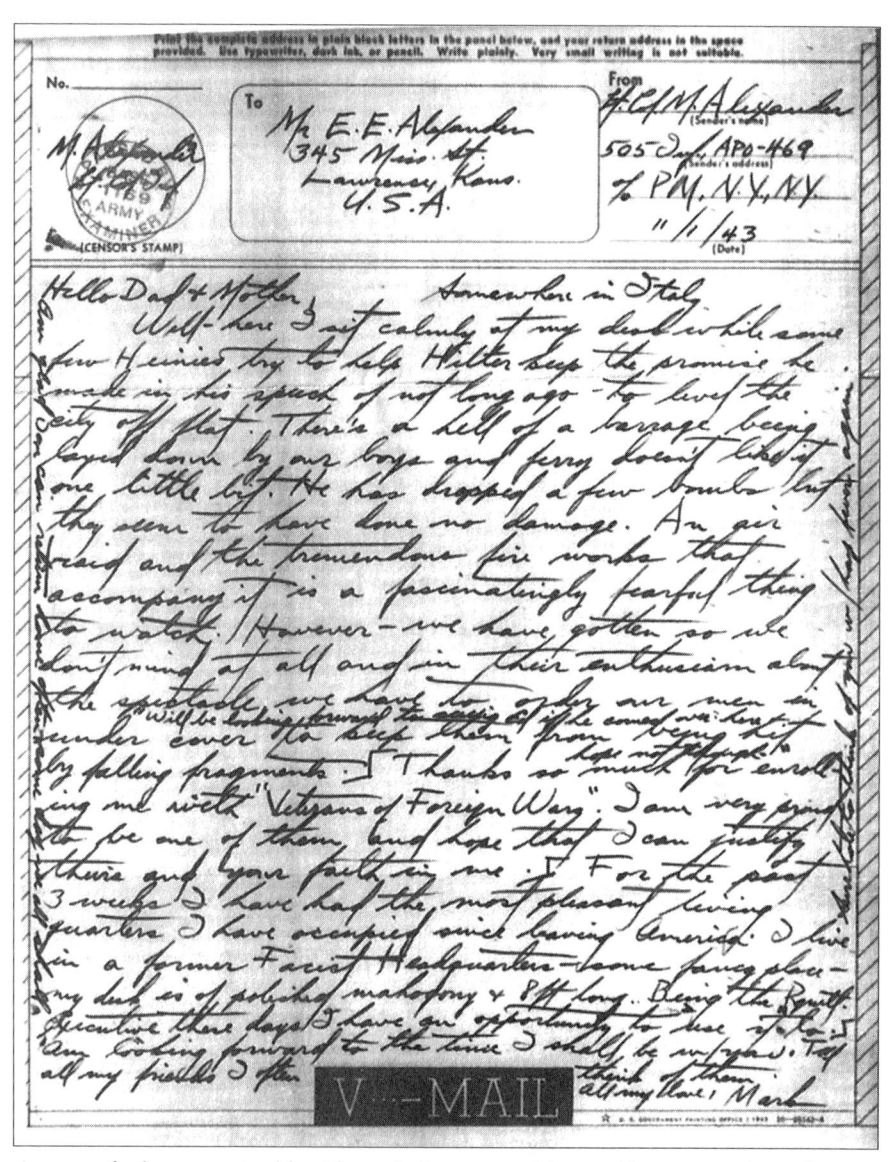

A copy of a letter received by Alexander's parents. Almost all correspondence from the troops was sent in the form of V-Mail. After a page was filled out and read by censors screening for classified information, a much smaller microfilmed version was shipped to the United States. Often the tiny writing had to be read with a magnifying glass.

reflecting the fact that letters were censored in the attempt to keep troop locations secret. Alexander, like every other soldier, however, did his best to let his family know where he was stationed, as in this letter to his brother Don, alluding to his recent trip to Capri: *Yes sir, not far from*

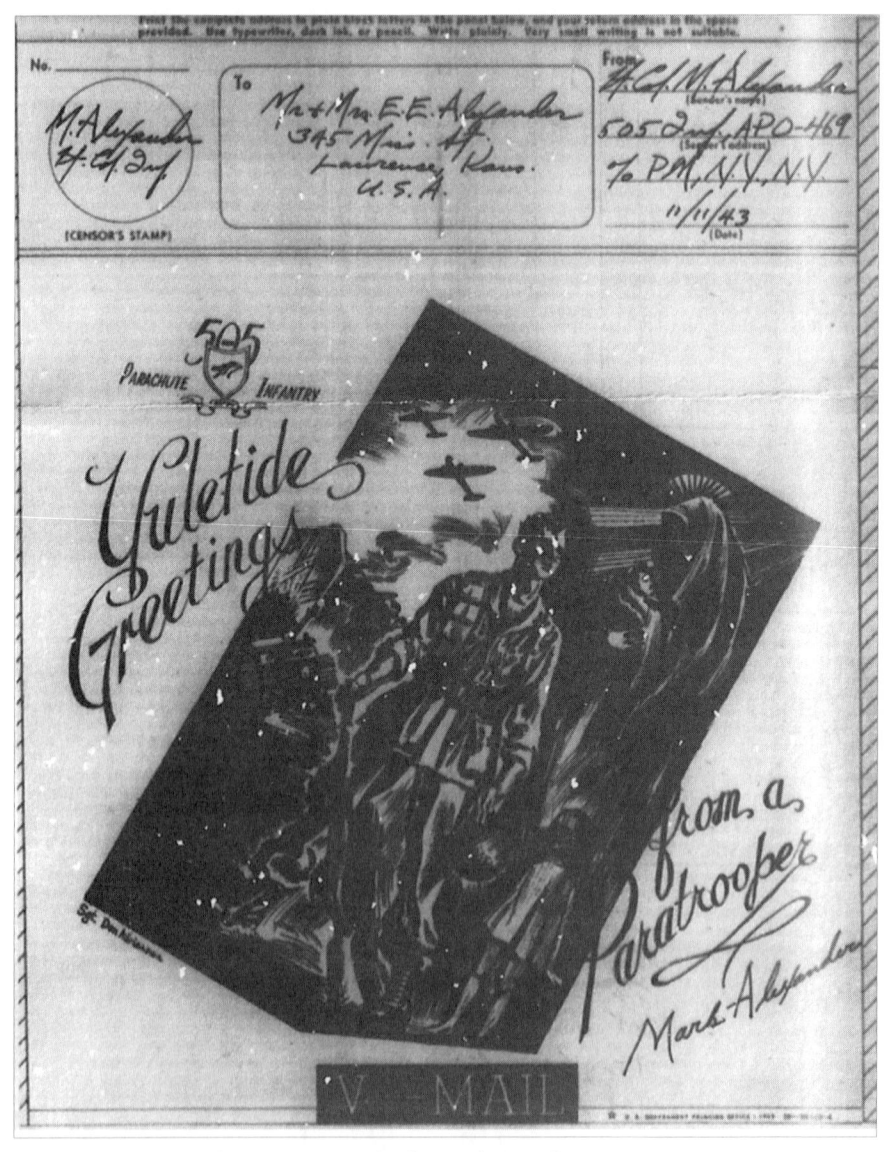

Even Christmas cards were sent in the form of V-Mail.

here Cesar used to woo and screw. He had an island where he carried on with the most of his loving-it's a beautiful spot too. [3]

Even on the home front, communication was spotty at best, and families were often in the dark as to the whereabouts and activities of their members. Although neither Alexander nor his parents knew it, his brother Ed had secretly joined the paratroopers and completed jump school. A letter on October 26 from Mary to her in-laws indicates that she was both concerned and proud. *Ever since I got Edwin's letter yesterday from Camp Mackall I've been thinking about you, wondering how you felt about having a second son in the Paratroops. I certainly admire his courage going through that tough course without a word to anyone. He's very proud to be a paratrooper and very much enthused about it. His greatest worry now is that you'll be upset about it, and he wants your approval in the worst way. I think he has wanted to do this a long time. He took me by surprise. I can't express it, but it's almost as if he grew from a boy to a man overnight. I'm right proud of him.* [4]

During his time as regimental executive officer, Alexander's letters home often veered between two underlying themes. On the one hand, he tried to reassure his loved ones that he was safe and sound, sitting behind a desk, and enjoying the best that army life had to offer, as in this letter to his brother Don: *We have a rather pleasant set up where we are now and, sitting back with my feet up on this 8 foot polished mahogany desk of mine, I speculate on what black shirt bastard must have done the same thing some four weeks ago. Right now I expect he's hiding out in Rome and sleeping in a dirty tunnel or an air raid shelter at night.* On the other hand, it was clear that he would have much preferred to be in the field with his men. As Mary noted in another letter to his parents: *In Mark's last letter [...] he says time goes too slowly on occupation duty. I'm afraid he craves action.*

Mary, of course, was right, although she hoped against hope that her husband would remain safe from the front, sitting behind a desk. *I had a post card from Mark last week and he said they are still awaiting their next combat operation. I'm hoping the war will end before they get to it, but I know that's wishful thinking,* she wrote to his parents. Mary did not get her wish, but it would still be many months before Alexander got the action he craved when the 505 jumped into Normandy.

CHAPTER ELEVEN

NORTHERN IRELAND

On November 18, 1943, the 505 loaded onto the USS *Frederick Funston* and headed out to sea. The other units of the 82nd Airborne Division, with the exception of the 504, also boarded navy transports and shipped off.

Although the 82nd was only supposed to fight until Fifth Army broke out of the Salerno beachhead, commanders were very reluctant to give up the elite and aggressive airborne units. General Clark wanted to hang onto the entire 82nd, even though they were slated to move to Ireland to begin training for the long-awaited cross-channel invasion into France. A compromise was struck whereby Clark was allowed to keep the 504, but he promised they would rejoin the division in time to gear up for D-Day. This would not be the case; after months of bitter fighting, the 504 arrived in England far too late to recover and integrate replacements.

Unlike the ship that brought the 505 to North Africa, the *Frederick Funston* was actually designed to carry troops. The rooms were larger and more comfortable and there was enough cafeteria space for soldiers to *sit down* and eat three meals a day. The convoy made its way from Italy to Oran on the coast of North Africa for a 48-hour stopover. "Luckily, I knew a quartermaster stationed there," Alexander recalled, "since I lost all my clothes except what I was wearing. He re-equiped me with a complete outfit.

"We re-embarked and set sail for Belfast. Our entire trip took quite a while because we swung way out into the Atlantic to avoid the German sub packs that were very active in the east Atlantic Ocean. We came into Belfast from the north. On board I didn't have any assignment other than to make sure my men were taken care of. I did practically nothing for ten days and I gained ten pounds. I got up to 160 pounds for the first time in my life. I would just eat and sleep and give a few orders." The food was the best the men had eaten since leaving the United States. Thanksgiving was celebrated on board and the turkey and pumpkin pie were delicious. [1]

With an abundance of free time on his hands, Alexander wrote several letters home from "somewhere at sea." He worried about his brother Ed, expressing surprise that he had had joined the paratroopers. *I'm glad in some ways, and again I could kick him in the pants for not staying with the engineers—for which he was best trained. I'm hoping now that he will show up wherever I go and that I can get him assigned to the 505 where I can see something of him*, he wrote to his parents in November 1943.

In a longer letter of December 8, the twentieth day at sea, his mind turns to Christmas, but he also warns his family that the war is far from over, and makes several accurate predictions about the future.

My prediction is that Germany will hold out until next October, so don't think we have won the war as yet. Germany still has the most powerful army in the world […]. The farther the German army draws back towards her center, the stronger she becomes strategically. Her defense problems are simpler and defense and supply lines are shortened. The one [thing] we are all banking on is that the bombings have weakened and demoralized the civilians until their production is seriously curtailed and their morale broken.

Anyways, we must consider that Germany will gain nothing by an unconditional surrender at this time. She must fight and brave it. Otherwise the Russians will be in on them like a pack of wolves. Well, I'm for letting the wolves at them. Perhaps they will utterly destroy that military group who have thru generations pushed Germany's cause as a conquering nation and aggressor upon the rights of weaker nations of Europe.

Russia will of course be a terribly powerful nation when settlements are completed. But Russia will have had enough of fighting for some time, and tremendous natural resources at her disposal will be occupied for years developing her own country. We cannot look far enough ahead to visualize what may later develop in the way of rivalry between the four major powers of the world, which will be China, Russia, G.B. and the U.S.

Now for us—my hopes are that your Xmas will be a grand one. You must have it so, as you are keeping the old home alive for us who are overseas. You must go on just as if we are there—for some day we shall be.

After unloading in Belfast, the 505 went about 30 miles northeast to Cookstown, where they had a training area set up. "It was pretty cold," Alexander recalled. "We got there in November and there was a little snow on the ground." Ireland was the complete opposite of North Africa. It rained practically every day and the land was lush and green. Quonset huts, corrugated steel structures shaped like a half-moon, with arced walls and ceiling, served as the regiment's new homes. "The latrines had what they called 'honey pots,' big cans they set below the seat. There were about 20 of them in one place. Every morning they sent guys in to haul them away and used it for fertilizer. I didn't like that idea at all."

In Northern Ireland, the disproportionate number of men who were absent without leave (AWOL) forced Alexander into trying court-martial cases for weeks on end, a task that he absolutely hated. "We had 146 AWOLs at one time out of the regiment. It was partly command's fault. I wouldn't say entirely, because you've got AWOLs off and on anyway, but not anywhere near 146 out of 3,200 men. The men thought, having fought in two campaigns, that they were really top-grade fighting men and they needed a break once in a while. I felt that way too. We had had no real leave since we went to North Africa, through Sicily and Italy and back up to training in North Ireland."

The men had a point. They had been through two campaigns and seen friends die in each. Other than a few days off here and there, training, combat or policing Naples had filled the majority of the nine months since they had left the States. It was also clear that they would soon be in very intensive training again, preparing for another invasion.

"Colonel Batcheller and I couldn't change anything regarding leave, because it had to come down from division headquarters. They would let just a few men go at a time. We should have had a rotation system where each guy was given a week or whatever it would be. But we didn't, so the men just went anyway. Then we would get them back again and I had to court-martial them. Lots of them. I hated this court-martial business, but that was part of my job. As executive officer, I had to handle a lot of discipline. I don't know how many god damn court-martial cases I handled." [2]

The enlisted men often had nicknames for their superiors. Alexander

Lt. Col. Herbert Batcheller became the 505 PIR regimental commander when Colonel Gavin was promoted to executive officer of the 82nd Airborne Division. Batcheller was later bumped down to command a battalion in the 508. He was killed leading an attack on June 6, 1944, D-Day morning.

caught wind of one of them. "Some of the guys—they didn't want me to know, but I heard it one time—were quietly calling Colonel Batcheller 'Horrible Herbie.' He was really a nice guy, but had some crazy habits. He'd go around making a noise, *huh-huh*, like he was half coughing or had something stuck in his throat. I don't know where he got a habit like that. He had made a name for himself as the crazy paratrooper back at Benning, because he had a motorcycle and would really speed up and down the streets on that thing. He had a lot of guts."

Brave or not, Batcheller got into trouble in Northern Ireland. He fell in love with an Irish lass. "He'd go off every afternoon and meet her somewhere, and spent a lot of time with her. I knew what he was doing, but I didn't want to know where he went, because I'd have to tell if asked where he was. Three times General Ridgway came looking for him. He'd come down and say, 'Where can I find Colonel Batcheller?'

"The first time I was in a room and had the door shut because I had a guy standing in front of me who had gone AWOL. I was giving him his punishment when Ridgway knocked on the door. He called out, 'Colonel Alexander?'

"I said, 'Yes, Sir,' and opened the door.

"'What are you doing?'

"'Trying court-martial cases, sir.'

"He asked, 'Can you tell me where I can find Colonel Batcheller?'

"I said, 'No, Sir, I can't.' And I couldn't. I was legitimate in saying that. If he had asked me if I thought I knew whom he was with or what he was doing, he would have had me over the eight ball. But he didn't and so he left.

"Then he came out again about a week later, looking for Batcheller. And I was still on court-martial cases. He asked me the same question, exactly the same way. I said, 'Sir, he's gone this afternoon. I don't know where he is.'

"He said, 'Well, he should be keeping me informed.'

"Batcheller was getting in a lot of trouble, plus we had all those AWOLs. I warned him. I said, 'The General's been looking for you. You better make yourself available.' But he didn't do it.

"I was spending all my time court-martialing these guys. We built a stockade on our own and everything. We had a big old barn and put guards on the doors. We had almost 140 men in there at one time. Each had a cot because it was really cold. Naturally, they didn't like it. The guards carried empty rifles and were supposed to club anybody who tried to get out, but I don't think anyone tried.

"Two or three times I asked, 'Colonel, shouldn't I go out and oversee some of the training programs?' I thought I should be out there in the field with some of the men, because he wasn't going. Norton was on it and handling it all with only the help of a captain and a lieutenant.

"He said, 'No, I want you to stay here and take care of these courts-martial.' I was stuck in the headquarters and spent all of my time for more than three weeks doing nothing else."

To make matters worse, Alexander came down with yellow jaundice, and this time no quinine was available to fight it. "The jaundice was part of the aftermath of malaria. To combat it, I started taking that yellow pill, Atabrine, again. My skin turned real yellowish from the combination of the sickness and the pill, about the color of a pencil.

"I felt terrible and was in bed for about a week. Although I was sicker than a dog, Batcheller made me handle court-martial cases from my bed.

"I said, 'Colonel, I'm sick.'

"He said, 'That's all right. You'll make out.'

"I was kind of tee'd off at him, but he asked me to do it, so I did it. These guys would come in and here I am, lying in a bed handing out punishments. Finally a captain was assigned to help me."

Although there were issues between the Northern and Southern Irish and often between the English and Irish, most of the Irish were extremely friendly and easy for the Americans to get along with. "In Ireland, I made some good friends," Alexander recalled. "Our headquarters was in an old castle. Every night at twelve o'clock the Irish heir would get up on the parapet and play his bagpipe. He and his family still lived in part of the castle. One of his ancestors had been a great hunter. In a hall that was about 75 feet long, brass plates hung all over the wall commemorating how many ducks he had killed that day. One day, they showed a picture of him with a cannon. He would put grape shot in a cannon and fire it at the ducks as they landed on a nearby lake.

"While I was there, I learned that there were no good feelings between the North and South Irish," Alexander continued. "In fact, right next to where we were lived a minister and his wife. I talked to the wife several times. She had three brothers in South Ireland and hadn't seen them in twenty years. When she married a northerner they severed her from the family. But that's the way it was in many cases."

Southern Ireland was off-limits to the Americans, who nevertheless found ways to get in and out of the country. "Colonel Batcheller, my boss, ordered me to send my jeep and a sergeant from our headquarters company across the border into Southern Ireland to get a load of liquor. This was fairly dangerous. If the South Irish caught you, they held you. It would take some diplomatic work to get you out. And any equipment you took over there, like a jeep, they kept. You would never get that back. In their opinion, letting Allied soldiers come and go would be collaborating with us and they wanted to stay strictly neutral.

"I sent Sergeant Dednum in Colonel Batcheller's jeep instead of mine, because I didn't want to pay for another one if it didn't come back. He crossed the boarder with no problem and got to the place where he would pick up the booze. He stepped out of the jeep and was about to knock on the door, when a South Ireland policeman pulled up behind the colonel's jeep and got out to take a look at it. Dednum said, 'Hey, I need to talk to you.' And when he got close enough, he punched the policeman in the stomach, jumped in the jeep and took off.

"It was no problem crossing the border south. The guards let you in, but don't count on getting out. They were under instructions not to let that happen.

"I was really sweating out the loss of Dednum and the Colonel's jeep. Part of my job as executive officer was to keep Colonel Batcheller out of trouble. If there was an investigation, however, I would have to tell them who had given the order, and then I would be in deep shit with my commanding officer.

"I waited in our service pool until 3:30 a.m., when Dednum finally returned. He had driven around for about an hour before finding a way to get back to North Ireland on some little mountain road."

By the end of January, Alexander was clearly tiring of his desk job. On January 23, 1944, he wrote home: *I seem to remember that this is my birthday and looking out the window above my desk, I am confused as to whether it is winter or spring time. First it snows big blotchy flakes, and then it rains. In 15 minutes for all I know the sun will be shining. Yes, North Ireland has the wettest, coldest, most consistently bad weather of any place I have ever dreamed of. We have been here for some little time now and are rapidly developing into a close proximity to garrison soldiers. It is very boring and I in particular am bored at having to spend so much time at a desk as executive officer.*

Alexander's personality would not under any circumstances allow him to do anything by half. His internal drive consistently won out over his dislike for office work, yet he would never be known as a great administrator, and administration constituted a very large part of an executive officer's work.

Lt. Col. Herbert Batcheller, commander of the 505 PIR (second from right), and Lt. Col. Mark Alexander, executive officer of the 505 (third from right), attend an evening tea given by Lady Montgomery (speaking to Alexander), the mother of British Field Marshall Bernard Montgomery, at the regiment's local Red Cross Club on January 23, 1944.

CHAPTER TWELVE

ENGLAND

AFTER TWO MONTHS IN IRELAND, the division made the short boat ride across the Irish Sea, and the 505 was stationed at Camp Quorn near Leicestershire, England. "We knew this was for the invasion of Europe, but knew not when or where we would invade," Alexander commented. "Even we senior officers did not know where we would land until about 30 days before D-Day." The regiment moved into pyramidal tents, each complete with a little coal- and coke-burning stove, and began a very intensive training program. [1]

In England, Alexander received a Silver Star for his leadership at the Volturno River. [2] He was also called to London to be decorated at a review before King George VI and General Eisenhower at Allied Headquarters. There was "an American and English combined guard of honor for five generals, a major and myself, " Alexander recalled. "We were decorated by the British commander-in-chief. The entire Allied staff was there and did us honors."

Alexander received the British Distinguished Service Order for Valor (DSO)—the highest award given by the British next to the Victoria Cross, and the highest any non-British citizen could earn—for leading the 2nd Battalion as part of the 22nd Armored Brigade in Italy. General Patton, awarded the non-combat Order of the Bath (an honorary order in the King's household), jokingly said to Alexander, "I'll swap my Order of the Bath for your DSO."

In contrast to Ireland, where Alexander was plagued by seemingly endless paperwork, England presented him with new challenges and opportunities. "General Gavin, a principal in planning for the invasion of France, took me to London twice to participate in planning sessions for

For capturing five bridges and a town in Italy as part of the British 22nd Armored Brigade, Alexander was decorated at a ceremony in front of England's King George. At left is Lt. Gen. George S. Patton. He is facing Sir Alan F. Brooke, Chief of the Imperial General Staff. Screened by Sir Alan is Lt. Gen. Manton Eddy. Next in line is Brig. Gen. Julius Holmes. General Dwight D. Eisenhower is walking toward Sir Alan. The next two men in line are unidentified. Lt. Col. Mark Alexander is in line behind Ike, second from right. The last man in line is unidentified.

the airborne operation. At one, about 20 generals and a few of us lower-ranking combat veterans were present. We sat around a 30-foot table."

The meeting was chaired by Sir Tafford Leigh-Mallory, who commanded all air transport to be involved in the invasion—British, Canadian and American. Leigh-Mallory was decidedly against paratrooper assaults on D-Day: as he had previously told Eisenhower, he expected 70 percent of airborne troops to be killed or wounded within the first few days. Only Eisenhower's insistence had brought Leigh-Mallory to the table, and everyone at the planning session was well aware of his views.

Gavin undoubtedly brought Alexander to the meeting because of his outstanding combat experience: at this point in the war, he was one of the very few Americans who had commanded a battalion in two campaigns. Probably more importantly, he was distinguished as the recipient of the British DSO. Gavin knew Alexander's views on airborne strategy matched his own, and that Alexander would speak up if and when the moment arose.

The moment did indeed arise when a dispute developed concerning the best altitude for the jump: Leigh-Mallory wanted the jump to occur at 1,200 feet to possibly limit damage to aircraft from enemy ground fire, but the American paratroopers argued for an elevation of 800 feet. The less time spent drifting to earth, the less they could be fired upon, and a drop at lower altitude also meant they would be less dispersed after landing.

Alexander made a rather passionate plea for the lower elevation. Leigh-Mallory listened, then said, "Colonel, I will call on you if and when I wish to hear further from you." Gavin, one of the lower-ranking officers at the meeting, did not come to Alexander's rescue, but the mild grin on his face showed that he approved. The argument to jump at 800 feet finally won the day.

Although he liked the British, Alexander was very annoyed by the exorbitant prices they charged the Americans for everything from a drink to the rent on British barracks, as he expresses in a letter of February 20, 1944: *Well, the British army is all right but these damned British civilians are sure gigging hell out of us at every turn. They charge us three to five times what everything is worth. A bottle of Scotch in London is $25.00. Also, what gets me is this reciprocal trade set-up wherein the British have built camps with money we loaned them and then they rent them back at prices much in excess of their worth, and we pay out a hell of a price for maintenance. Even if you take a rock from the hillside, you pay for it.*

Given Alexander's position as second in command of the 505, the regiment's finances were much on his mind. His next letter home, written on February 21, deals uniquely with this topic; his aggravation is such that it is the only existing letter to his parents that does not sign off with the word "love." *I contracted with the British maintenance officer the other day for enough 4-inch and bigger rock and shale from a coal mine dump to lay down about 400 yards of road, 10 feet wide and 8 inches thick. We were to furnish all the trucks and all the labor [...] and also about six sacks of cement were called for to build a service rack for our motor pool. All together the British maintenance engineer said it would be at a cost estimate of $1,600. What makes me so damned mad is that our own engineers who receive these services and materials* *from the British have nothing whatsoever to do with getting a fair estimate of the cost, and yet are the only representatives of ours who know what we are getting. No one even looks the materials over to see if we even get what is specified in the contract. The other day we got 120 fence posts and 15 hundred weight of wire—cost $320. [...] This reciprocal trade business [as it] is now being done will put us in debt to the British at the end of the war. I want some of you [armchair] politicians to think it over.* [3]

A major change in leadership occurred when Colonel Batcheller, the commander of the 505, lost the confidence of Ridgway and Gavin, and was subsequently replaced. On March 1, 1944, he was relieved and replaced by Col. William "Bill" Ekman, a West Point graduate. "I think part of it was when Ridgway couldn't get track of him, but a lot of other things were not going well either," Alexander commented.

Ekman possessed no combat experience as yet, but certainly knew the airborne inside and out. He had served as a company commander in

Lt. Col. William Ekman, the new commander of the 505 Parachute Infantry Regiment, celebrates at his "prop blast" in Leicester, England. The senior officers of the 505 are from left to right: Hagen, Alexander, Gavin, Ekman, Winton, Krause and Vandervoort.

the 501st Parachute Battalion, America's first paratroop unit of that size, and more recently as executive officer of the 508th Parachute Infantry Regiment. Alexander stayed on as Ekman's XO.

Meanwhile, it had become apparent that the 504, still fighting in Italy, would not rejoin the 82nd Airborne Division in time to recover and incorporate replacements before the upcoming invasion. The 508 RCT took its place as a new addition to the division, and another parachute regiment, the 507 was also added, bringing the total to four, including one glider infantry regiment, the 325 GIR. Batcheller received an extraordinary second chance: when the promotion of a battalion commander to fill Ekman's old executive officer position created another opening, Batcheller then became the new battalion commander in the 508.

Norton and Alexander, good friends since Sicily, maintained their outstanding working relationship. "He read the letter informing us of the change in command and said I should have had the 505. He also said, 'Don't worry about it. You'll have a regiment soon.'

"I said, 'Jack, it doesn't worry me a bit. I'm happy where I am.' I didn't resent it at all because, hell, I was still learning. I had only been in the service a short time and was worried I was moving too fast. I didn't want to get in over my head. In fact, I went into Sicily with two years and nine months of military training. That's not very much for a battalion commander.

"Ekman was two years younger than I was, but he had nine more years of military experience, plus a year in the paratroopers down in Panama, and was an Academy graduate. He was also far senior to me in his promotion to lieutenant colonel, so it only made sense that he be promoted ahead of me.

"The Academy men took pretty good care of their own people, and I didn't blame them. They had all gone through four years at the Academy together. When you go through something tough together you become very close associates. You also understand what training they have gone through and have a better idea of their capabilities. Knowing a guy and what he's apt to react to is a hell of an advantage when you are at war. You normally know what you're getting with an Academy man."

Colonel Ekman started his new job with the deck stacked against him. The first time he addressed the troops, he accidentally said, "men of the 508" instead of "men of the 505." A groan rose from the regiment. Alexander thought, "the poor guy."

The 505 was full of confident, cocky veterans of two combat jumps and two campaigns. Ekman hadn't had any combat experience yet and every man in the regiment knew it. Things had been running a little loose and he needed to get them focused and firing on all cylinders again. He tightened the screws.

"When he first took over, he got kind of rough," Alexander noted. "And he probably had to do it. I was his exec. He did have me do things I didn't want to do. He would play recall on the bugle at any time of the night. You never knew when he was going to do it. What he was trying to do was get control of the regiment. Initially, a lot of men didn't like him."

Camp Quorn was within eight miles of several sizable towns and the large city of Leicester. There were lots of pretty English girls around and the men liked to spend as much time as they could with them. Some of the rowdier paratroopers got into fights with other American soldiers in the area, and Ekman restricted the entire regiment. A high wall ran around the perimeter of the tent area, but even with that, it was hard to keep the men from sneaking off.

Alexander was walking outside along the wall one evening, and "some guy dropped off it right in front of me. He turned around, saw me, and said, 'Oh, my god!' I kind of growled at him, 'Okay, just see how fast you can get back over that wall.' And he made it. I didn't know if he would be able to or not. It was pretty high. There were a lot of things to do and a lot of English girls around there. So it was hard to keep the guys in."

The top military brass also indirectly added to Ekman's SOB reputation with the troops. A crackdown throughout England took place to find and return AWOL soldiers. Several 505ers were caught in the sweep and given extra duty. Not knowing where the crackdown originated, the men put the blame on the new commander. [4]

"One morning I walked in the office and he had a big black eye. I said, 'Bill, what happened to you?'

"He said, 'You won't believe it.'

"'Well, tell me anyway.'"

He had been to the White Horse, a bar popular with the soldiers. It is likely that the 505 was on restriction and he was making sure none of his men were there. He waited outside and monitored people coming and going for a while before heading back to camp. Everything was blacked out for fear of German air raids, except for a few very dim lamps on the corners.

As Ekman put it to Alexander, "I was coming home through the church square. Just as I got to a corner, a voice says, 'Colonel Ekman?' I said, 'Yes.' And as I turned, a big fist hit me in the eye and knocked me flat on the ground. I heard feet running and a voice called back, 'I just wanted to be sure!'"

"So the next morning," Alexander continued, "Ekman had a formation and challenged whoever it was that hit him to meet him behind the mess hall. Well, who in the hell is going to admit to doing that? I said, 'If you think any of those guys are going to admit to hitting you in the eye, you're dreaming.'"

One of Alexander's duties as executive officer was to hand out disciplinary measures. He severely disliked having to court-martial AWOLs in Ireland and handing out punishments as directed by Colonel Ekman, but it was part of the job. On one particular case, however, he went out of his way to ensure justice.

"One of our men had beat the hell out of a woman in the park. She came in and she was all beat up, black eyes, broken nose and bruises all over. I saw her. She told us the guy who did it was named Mac. I had everybody with Mac in his name line up, so she could point him out."

Don McKeage was one of the soldiers who had to line up. "She heard his buddy say, 'Hey Mac, let's get the hell out of here.' Well, hell, everybody was Mac. We all dressed in our Class A uniforms and had to go down to Regimental. And they've got this girl walking up and down in front of us. She's stopping and looking at each one of us. Sure enough, some guy had beat the shit out of her, but she pointed him out." [5]

"About that time," Alexander continues, "an English police officer from Scotland Yard showed up. He said, 'I hear you've got a problem here.'

"I agreed and he said, 'You should know we've investigated and found that she was a street walker. I might as well warn you. In English law if someone mistreats a prostitute, we never bring charges. I'm not going to do anything about it.'

"I thought, 'Well, that's a hell of a law.' So I had the soldier who beat the girl sent back to the States and forwarded his records along with him. Then he was tried back there. I don't know whatever happened or became of it. He was a nut. And I found that he had been kind of nutty in other ways as well. You didn't know everybody in the regiment. You knew quite a few of the characters, but a lot of them would get by with something and you would never find out about it."

In England, Alexander was also forced to deal directly with the feisty

Lt. Col. Alexander in England four months before the D-Day invasion of France.

nature of Ed Krause, the commander of the 3rd Battalion. "I found out Ed Krause was feuding with Vandervoort, who commanded my old 2nd Battalion. Krause had just been promoted to lieutenant colonel. So he goes over and starts jumping on Vandervoort, who was still a major. He was saying things like, 'You didn't salute me when I went by,' that kind of stuff. Vandervoort was kind of argumentative too, so they fought about it.

"I had to have them both in and I shook them down. I said, 'Look, you've each got your own battalion. You've got plenty to do there. Stay the hell away from each other. Your quarrelling is bad for the morale of the regiment.' Vandervoort was a good man and became a hell of a good battalion commander. But he was hard-headed as hell." [6]

All the while, the entire division was involved in very heavy training under the "merciless" General Gavin. In Gavin's own words:

> All maneuvers in which decisions were required were preceded by a long grueling physical test, usually an overnight march of about eighteen to twenty miles with full combat equipment. Then when the men expected a rest, they were presented with difficult combat situations. After an all-day maneuver, when they were tired and hungry, a night march was ordered. After a couple of hours of marching, at about midnight, they would be ordered to halt and go into a dispersed bivouac, in anticipation a night's rest. After about an hour of sleep, which was just enough to cause them to lose their sense of orientation to events and environment, unit commanders were suddenly awakened and given a new set of orders requiring immediate movement. They marched until daylight, when a new situation was given to them, usually a final attack order. [...] It was exacting training, but it gave me an opportunity to get to know a lot about them and for them to learn much about themselves. [7]

Nor did the workload let up outside of the field. Alexander described "a continuity of classes going all the time in the evenings. Primarily, battalion commanders and some of the company commanders taught them, and I taught a few. They were being taught to all of the officers in the regiment, then we had another set of classes for all the non-coms. Usually everyone was eager to learn because it might make the difference between living and dying.

"French maps weren't easy to read, because they were in meters, and you had to learn to convert them to yards and miles. Colonel Krause was going to teach a map class one night. He got up at the podium and he explained what he was going to teach. Then he says, 'By the time I get through, you're all going to think I'm a son-of-a-bitch.'

"A mild voice from the back of the room says, 'That'll be no change.'

"I laughed like hell along with some of the others that were not afraid to laugh, but a lot of them were scared to because Krause would get them later on. He turned around like a damn fool and said, 'Who said that?' Of course no one was going to admit to it."

Alexander received a break from his regular duties when General Ridgway pulled him away to set up and umpire proficiency tests and a night jump for each of the nine parachute infantry battalions in the division. This included the three battalions of each of the three regiments, the 505, 507 and 508; the three battalions in the 325 GIR went into combat via glider and were therefore exempt from the exercise. The 504, recently arrived in England from Italy, was not included, because it would not be participating in the cross-channel attack.

For Alexander, working with men in the field was far preferable to working at a desk. "I scheduled every battalion in the division for a night drop. I jumped with the first five. For the last few I decided there was no sense in me standing up there freezing my butt off every night in the open door of the plane, so I met them on the ground. By the end of it I had fifteen night jumps, including those in Italy, Sicily, North Africa and the United States.

"We had one bad night drop where some fog came up and a plane from D Company collided with another one. It killed a whole planeload of troopers. After that, if there was any fog, we didn't jump. These things were not made note of. I mean, it's on the records, but you don't see any publicity on that type of thing."

When Lt. Col. Krause's battalion showed up to jump, Alexander found they didn't have working batteries in their radios. "I was chewing him about it. I said, 'Ed, you should have radios that are operational out here, so you can communicate with your men.' He was giving me a bad time about it." Unknown to either man at the time, Ridgway showed up. He listened for a minute and then left, figuring things were well in hand.

The General seemed to take a particular interest in the battalion test jumps; this was not the only time he showed up to check their progress. "Colonel Batcheller was given a battalion in the 508 as a chance to recoup himself. Apparently though, they were having some trouble. Batcheller got me on the radio and said, 'Mark, cancel the jump for my battalion. We're not doing well at all.'

"I said, 'Colonel, I can't cancel it. It has to come from division to cancel this exercise.' Well, he got *mad* and let me hear it. About that time Ridgway walked up behind me and I think he heard the tail end of the conversation. He didn't say anything, but he was grinning." Ridgway apparently liked the results of the tests: he later gave Alexander a rare written accommodation for directing the training exercises.

Alexander notified friends throughout the airborne that his brother Ed was now a paratrooper and asked if they knew his location. He

Officers at Camp Quorn, England, 1944. Alexander, second from the left, vastly preferred directing training exercises to administrative tasks.

discovered that Ed had recently arrived in England as part of a group of replacements to be used to fill holes in the airborne regiments. "Ed reported in and wanted to be in my unit. I said, "No, I'll not take him. Let him have the regular channel.' I didn't want to be accused of favoritism."

Alexander did pull a few strings for his brother, however, although the arrangement did not work out. "I knew he had three and a half years of engineering in school, so I figured he belonged with the military engineers. Well, the G-1, Col. Walt Winton, needed a man for the division to work on his map section. Ed was good at that, so instead of asking first, I thought I'd just assign him over there. It's a safer assignment anyway, because if you're with division headquarters you're probably not directly on the front lines.

"Well, Ed wouldn't take the assignment. Then my friend Colonel Winton got mad at me because he cut order on him. He said, 'I had to go to a lot of trouble to get him transferred.'

"I said, 'Sorry. I thought he would be happy to take it.'" There was no way of knowing where Ed would be ultimately assigned.

Time before the invasion was growing short. The usual rumor mill often foretold of combat just days or weeks away, but no one gave it much credence. Obvious clues, however, clearly showed the fight was close at hand—including clues at the mess hall. "For about 30 days while we were training in England prior to Normandy, we got nothing but lamb, shipped out of Australia. When it was cooked you could smell it in the air a mile away. The guys would line up for the mess hall and they'd start going, *Baaah! Baaah!* You could hear it all over. But one day, there was beef at the mess hall. And so right away the rumor starts, 'They're getting us ready to ship out.' And they were right."

Those on the home front also knew the invasion was imminent. The knowledge weighed heavily on Mary, as it did for thousands of other soldiers' wives, but she bore it with love and courage, as her letter to Alexander of May 11, 1944 attests.

We just received your airmail of May 6th and each of us thought it was a wonderful letter. There's a lot of love and kindliness [...] of which you spoke waiting for you right here. The day when we are again living together is the day I'm waiting for. You and I have most certainly changed a little in the past year, but I don't think our love has, except to grow bigger. And I don't think our ideals have changed [...]. Mary Jo and I are ready and waiting. We are sweating out the invasion, but we're the most optimistic cusses you ever saw. [...]

It must be a funny feeling to have a child that you've never held in your arms or even seen in the flesh. It won't be so much longer when you two can really get together. I still believe—probably because I want to—that the Germans won't last long after the invasion really starts. The strain of waiting must be terrific, especially for you who likes to get things done fast and thoroughly.

It's going to be fun to relax completely again when you are back. In the meantime and always, I love you, darling, with all my heart.

At the end of May, the paratroopers were restricted to base. On May 29, the 505 bused to the departure airfields, where they were sealed in and the next day shown large sand tables displaying the Normandy countryside and the airborne objectives. Remembering Sicily, and knowing that they might be dropped miles from the intended target, they memorized not only their own drop area, but those of the other units in the 82nd, and even those in the 101st Airborne Division. The 505ers also learned at this time that their sister regiment, the battle-hardened 504, would not join them. [8] The 505 was hence the only regiment with combat experience out of the entire Allied airborne force, which included the American 82nd and 101st Divisions and the British 6th Division. Much was riding on their capable shoulders.

The 505 battalions had the following missions: the 3rd Battalion to take Ste. Mère-Eglise, a major crossroads on the Cotentin Peninsula behind the American landing beaches; the 2nd Battalion to take the village of Neuville-au-Plain and set up blocking positions to the west and east; the 1st Battalion to clear the area between Ste. Mère-Eglise and the La Fière Bridge on the Merderet River, and serve as regimental backup. [9] If the airborne assault became a disaster, all units of the 82nd were to fall back on Ste. Mère-Eglise to make their stand.

Cooped up at the airfields, the troopers had plenty of time to read, play cards and think. Every soldier must at some point consider his own mortality before entering combat, especially troops like the paratroopers, who dropped behind enemy lines. Alexander's last letter before the invasion betrays these thoughts while simultaneously seeking to assure his family that everything will be all right.

June 2, 1944
England

Dearest Mother and Dad,
Every day I think of my sweet family of Alexanders back there in Lawrence and always I am very proud of you and looking forward to those delightful times we will have together. I try very hard to picture you all together, how you look, how you laugh, how you like my Mary Jo and Mary, how the new kitchen looks, and a million little memories of home go tripping thru my mind like the frames of a motion picture.

Well, here it is, the day before we take off again and I'm about to jump into the roughest one of the lot. We paratroopers are going in ahead of everyone else as usual, to try and soften it up a bit for the beachheads. And I'd much rather be going in this way than coming in with the amphibious forces. Yes, I still feel pretty lucky and shall of course take very good care of Mark.

By the way, Ed is still at a replacement center here, and there I want him to stay until this thing gets going.
Remember that I love you always.
Your son,
Mark

CHAPTER THIRTEEN

D-DAY: JUNE 6, 1944

OPERATION OVERLORD, THE ALLIED AIRBORNE mission, called for the paratroopers to jump into Normandy in the very early morning hours of June 4-5. It was to be followed a few hours later by Operation NEPTUNE, where beaches on the Cotentin Peninsula were divided into American, Canadian, and British sectors in anticipation of the amphibious assault scheduled to take place at dawn. Seizing the beaches and control of the Peninsula would cut the enemy off from the sea; a rapid Allied thrust into the French heartland and deep into the continent would then deliver a fatal blow to the Wehrmacht, pushing the Germans out of occupied territories and all the way back into Germany.

Training and timing an invasion of this magnitude was a tremendous undertaking involving thousands of ships and hundreds of C-47 airborne troop transports that placed 150,000 Allied troops on shore by the end of the first day. [1] Among the 821 C-47s used in the invasion were 20 pathfinder aircraft carrying specially trained paratroopers assigned to set up lights and homing beacons on designated drop zones. The pathfinders were to jump 30 minutes ahead of the regimental drops.[2] Waco gliders carrying glider troopers, artillerymen and engineers, as well as jeeps, anti-tank guns and supplies were also slated to land on fields amidst the crisscross maze of hedgerows.

As time ticked away, General Ridgway approached Alexander to say he had decided to jump into Normandy with the 505 rather than go by glider or ship. "He said, 'I want to be there on the ground right from the start. And I want you to pick a plane for me where I'll have the best chance of landing on the drop zone.' We were the only combat-seasoned regiment that was jumping into Normandy. He knew we gave him the

D–Day: 6th June, 1944

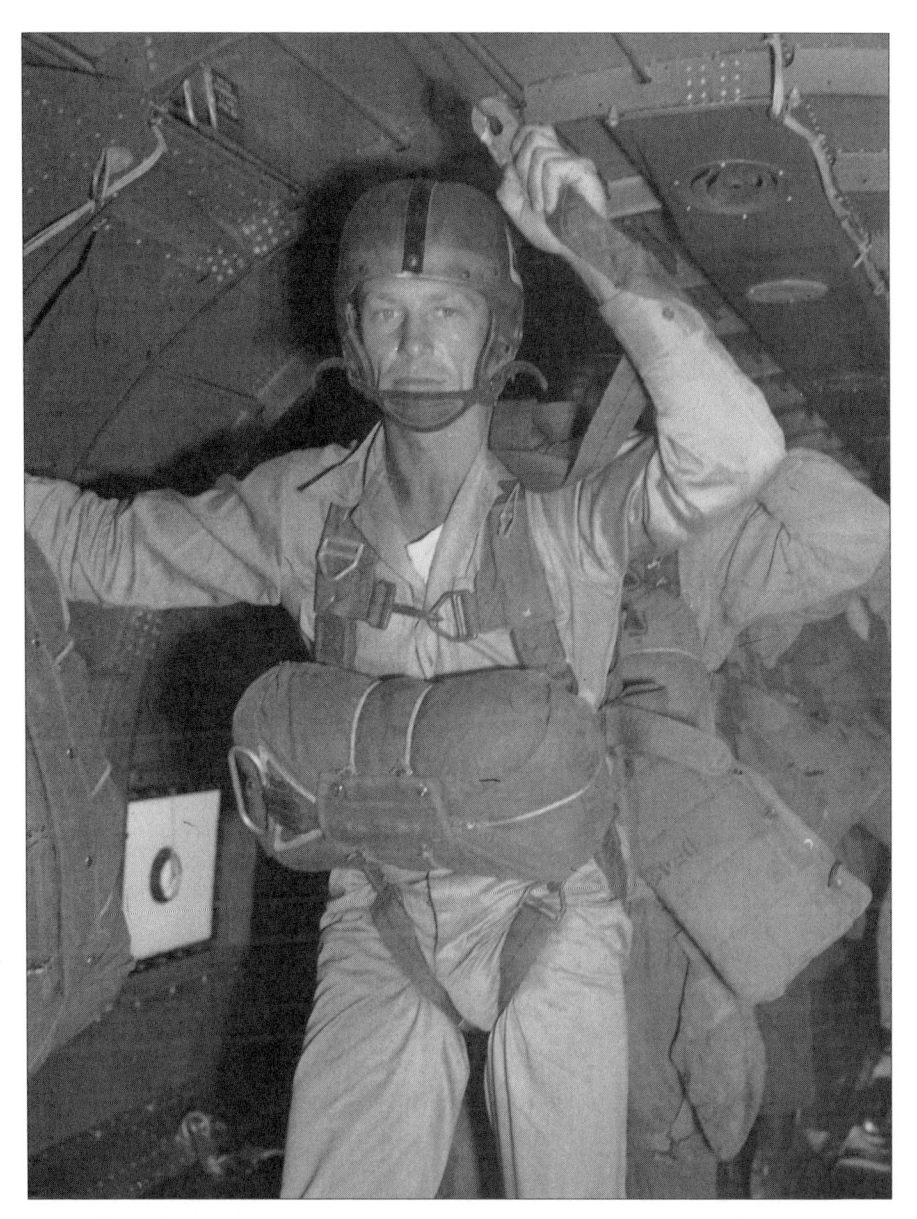

Lt. Dick Garber, a very experienced jumpmaster, was selected to parachute General Ridgway on D-Day morning. He is pictured here before a training jump—notice the football-type training helmet. His left hand is holding the static line that will release his main parachute upon exiting the aircraft. His reserve parachute is strapped over his stomach. If the main chute fails, the spare can be released by pulling the ring shown on the left side of the bag.

best chance of getting on the ground in the right place. He also decided to put his command post near ours. Our experience would be important if the command posts were attacked.

"I chose a C-47 with Lt. Dick Garber from the 505 Headquarters Company because he had jumpmastered at least 50 times as a trainer before he joined the 505. He had a lot of experience and was solid. Garber's plane was on the right side of the flight as well. Standing in the door on the left side of his plane, he could best see the beckoning lights of the pathfinders. The General sat in with Headquarters Company for loading and jump instructions on the 4th of June. This, I believe, would be his fifth jump. I didn't take him in my plane because it would be way out on the left side of the formation and it was a tough place to see the beacon lights if the plane flew the correct route."

Ekman, Alexander and the 505 headquarters staff divided up. Alexander and regimental intelligence officer, Capt. Patrick Gibbons, were assigned with half of the group to a plane flying on the left; Ekman, Norton and the others were to fly in a plane on the right. This increased the odds of at least one planeload landing near the proposed command post, enabling a working headquarters to be established. It also decreased the danger that both the commander and executive officer would be killed that morning. Being the commander, Ekman would ride in on the right side of the formation, giving him and his stick the best chance of seeing the drop zone before landing, making it quicker to locate once they were on the ground.

The 52nd Group Carrier Wing again carried most of the 505, but because Alexander had been promoted out of the 2nd Battalion and into Regimental Headquarters, he did not have his favorite pilot, Tommy Thompson. Orders for all flight crews stated that no paratroopers were to return home. All would be dropped. Clearly implied, although not said, was that they would jump whether or not the pilot found the drop zone. And men who jumped too far away into enemy territory would almost certainly be captured or killed.

Stormy weather over the English Channel caused General Eisenhower to delay the assault. The men were ready to go, and the delay was a letdown. He finally gave the anxiously awaited order to launch the invasion in the early morning hours of June 5-6, 1944. The paratroopers had nervously stood by at the airfields for some 36 hours before the "go" signal once again rocketed morale to the sky.

Paratroopers weighed down by as much as 150 pounds of gear and weaponry, laboriously climbed through aircraft doorways with a push from the man below. Once loaded, the C-47s lined up on runways, revved engines, and one by one rolled away, accelerated and climbed into the sky. Assembling into formation took quite some time. They circled for half an hour before heading for France in a flight of V's.

"After assembly in formation we headed for Normandy." The planes flew down along the west coast of France for some distance before turning east at the islands of Guernsey and Jersey. This roundabout approach ensured there would be no friendly fire disaster like the one in Sicily when the 504 flew in over the invasion beaches.

"There was a quarter moon and an occasional cloud. The flight was beautiful. Standing in the open door of the C-47, I could see hundreds of ships below. We received no fire until we passed over Guernsey and Jersey. Then we received a great deal of spectacular anti-aircraft fire, the tracers seemingly coming right at us and then falling off below. The formation turned left at the islands and started across the Normandy peninsula, going from west to east. There was more fire as we reached the coast.

"We immediately hit a scattered formation of cloud that covered the 1,200-foot approach elevation at which we were flying. We were supposed to fly lower to an elevation of 800 feet for the jump, but the reduced visibility caused the formation to begin to disperse—some aircraft went higher, some lower.

"In my plane, we were in the clouds for almost the entire flight across the Normandy peninsula. The red warning light came on. We stood up and hooked up and I waited for the green jump light as we flew through the clouds. I was afraid to jump without the green light for fear other aircraft might be just behind us and at a lower elevation. I remembered the C-47 flying through a stick of jumpers back at Fort Benning and killing several. The pilot probably felt the same way about it, and that's why he hadn't yet given the jump signal.

"The guys were pressing me to get out of the plane. I couldn't see the ground. I waited and was about to jump without the green light because I knew we had passed over the intended drop area. We were still flying in the clouds and rapidly approaching the east coast of Normandy, bringing us back over the ocean. Just then the green light flashed on. We were traveling at an excessive speed as I led the jump into the clouds. Because we were going so fast I experienced a hard opening shock as our parachutes caught the wind. I estimate our jump elevation was at

800 feet, as we landed very quickly."

Alexander had very little time to look about for familiar landmarks before the ground rose up and hit him in the mouth. "I landed on a stump in a small clearing in a lightly forested area. The stock of my carbine, carried slung across my chest, hit the stump first, popping it up, and the gun sight raked across and cut a small gash in my left jaw. But I landed pretty well. I was about 200 feet from a small house and barn." By British double daylight time, it was between 1:30 and 2:30 a.m.

Normandy was covered with hedgerows surrounding every square of farmland and lining nearly every road. Planners and parachutists alike knew they were there from observation photos and detailed sand tables, but as they had often encountered hedgerows during training in England, no one worried. This was a huge oversight, for the hedgerows in Normandy were very different from those in England. Wide and tall, built-up with earth and rocks, they were as intertwined as a bird's nest. Only the British took them seriously: the 79th Armoured Division and the Royal Engineers brought in tanks with sharp, strong cutting edges mounted to the front to knock holes through the thick growth. Called "Hobart's Funnies," after the British armored warfare expert Percy Holbert, these and other inventive adaptations that Holbert was responsible for developing, including amphibious DD tanks, were ignored by the Americans.

This was all the more unfortunate in that multiple hedgerows often separated the members of a single stick of paratroopers immediately upon landing. Because France was not built on a "grid," unlike much of the United States, the roads and hedges weaved and turned. German machine gun nests, nearly invisible to the naked eye, could be anywhere and often were.

Alexander was one of the "lucky" ones, to use his own word. "My entire jump stick of 18 men rounded up their equipment, rolled back along the line of flight and soon joined me. Captain Gibbons spoke passable French and after talking to the family that owned the farm nearby, we figured out where we were, or thought we were." Alexander had landed several miles northeast of the intended drop zone. "Our calculations placed us about two and a half miles north of Ste. Mère-Eglise and to the northeast of Neuville-au-Plain.

"Our objective was to establish the 505 command post on our intended drop zone between the little French town of Ste. Mère-Eglise and the Merderet River. We picked up all the equipment we could find

D–Day: 6th June, 1944

and moved out in column toward Ste. Mère-Eglise. In route we gathered a few more men who had been dispersed." It was still dark, but dawn was fast approaching.

"As the sky began to lighten, we met Major Kellam, the 1st Battalion commander, with about 40 of his men who had also been dropped north-northwest of the drop zone, so we joined up. They were headed for their 1st Battalion objective on the Merderet River at La Fière Bridge. We had not gone far when we came to the main road leading northwest toward Cherbourg and southeast to Ste. Mère-Eglise. I definitely knew where I was at that point.

"We heard motor vehicles approaching from the northwest and quickly set an ambush. Preferably you want your men all on one side of the road. In this instance, a few ended up on the other side. The trouble with that is you can shoot your own men if you're not careful. A small convoy of two big trucks and eight or ten motorcycles rolled into view. There were 20 or so Germans in it. We knocked them all off except for two motorcycles toward the back, which quickly turned and escaped. One of the trucks was loaded with communication equipment.

Maj. Fred Kellam, commander of the 1st Battalion, helped set an ambush soon after jumping and gathering a small group of his men. He faced far heavier fighting later in the day.
Photograph courtesy of Bob Murphy

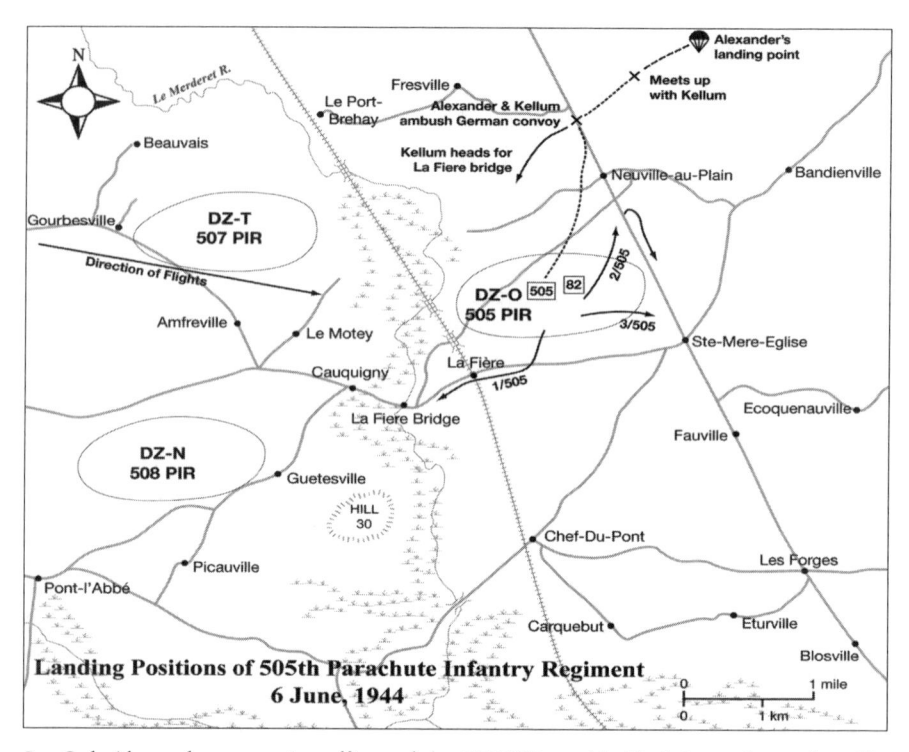

**Landing Positions of 505th Parachute Infantry Regiment
6 June, 1944**

Lt. Col. Alexander, executive officer of the 505 PIR, and half of the regimental staff landed northeast of Neuville-au-Plain, several miles northeast of their intended drop zone, Drop Zone "O."

"We initially didn't try to take prisoners. We had no place to put them. They would have tied our men up. If we had wounded Germans, we eventually took them into our aid stations. But we didn't take many captive. The Germans didn't take many prisoners either, I'll tell you that. It was brutal. Later on, we took some prisoners, but in the first few days we were just fighting for survival." [3]

Alexander's job as regimental executive officer was to run the 505 command post, freeing Colonel Ekman to command the business of fighting. "At this point in time and distance, Chick Eitelman, the headquarters men from my plane and I headed for our regimental and division command posts just southwest of Ste. Mère-Eglise. Major Kellam and his group of 1st Battalion men continued toward their objective at La Fière Bridge. When I arrived at our regimental command post, I found that Major Norton, the 505 operations officer, and a limited staff of three or four regimental headquarters men already had a tent set up and were in action with a radio. It was located on our original drop zone. Norton was lucky and landed nearby. I was late coming in."

Ekman had been at the CP earlier in the morning before heading for Ste. Mère-Eglise and La Fière Bridge, the main regimental objectives. Norton had radio communications with Lieutenant Colonel Vandervoort and Lieutenant Colonel Krause. Krause's 3rd Battalion had seized the critical town Ste. Mère-Eglise, making it the first town liberated in France. Almost immediately, German forces launched a counter-attack. Ekman ordered Vandervoort's 2nd Battalion to move into Ste. Mere-Eglise to help hold it. [4]

Major Kellam reached La Fière Bridge; he had no radio contact with headquarters, but sent a messenger to report the 1st Battalion was being attacked by strong German forces backed by Renault tanks. Kellam, the 1st Battalion and a hodgepodge of scattered 507 and 508 men held the

General Matthew B. Ridgway, commander of the 82nd Airborne Division, talks to some of his staff in Normandy. He chose to have his headquarters established near the 505 headquarters on D-Day morning because the 505 was the only Allied PIR with combat experience in the invasion.
Photography courtesy of Bob Murphy

east side of the bridge. The 507 was supposed to hold the other end of the causeway, but they were so badly dropped, the few defenders who managed to find their objective that morning were pushed aside by overwhelming enemy numbers. Kellam would have to hold on.

"General Ridgway jumped with 505 Headquarters Company as planned. Although I dropped a few miles away from where I was supposed to, in a way I was lucky, because I had picked Ridgway's plane and he landed within 150 yards of the proposed drop area. That is a really good drop. He later told me that his first encounter upon landing was with two dairy cows that scared him in the dark."

The first wave of gliders supporting the 82nd Airborne Division landed in the dark a few hours after the paratroopers hit the ground, carrying most of Ridgway's division staff. Crucially, they had on board two batteries of the 80th Antiaircraft Battalion (who were equipped and served as anti-tank and artillery units), 16 much-needed 57mm cannons and the jeeps to tow them, plus five jeeps with loaded ammo trailers and one with a command radio. The hedgerows were hell on the gliders, which were constructed of plywood, aluminum tube and canvas. Most of the fields were too small to land on, so the gliders slid right into the hedgerows. There was nevertheless no other way to bring in jeeps and anti-tank guns like the 57mm, which were too large for a parachute. In addition to the 52 gliders described above, a larger dusk landing brought in 1,200 troops (mostly 82nd artillerymen) and vehicles, ammo and howitzers. On the morning of D+1, the 325 GIR came in on 200 gliders. [5]

Glider landings were dangerous even when soldiers were the only cargo, but when there was heavy equipment or vehicles onboard, the danger greatly increased. Jeeps and other equipment had to sit forward right behind the pilot and co-pilot to establish the correct center of gravity in the glider. "Something that's in motion tends to stay in motion. When the gliders hit those hedgerows, the jeep or whatever else it was carrying would continue forward after the glider had stopped and wipe those guys out. People riding in front were in a very bad position.

"Several men with the division headquarters had really been hurt bad. Colonel March, who commanded the artillery, was really banged up in a glider landing. He would have to be evacuated as soon as possible. The chief of staff, Colonel Eaton, hadn't made it in yet. Although it was unknown at the time, he was also badly injured in a glider landing. Five or six key members of the division staff were still missing. Almost all of them chose the glider route in."

D–Day: 6th June, 1944

A Waco glider loaded with ammunition, a jeep and its crew from the 320th Field Artillery Battalion, 82nd Airborne Division. A jeep could be backed into the hold of a glider, but the front section, where the pilot sat, was connected to the rest by hinges and rotated up and out of the way. A large number of gliders crashed during the Normandy invasion, often resulting in the cargo breaking loose and injuring or killing pilots and other occupants. *U.S. Army photograph courtesy of Bob Murphy*

The bodies of 17 men from Company A, 325th Glider Infantry Regiment lie near their glider, which crashed near Hiesville in Normandy on June 7, 1944. *U.S. Army photograph courtesy of Phil Nordyke*

    The uninjured members of Ridgway's division staff set up the 82nd Airborne Division field command post about 100 feet away from the 505 headquarters, and set about tracking elements of the entire 82nd. "A small group of Germans had passed from east to west just to the south of our command post. They fired through the hedgerow in our direction, generally shooting over our heads and causing leaves to fall around our area. About 60 glider pilots from the early morning flight had collected and were lying around near the division HQ. Each had a carbine or rifle.

    "I went to Ridgway's CP and said, 'General, can I have those glider pilots?'

    "He said, 'What do you want them for?'

    "'To put up a perimeter defense around the two headquarters.'

    "He said, 'Go ahead!'

    "Even though we were only 100 feet apart, that was the last time I saw Ridgway for quite a few days.

    "The pilots were very enthusiastic to cooperate and get into a position to defend themselves. I divided them into four small squads, put them under command of a major pilot and had them take up defensive positions, with three units on the perimeter and one of about ten men in reserve near the tents. I wanted the three units to be like small platoons and the reserve would go to any area that was attacked. Later on, another small group of Germans passed near us, trying to join up with more of their forces to the north.

"Norton was on the radio. We started receiving reports that the 2nd and 3rd Battalions were being attacked at Ste. Mère-Eglise, our main regimental objective, the 3rd Battalion from the southeast and the 2nd Battalion from the northwest along the main road from Cherbourg."

There was still no radio communication with the 1st Battalion, and their status was unknown. "Before noon, a runner came in with the information that the battalion commander, Major Kellam, the executive officer, Major McGinity (who had been my executive officer in Italy), and the operations officer, Captain Roysdon, had all been killed. These were the three senior officers in the entire 1st Battalion. We couldn't get any more information except that they were dead and La Fière Bridge was being attacked by tanks. We also couldn't reach Colonel Ekman. About noon, after we kept getting these sketchy, but very bad reports from down at the bridge, I talked it over with Norton and decided I should head for La Fière Bridge."

As Alexander's job was to stay and run Ekman's command post, he should have stayed and done just that, unless given permission by Colonel Ekman or one of the generals to do otherwise. However, one of the many lessons the 505 had learned, and that other regiments would quickly learn as well, was the need to be flexible once the shooting started. Some of the inexperienced regiments had planned down to where each man would dig his foxhole. The 505 also planned, but knew better than to go into that level of detail. They trusted the officers and NCOs to deal with each situation as warranted.

Alexander had proven himself in Sicily and Italy as an excellent battalion commander, and Norton had certainly shown that he was more than able to run an under-manned headquarters. "I took my orderly, Corp. Chick Eitelman, with me. On the way we had a short skirmish with a couple of Germans. They shot at us, we shot back, and they moved on out of the way. I don't know whether we hit any of them or not, but Chick got hit right square through his kneecap. He was limping like hell and that type of an injury will swell up on you. So I said, 'Chick, I want you to go back to the aid station.'

"He said, 'No, I don't want to do that.'

"I said, 'Look, you're going to have a lot of swelling in that leg and I don't want you to end up a cripple. I'm giving you an order to go back to the aid station.' He was mad at me for sending him back, but I think I did the right thing. I lost my right hand, Chick, and never got him back.

"I proceeded to La Fière. On the way, I found a mixed group of 40 or so 101st and 508 men lying in a ditch along the road. Supposedly someone had held them as a reserve. I did not know who, so I rounded them up and took them with me. We arrived at the railroad crossing above the bridge at about 1:30 in the afternoon."

The German push was over, but they were still hitting with lots of mortar, machine gun and occasionally 88mm cannon fire. Alexander scouted the position, which consisted of the east side of the river around the tiny La Fière Bridge. This, and the small bridge at Chef-du-Pont, a village a few miles downstream to the south, were absolutely key to the entire battle for Normandy, for they were they only routes to move off

Arial view of the manor house (or Manoir) and La Fière Bridge after the battle, taken from the west. The area in the bottom of the photo was flooded during the fighting. A platoon of A Company, 505, was situated just to the right of the bridge in this picture. The rest of the company was to the left. Other understrength units were positioned in and around the manor buildings. Near the top-left of the picture, the railroad track crosses over the road. The 57mm cannon was slightly closer to the bridge from that point. Two gallant bazooka teams of two men each were at the foot of the bridge (bottom left of photo) and caused great damage to approaching enemy tanks. *Photograph courtesy of Bob Murphy*

D–Day: 6th June, 1944

La Fière Bridge photographed in 2001, facing east. The church in Cauquigny is visible at top left. *Photograph courtesy of Barry Nichols*

the Utah Beach area and into the interior of the Normandy peninsula. Likewise, these two tiny bridges were the sole means of passage for German armored units moving out of the interior in the attempt to push the Allies back into the sea.

The importance of the bridges was magnified because Gen. Erwin Rommel, in anticipation of an upcoming Allied invasion, had purposely closed the dykes that controlled the floodwaters in the surrounding marshy areas. This defensive measure caused the creek-sized Merderet River to swell past its banks and submerge flood plains on either side. Reeds and grasses growing up through the water gave the appearance of soft, grassy land to photo reconnaissance aircraft and descending paratroopers alike. As Alexander scouted the area, parachutes were still visible floating on the water, often marking the watery graves of surprised and overloaded troopers who had drowned before they had been able to shed their parachute and gear.

The bridge at La Fière was closer to the American-held side; a causeway ran from it over to the Germans near the little town of Cauquigny some 1,000 yards away. On the left of the road, a mixed

The commander of A Company, Lt. John "Red Dog" Dolan, sitting among hedgerows in Normandy. Dolan found himself the ranking officer of the 1st Battalion after the senior officers had been wiped out early on D-Day morning. *Photograph courtesy of Bob Murphy*

group of 30 or 40 C Company, 505 PIR, men occupied a stone manor house locally called "le Manoir," and a few smaller outbuildings grouped around it. Badly misdropped, they represented their entire company, and had been in this position since running the Germans out earlier that morning. Some 507th men were on the ridge above the manor. The few B Company soldiers that been able to make their way to the bridge were held in reserve. [6]

Only about half of the 1st Battalion, 505, had made it to the bridge at this point; with most of the command structure wiped out, Lt. John J. "Red Dog" Dolan was the senior officer. "I found that most of A Company under Dolan, a really good company commander, were well organized and mostly on the right side of the road facing the Merderet River and bridge," Alexander recalled. "One platoon from A Company was on the left of the bridge, also in a very forward position (just left of the manor house). I think Dolan had 126 men earlier that morning. It was almost a full company. They had experienced the best drop of our whole regiment. But in the fight, quite a few of them had been killed or injured.

"On the bridge was a broken truck our men had pushed out there to use as a roadblock. Just past it, on the causeway, was a small anti-tank minefield, then a disabled Renault tank from the earlier fighting." That fighting had been brutal. Tanks and German soldiers made it down the causeway almost to the bridge before being driven back. The mortar and cannon fire took a heavy toll across the defending positions. Major Kellam was killed attempting to resupply forward troops with ammunition. A Company received the worst of it. Lines thinned and the wounded were forced to stay and fight.

Although the enemy retreated, mortar, machine guns and artillery continued to pound away. "Our whole position was receiving heavy fire from the west bank around the village of Cauquigny. Through my binoculars, I spotted two German tanks screened behind the buildings. I approved Captain Dolan moving his men on the right side of the bridge back some distance because they were getting their ass shot off. They were dug in right up on the banks in a low rise of mostly shale and were very visible to the Germans, who were hitting them with intense mortar and machine gun fire along the riverbank." After the move, however, "they were in a good, tough position to repel enemy attacks. They could see and bring fire on the bridge and causeway.

"I located one of our 57mm anti-tank guns abandoned in a defilade position, in kind of a drainage area about 75 yards above the bridge and on the left side of the road. There were two holes through the shield, apparently from an earlier duel with the Renault tanks, and there was no gun sight. Six rounds of armor-piercing ammunition were all that remained. I put three men on the gun. [7]

"I said, 'The sight is missing, so bore-sight it.' You can do that—look down the barrel to line up your shot—at short distances and do pretty well. We learned that down at Fort Benning before going overseas. When you run out of ammunition, get the hell away from the gun. It's going to draw fire." Indeed, the gun already had drawn fire: the first tank in the attack had hit it twice. Fortunately this action temporarily deflected attention away from the two bazooka teams very close to the bridge, one on either side. As the most forward Allied positions, they put themselves at great risk and managed to knock the French-built tank out of action. [8]

Alexander determined that although things were far from ideal, the defenses were set as well as they could be, and had good leadership under Dolan and the other officers and non-coms. "I went around and checked things and ended up back by the railroad and dirt road junction (near Kellam's command post) just as General Gavin came in from Chef-du-Pont. He had 507th men following some distance behind because he heard our men at La Fière were having a bad time. I assured him that the men were in good position and had weathered the attack. He instructed me to take command of the position."

"I said, 'Do you want me on this side, the other side, or both sides of the river?'

"He thought for a minute and said, 'You better stay on this side because it looks like the Germans are getting pretty strong over there.' He was worried that if we attacked them and things went badly, we might lose the bridge altogether. He added that I should hold fast, not allowing passage to the Germans. At that time he was more concerned about the situation at Chef-du-Pont.

"While General Gavin and I were discussing, Lieutenant Colonel Maloney arrived with about 75 men from the 507th from the direction of Chef-du-Pont. Gavin attached them to me and I instructed them to take up a position on the left side of the road, facing the bridge above the manor. General Gavin took the 508th and 101st men I came across on my way to La Fière and headed for Chef-du-Pont."

To take and hold the west end of the bridge at Chef-du-Pont, another hotly contested piece of real estate, was the objective of the 508 PIR, which had also been very badly scattered during the jump. Gavin and Ridgway were doing their best to juggle their men, and take and hold the most critical objectives. Ste. Mère-Eglise was controlled by the 2nd and 3rd Battalions of the 505, although they were under heavy attack from two sides; the east ends of the La Fière Bridge and the Chef-du-Pont Bridge had to be held at all costs to prohibit the enemy from crossing to attack the Americans at Utah Beach.

The generals also wanted the west ends of the bridges, which would allow American forces to go on the offensive and move across the peninsula. Gavin ordered Alexander to remain on the east side, because he knew if Alexander attacked and failed, the disciplined, well led Germans would likely launch an immediate counter-attack before the Americans could regroup.

Alexander reorganized the defensive position of miscellaneous men on the left side of the road. There were still some 505 C Company men in the manor and the 507th soldiers, under Capt. Robert Rae, were to the left and high ground above the manor. "Two of them were dug into the side of the hedgerow on the higher part of the ground near the road. The hedgerows consisted of a lot of growth with dirt built up inside it. About that time an 88mm round from the other side of the river hit right alongside, and almost completely buried them. The Germans were firing right smack into the area. They were together in a big foxhole on a forward slope. An enlisted man and I dug them out. The men were still alive, but had been hit with shrapnel. We sent them back to the aid station after giving them a shot of morphine."

Random but steady shelling continued across the entire position. Alexander took medic Kelly Byars to check abandoned foxholes for wounded possibly left behind. Dug along the bank of the marsh, the foxholes had housed a platoon of Dolan's men before they were pulled back to a safer distance.

They were empty with one exception. "We found a man in a big foxhole dug in a mound of shale. A silver dollar-sized piece of his skull had somehow been blown out. Yet he was still alive. His brain was exposed, but hadn't been cut at all. I could see it pulsating with blood pressure. The wound wasn't bleeding.

"We got in there and were about to pick him up and carry him out. Our area had been getting hit all day, but when the Germans saw Byars and me moving around, they laid down a prolonged concentration of shelling to get us. They really schlacked the area. Dirt and rocks were blowing in on us. Kelly and I sat there in the bottom of that foxhole with that wounded guy. My left ear was turned towards one of the blasts that landed very close, and it rang for days. We had to stay there for about 25 minutes while they bombarded us. Their bombs landed every place except in the foxhole.

"I finally said, 'Kelly, if we take him out of here, we're going to have to run like hell or we're going to get hit. Wait until dark and come back and get him with a stretcher. That way you don't jar him around.' Byers fixed him up as best he could and left him there. When there was a lull in the mortaring we ran like hell. I inquired later, but never could find out if the wounded man lived or not. That always bothered me. That Kelly was a heck of a good medic.

"Later in the afternoon, General Gavin came back and took the 507 men on the double to strengthen the weak position being held at the Merderet crossing near Chef-du-Pont. The 2nd and 3rd Battalions of the 505 were still having a rough go as well. Lieutenant Krause was temporarily in the aid station after receiving several wounds. B Company was taken from us and attached to the 3rd Battalion in Ste. Mère-Eglise. I objected to that when it happened, but Ste. Mère-Eglise was being attacked from two sides and they had ongoing fighting while we were being shelled. No Germans were coming across the causeway right then."

The incoming ordnance remained bad all over Alexander's position for the rest of the day. Although it slowed after dark, mortars continued falling throughout the night. At first light, the barrage increased to become as heavy as it had previously been. No one, not even Ridgway or Gavin, could know how costly La Fière Bridge would be over the following days.

CHAPTER FOURTEEN

LA FIÈRE BRIDGE AND CAUSEWAY

"ON JUNE 7 WE WERE constantly under fire. I could occasionally see German infantry moving about in the village of Cauquigny across the flooded plain. We had no long-range firepower other than machine guns. Well, we had one 57mm gun with six rounds of ammunition and a limited supply of mortar rounds, but this all had to be held in reserve for any serious effort the Germans might make to cross the bridge."

Alexander, Dolan and everyone else were forced to lie low and do nothing while the Germans threw punch after punch. They waited in foxholes, hearing the screams of dying, unable to fight back or help their agonized comrades torn apart by tree burst shrapnel.

About this time a squad from the 307th Engineers was brought in as riflemen along with two 1st Battalion headquarters machine gun crews who had finally made their way to the bridge. Alexander sent them to Lt. William Oakley, whose 1st Platoon, A Company, situated just left of the bridge, had taken very heavy casualties the day before. It was now down to only six men, some of whom were walking wounded.

The mortar barrage continued throughout the redeployments, but at about 8:00 AM, the exploding ordnance came down like rain. Heavy artillery and mortar fire hammered at the Americans, spraying jagged metal throughout the bridgehead. [1] Two hours into the bombardment, four German tanks rolled out onto the causeway, followed by a large number of infantry. Bushes and trees lined both sides of the causeway, allowing only glimpses of the advancing force. Muzzle flashes were often the only sign of them. [2]

The lead tank drew fire from the 57mm gun as it advanced. When it was close enough, the bazooka teams scrambled out of their foxholes

193

and opened fire. Just as it reached the bridge, a shot from either the 57mm or a bazooka disabled it. A second tank was also quickly knocked out. These, combined with a dead tank from the day before and a wrecked truck the paratroopers had earlier pushed onto the bridge as a road block, provided cover for the attackers.

The fire from 88s, mortars, machine guns and rifles was so intense that men all over Alexander's position rapidly became casualties. Alexander repeatedly came forward into the fight to check positions and the attrition of his men, continually assessing and making adjustments. Private Bob Murphy, with A Company's 1st Platoon just to the left of the bridge, captures the horror and intensity of the battle:

> The Germans crouched behind their tanks and in the causeway foxholes, and the Americans made the most of their ground cover. Suddenly, the mortar fire from the west bank doubled in intensity, most of it falling among Oakley's men until they could scarcely raise their heads. Second Lieutenant Oakley was hard hit by a mortar burst, and spouted so much blood from a big hole in his back that they had to get him out in the middle of the fight. Sergeant William D. Owens, a squad leader, gave him a morphine shot and took command of what was left of the 1st Platoon. Oakley died behind a hedgerow; he was a heroic leader, who had led in combat in Sicily and Italy.
>
> Our platoon strength was dwindling so rapidly from the bullet and mortar fire that Owens found it difficult to know whether any defensive line remained. First Sergeant Robert M. Matterson, who was slightly to the rear of the rifle line, was trying to steer the wounded back. He found them coming back in such numbers that he "felt like a policeman directing traffic." Sergeant Russell O'Neal saw a new replacement trooper to his 3rd Platoon get half of his head taken off by an 88. O'Neal did not even know his name. Private John Ross also took a direct hit from an 88. There was nothing left of him but body-parts and dog tags. [3]

Men died, machine guns overheated and jammed, and ammo was getting low. A brave supply sergeant, Edwin F. Wancio, scurried around delivering extra ammo as quickly as he could. Sergeant Owens' original squad was down to three people, and there were only 15 left in his platoon. He sent Bob Murphy as a runner to Lieutenant Dolan with the 1st Battalion's 3rd Platoon on the right side of the bridge, who was also taking a beating. The message said they were out of ammunition and could not withstand another tank and infantry attack. What should they do? Dolan sent Murphy back with a piece of paper that read, "I don't know of a better place than this to die." Verbally, he told Murphy, "No, stay where you are." They fought on. [4]

As bad as things were for the Americans, they were probably even worse for the Germans out on the causeway. After almost an hour of close-quarters combat, one of them raised a Red Cross flag and asked for a half hour truce to remove their wounded. Alexander was more than happy to grant it, as were the rest of the paratroopers. One of the enemy tanks had lost a tread and another one or two were also out of commission. The others were able to turn around and go back. "Later, a battalion of the 325, which had landed by glider that day, moved into a reserve position to our rear. They were eventually attached to the 505."

There was yet another tank up there that had been knocked out the first day. "The Germans were good at recovering equipment. That night I heard a clanking and went down to see what was going on. By the time

Disabled French Renault tanks, manned by German soldiers at the bend on La Fière Causeway. The tanks were put out of action by A Company, 505 PIR bazooka teams and the 80th AA Battalion's 57mm gun. *Photograph courtesy of Bob Murphy*

I got there they had already driven a tractor out onto the causeway, hooked it to one of the disabled tanks and pulled it out. They brought it back into Cauquigny and repaired it. The next day it was back in action.

"On June 8 (D + 2) the Jerries kept up the mortar fire, but didn't try any more attacks to get across the bridge. We remained in position until we were relieved that evening by elements of the 507th." The 1/505 was finally off the front line. They had been chewed up badly, but held their own under immense pressure. "I stayed in command of the 1st Battalion, which now had only 176 men. A battalion is normally 525 men."

Meanwhile, the 2nd and 3rd Battalions had successfully defended Ste. Mère-Eglise. Reinforcements arrived from Utah Beach, and Ekman put both of his battalions on the attack to the north, creating a little breathing room. Alexander and the 1st Battalion moved northeast to take the position of the 3rd Battalion, 505, at Granville, and were put into reserve. He asked to have B Company returned and Gavin sent them back. For the next 24 hours, his men rested and stocked up on ammunition and equipment.

The battle for La Fière Bridge and Causeway, however, was far from over. The night of D + 2, troops from the 325 crossed the river at a ford upstream, contacted and joined a pocket of 507 men and attacked Cauquigny. The Jerries hit back hard, killing many and forcing the Americans to back off. The following day General Ridgway ordered a charge straight across the bridge and over the 750-yard causeway into Cauquigny. He called for smoke, but it was misplaced and blew away almost immediately. The attack went ahead in broad daylight without benefit of concealment.

The green 325 GIR led the charge. About 30 men from E and G Companies made it across and started the attack, but were at the mercy of the heavily armed Germans. Many others stopped on the causeway, frozen by the sight of their numerous comrades piling up at the bend in the narrow road. Gavin and Ridgway, again leading from the front, went out onto the causeway, urging the stalled men on. Ridgway called for his second wave. Gavin gave the order to Captain Rae, who led his group of 80 to 100 men from the 507th into a hail of bullets and artillery in a perilous course over the bridge and causeway, making their way around dead bodies and wrecked tanks. Many of the men who had previously frozen stood and followed. They and the ad-hoc force that shortly followed together managed to take Cauquigny.

Looking back on the battle at La Fière Bridge, Alexander expressed frank relief that he was no longer present on D + 3 for the final charge over the causeway. "Man, did they have casualties. And I was glad I didn't have that assignment. I thought afterwards how lucky I was to no longer be there, and have to lead that daytime attack.

"They lost a lot of men, but got across and established a bridgehead. They found a 20-foot pit where the Germans had their mortar battery set up. Their men had a good view of our side of the bridge. They also had a couple of cannons, and I know there were at least two tanks because I had seen them through my field glasses.

"I didn't think they should have gone across there at all. They should have waited for night and tried—gone the next night [D + 3] if they couldn't do anything else. At the time, in my mind I criticized Ridgway for that. A daylight attack straight across that open place was no good at all. But you don't go down and tell a general that he's not doing very well.

"Later I learned that General Collins, the corps commander responsible for cutting off the Normandy peninsula and taking Cherbourg, put a lot of pressure on Ridgway to get that bridgehead. He wanted it right away. If Ridgway didn't do it, Collins would send another division across that very day. Ridgway knew that it was one of the 82nd's original objectives. It was our job."

Omar Bradley had already ordered the 90th, a green division unloading at the beach, to move up and cross at La Fière. They had much heavier armor than the paratroopers, and it in fact made sense for them to make the crossing. But Ridgway thought it would be bad for his troopers' morale to let the new 90th establish the bridgehead instead of his seasoned paratroopers. There was also the chance that the 90th might fail in their first fight, setting back Allied plans and becoming demoralized as a fighting unit. If the 82nd was going to do it, they had to do it immediately. Gavin agreed with Ridgway that the 82nd should make the crossing. [5]

Although ordered to attack immediately, Ridgway delayed the charge for two hours to bring more artillery pieces into position for the pre-attack barrage. Many years later, Ridgway and Alexander were still going over the events. "Ridgeway wrote to me in May 1972 and said the taking of Cauquigny on June 9, 1944, was, and I quote, 'the hottest single incident I experienced in all my combat service both in Europe and later in Korea.'

"Looking back, it's a lot easier to see what should have been done. I was there on D-Day. I knew the best time to go across was right then, before the Jerries got set. I'm sure we could have gone across that night and taken that village and held it. I'm positive of it. And the 507 had pockets of men holding up at a couple of places across the river, who could have moved over and helped us hold the bridgehead. It would have been better to go across. I would either have had a definite smoke screen or gone at night. One of the two."

Although Alexander initially questioned the tactics and plan to take Cauquigny, he always maintained the highest respect for Ridgeway and Gavin, both during and after his military career. Alexander may have been able to capture and successfully hold Cauquigny, but if he had tried and failed, it could have proven disastrous. Gavin likely made the right decision to hold only the east end of the bridge during the perilous first days when *all* of the 82nd positions were still tenuous.

CHAPTER FIFTEEN

MONTEBOURG STATION

AFTER REGROUPING AS WELL AS POSSIBLE, the 1st Battalion was placed along a front extending from the Merderet River toward the ocean far to the right. The 505 was on the left of the line, against the Merderet River. To its right was the untested 8th Infantry Regiment, then the 12th Infantry Regiment and the 22nd Infantry Regiment. This line readied for a push north toward the strategically critical city of Cherbourg and its deepwater port.

The 2nd Battalion of the 325 Glider Infantry Regiment was attached to the 505 to replace Ed Krause's 3rd Battalion, which hunkered down in a reserve position guarding a river crossing. [1] The units within the 505 prepared to advance as such: the 2nd Battalion on the left, closest to the Merderet River and railroad track, which nearly paralleled the river; the 325 men to the right (east) of them; Alexander's 1st Battalion in the rear, following as reserve.

"They started us on the attack north. During the advance that day we ran into spotty resistance that the 325 had either missed or bypassed. We attacked halfway up to Montebourg Station and set down for one night. In the meantime, the 8th was coming up on our right, but always lagging behind." The 8th Infantry Regiment had a tough row to hoe to keep up with the aggressive, battle-tested paratroopers. The fact that they were green troops made it that much harder.

Before noon, the 2nd Battalion and the 325 advanced to within 200 to 300 yards of a small canal running southwest toward the river about halfway between Fresville and Montebourg Station. Just beyond it was a hill on which the enemy had a strong defensive line. The 2nd Battalion and 325 were taking heavy fire and there was sparse cover ahead. When

Colonel Ekman learned the 8th Infantry was settling into a defensive position, he had his men "set down for the night."

The next morning, June 10, the Americans went on the attack again. The plan called for the 505 and the 8th Infantry to break through the German defensive line and drive the enemy back a mile, taking the Montebourg-Le Ham road. Ekman ordered Alexander to bring the 1st Battalion around the right side of the 325 and hit the enemy positions. Circling around the 325 brought the 1st Battalion through some of the 8th Infantry's area. Unbeknownst to Alexander and Ekman, the 8th Infantry had already had a hard fight in this area the previous day before backing off. [2]

According to Alexander, "the 1st Battalion now had a strength of 276 men. (A full parachute battalion numbered about 525 men.) I was taking them in column up to a new position. On the way we passed over the knob of a hill. The trail went right close to the top of it where it was bare. There was a dead German lying there with a P-38 pistol right on top of him.

"Well, I knew right away it was a plant. A booby-trap. I looked closely and there was a wire going from the gun. It was hooked up to a grenade, I imagine, just waiting for someone to pick it up. So I stationed a man to keep anybody from touching it until our battalion got clear by. We didn't have time to fool with it right then. The Germans did a lot of things like that. They put booby traps out for us, but mainly they did it with trip wires. They would run wire along the ground, and if you stepped on it, you would trip it. A bouncing betty pops up about five feet off the ground and explodes. Man, those were nasty. You had to watch for them."

Continuing north, they knew the Germans were somewhere in front of them, but didn't know exactly where. Alexander was up with the front elements as they moved. "As we were going forward, I heard a little voice. I went over and here's this wounded man from the 8th Infantry Regiment lying close to the trail. He had been shot through the groin and I got a medic to take care of him. We found out the 8th had fought there the night before. Evidentially, they had withdrawn not realizing they left a man behind. We picked him up and sent him back to the rear.

"It turns out the 8th made an attack and ran into a real strong German fortification. It was about 20 feet long and dug in three feet deep. Then they put timbers and dirt on top and made slits for fire ports. It was very well concealed and I was pretty close to it before I saw it.

Montebourg Station

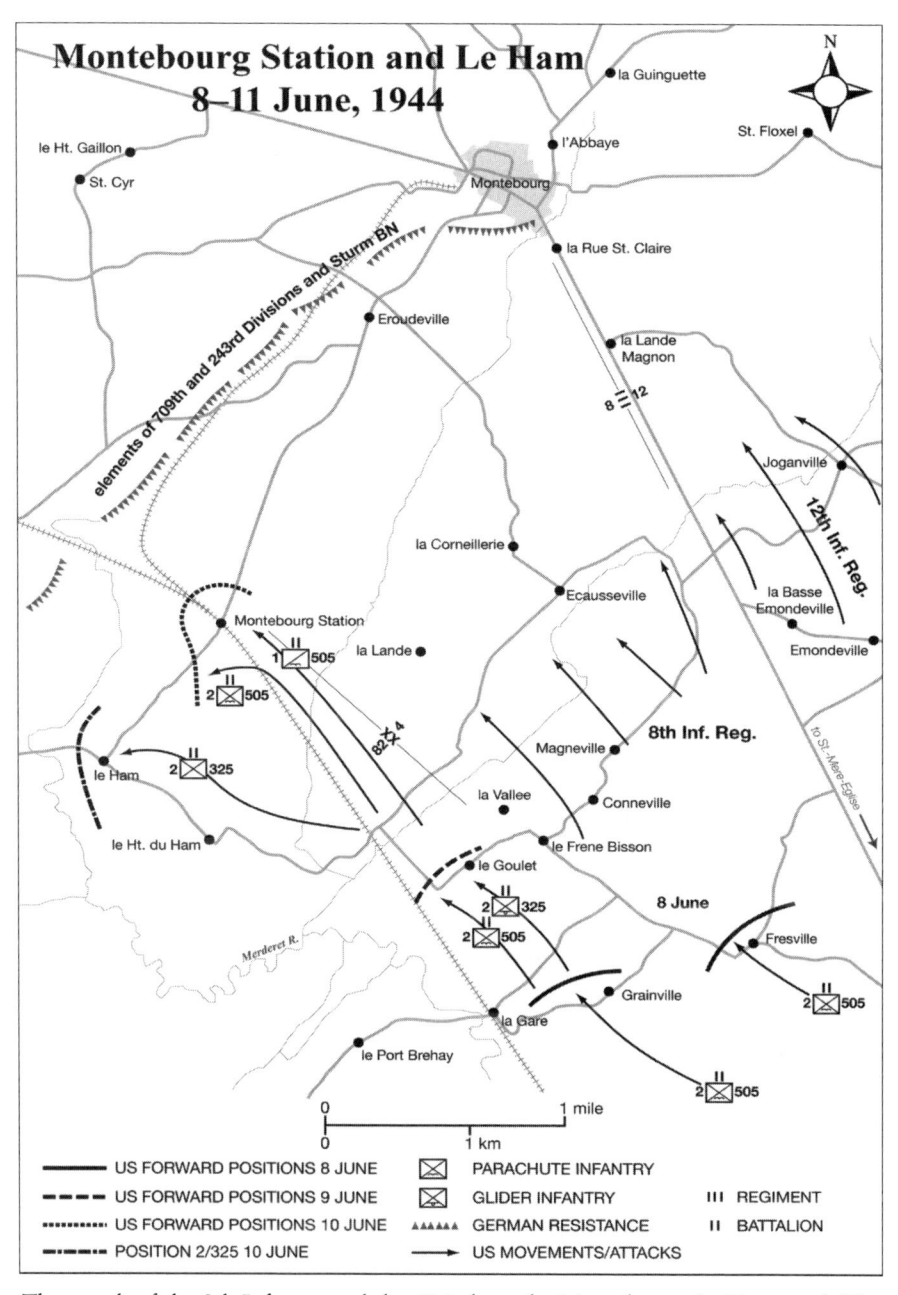

The attack of the 8th Infantry and the 505 along the Montebourg-Le Ham road. The 12 Infantry Regiment advanced to the right of the road going from Ste. Mère-Eglise to the city of Montebourg.

"The Germans were good at placing them, too. They would put them at the far end of a big field, so anyone who went out into the field was usually killed. You had to come around from the sides to get to them. This one was just at the back end of an open field. There were trees on the left that you had to work up through. Working your way around and pressing was the best way to fight them. If you go across the field, you're asking for trouble. It's hard to take a position like that.

"At the time of the fighting there were probably eight or ten Germans in there, so they really mowed some people down from the 8th. That's where this guy had been hit, out on one side taking a fire port. The 8th had fought with them and backed off the night before. They didn't take it. So we approached, but the Germans had already pulled out. They left in such a hurry there were still five or six dead lying inside."

"We attacked and the 325, on our left, was soon left behind. I think they had not been given the attack order at that point. The 8th Regiment on our right was slow and about one fourth of a mile behind. The 1st Battalion was wide open on our left and right flanks, with the 2nd Battalion in the reserve position following in column.

"Lieutenant [Gerald 'Johnny'] Johnson, the commander of C Company, a runner named Bob (I usually took a runner with me or a radio man) and I were walking down the road, and there was a tree nearby on the right side. The Jerries spotted us from somewhere and put an 88 round into the tree. The canister exploded and sent shrapnel everywhere. [3]

"I was on the right, closest to the blast. The runner was in the middle and Lieutenant Johnson was on the left. I got powder burned on the side of my face from the blast, but was not hit by shrapnel. The poor guy in the middle got a big scoop out of his back. A big piece of shell fragment just scooped it away. You could see the bones and sinews on a big wide area. He could still walk. We gave him a shot of morphine. I grabbed an aid man and had him take this guy back to the station. Johnson was completely untouched. One guy out of three got hit."

After taking care of the injured man, they tried to locate the enemy troops. Alexander saw a mound quite a ways off down the road and surmised the 88 was likely there. "I crawled up on top of a nearby two-story house that had a straw roof on it. Straw roofs are pretty thick. They laid slats across and then put the straw in and over the slats. The old farmer and his family were there. Our advance had been so fast, a lot of the families just stayed in their homes while we went by. When I started climbing up on his roof, he said something to the effect of, 'No good. You may fall through.' I said, 'I'll chance it.'

"I got up there and had a piece of thin board with me. I knocked a hole in it and slowly slid it up at the peak of the roof to make it look like a chimney while I looked through the hole. There was a position ahead where I thought there might be Germans, but I still couldn't see any of them, so I slid back down off the straw roof. I think that old farmer was glad to see me get down.

"Sometimes commanders didn't go out and look at what their men were up against, which to me was a crime. You should do enough reconnaissance to know what you're throwing your men into, or you shouldn't throw them in there."

The advance proceeded to just short of the town of Montebourg Station. The 505 was in a small wood. All along their front, separating them from the town, ran a road followed by a wide, open field about a quarter mile deep. "General Ridgway came up and wanted us to attack immediately and hit Montebourg Station. I looked it over from behind the trees. By this time Norton and our regimental headquarters had moved up. Ekman was also there and the 2nd Battalion commander, Ben Vandervoort.

"We were screened from the enemy's sight by the clump of trees. Ekman told me, 'You give the order.' So I did, which was for the 1st Battalion to lead, followed closely by the 2nd Battalion. After my 1st Battalion took Montebourg Station, the 2nd Battalion was to take the lead by turning to the left by 45 degrees to hit the village of Le Ham.

"We needed smoke to cross that field. I was a little reluctant to ask for it because a big storm had hit the English Channel and washed out the makeshift American harbor platforms that had been installed off Omaha Beach. They couldn't get any supplies through for about three days. So the order came down that we were not to use smoke and a few other things until further notice because they could not be replaced.

"But if I could get smoke, I wasn't going to go without it. I talked our artillery observer into giving us some. I took him with me and he put it right where I wanted it. He gave me a beautiful smoke screen. We attacked and got into the village and hit the Germans before they even knew we were there. I wondered afterwards if I was going to get called on the mat for disobeying a directive. Fortunately, I never did get in trouble for it. Without that smoke we would have lost a lot of men going across that open ground. It helped a great deal, but we still had a pretty good fight taking the town."

The first part of the attack went according to plan. The 1st Battalion got across the field, knocking out enemy machine gun nests and riflemen, and forcing many back. In spite of stiff resistance, ground was quickly and steadily gained as Alexander's men set and expanded their lines. "As we got in a little further, artillery rounds came over and I lost two men. They were American rounds. I heard the call for fire over the radio and could tell by the voice who it was." It was an officer junior to Alexander. "I called up and said, 'Lift that fire. You're dropping on my position and you've hit two of my men.'

"'Oh,' he says, 'I'm not dropping it in that area.'

"I said, 'Just lift the god damn fire and don't argue with me!' In war things happen like that."

The artillery fire was immediately called off, but unfortunately there were many other incoming projectiles. In addition to German infantry, the left side of Alexander's perimeter had to contend with a multiple-firing gun that proved to be very effective killing machine.

Orienting himself by the sound of the gun, Alexander took his artillery observer out as far as he could to try and spot it, moving very close to a large bridge that crossed over the railroad tracks. "This multiple-firing gun was giving us a bad time. I started up and peeked over the crest of the bridge, when an enemy machine gun down the road on the other side opened fire on me. I backed down, out of direct fire.

"From near the bridge I looked and spotted the gun mounted on a railroad car north of the village. I think it was a 40mm pom-pom. We also called it a boofer. It was designed as an anti-aircraft weapon and fired about 700 rounds per minute. It even had explosive rounds. It was a nasty weapon against infantry. We brought in artillery fire on the gun and silenced it." Unfortunately, it didn't do enough damage to permanently take the boofer out of action. Two days later it was back and took an ugly toll on the 325 GIR.

"I returned to directing my men. While we were still clearing the village, Colonel Ekman came up and wanted to know the situation and what I was doing there. I explained the situation and told him I was waiting until the battalion had cleared the village and I didn't want to get pinned down. You avoid getting into positions like that if you can help it, because you're supposed to be running the show. You can't do it when you're pinned down on your ass."

The village of Le Ham lay a short distance on the other side of the railroad tracks near Alexander's left flank. It was to be taken upon

A wounded German soldier awaits treatment. His dead comrades lie in a ditch on the right side of the photo. *U.S. Army photograph courtesy of Phil Nordyke*

arrival by the 2nd Battalion. Gavin's officers were trained to lead from the front, and Colonel Ekman wanted to scout. "Come on," he said to Alexander, "let's have a look."

Ekman and Alexander made their way out by the bridge Alexander had earlier tried to cross. Ekman wanted his own lay of the land, and the bridge gave the best vantage point. In spite of Alexander's warning about the enemy machine gun sighted on the bridge, Ekman said, "Well, I'm going on up." He got about halfway before the Germans cut loose. Luckily the Colonel was fast and made a running jump off the near end of the bridge.

Ekman then left to check on the 2nd Battalion, which was expected to arrive closely on the heels of the 1st Battalion. Alexander continued his own personal reconnaissance. "I went up into a two-story house to see if I could view that machine gun and get some artillery fire on it. But there were trees in the way and I couldn't see down the road. I came downstairs, stepped out the door, and another officer in the area fired his rifle, putting one right in the damn door frame about two inches from my shoulder. He got nervous and thought I was a German. I was glad he was a lousy shot, and told him that he was more dangerous than the Germans." This was the most polite of the expressions Alexander used. The officer got an earful and wisely made himself scarce.

Even though resistance was stiff, the 1st Battalion took the town of Montebourg Station with light losses. The front line ran west to east and curled around on each end in an uneven semicircle. Alexander was worried about his flanks. They were way out ahead of the 325 GIR, which was beginning an attack on his left near the river, and even further out in front of the 8th Infantry on the right. A German counter-attack on either side could be disastrous.

Vandervoort's 2nd Battalion arrived and went on the attack. Unfortunately they had gotten hung up, and the extra half hour was all the Germans needed to dig in. Good on offense, the Germans were also masters of defensive strategies and made the most of time. Vandervoort's men gained ground, but were stopped cold before entering the village of Le Ham. Primarily facing west, Vandervoort then positioned his men from Alexander's left flank, running south in front of Le Ham.

Ekman was not pleased that Le Ham had held out. He wanted Alexander's 1st Battalion to pull south around behind Vandervoort's men and attack Le Ham from that direction. Alexander thought it would be asking for trouble. "I said, 'Bill, I don't think that's a good decision. There are Germans on both sides of me.' This would have left Vandervoort's backside open, and I would be moving in front of the 325, which was coming up on my left." Crossing in front of another unit, even if it's friendly, is a bad idea. Ekman listened and agreed.

Alexander, too, always made it a point to listen to his junior officers, and thought that the few "rank-conscious" commanders who did not do so handicapped themselves by ignoring one of the best possible sources of information. "The guy may be wrong, but at least hear him out. You can learn a lot that way." Alexander later noted that Ekman not only got the 505 focused and firing on all cylinders after taking over in the toughest of circumstances in England, but very quickly acclimated to live combat, leading his regiment well.

Alexander picked a nearby house to use as his command post. It wasn't too far from the bridge and must have been in the view of the Germans, because a few minutes after he moved in it was heavily fired upon. He and his staff made a quick exit and picked another little house some distance east of the bridge that was "central to the perimeter" for his new headquarters. "I was concerned about having Germans on both our flanks. We were ahead of the 325 on our left and the 8th on our right. I knew where they were because I could hear them fighting. You went a lot on the basis of what you heard, but there were also plenty of times you couldn't hear anything helpful. It was possible that enemy troops could come around the ends of our position. We were in a very vulnerable spot.

"I knew there were no American forces on our right (the east). The 8th was new, and the first day or two when a unit enters combat, green troops always have some problems with direction and a few other things. Also, they were trying to keep up with a seasoned airborne regiment, and the airborne was very aggressive and advanced quickly. I also knew there were no American forces on our front (north) or to the left (the west past Vandervoort's 2nd Battalion).

"Lieutenant [Claiborne] Cooperider and I went down the railroad track to the south. The 325 was moving up in that direction, but was way behind. I wanted to know what was going on in that area because we were not set up to defend any attack from there. After walking a few hundred yards, we saw three Germans ahead of us run across the track from west to east to get in behind us. Cooperider said, 'Colonel, let's get the hell out of here!' We did. We went back to Montebourg Station."

Although the railroad gun had been knocked out, other nasty weapons were blasting away at the entire position. The right flank was under pressure from infantry, and from somewhere behind them several screaming meemies fired away. "A screaming meemie is basically a launching device that throws up big ash cans about the size of a five-gallon bucket filled with explosives and shrapnel. These flying canisters make a wailing noise as they come down, exploding into deadly fragments. The sound of it was very discomforting to a lot of the men. It's a psychological weapon as much as anything.

"These big chunks of explosives were dropping all over our area. My runner/bodyguard and I moved to the right portion of our perimeter and climbed up inside a three-story mill with sheet metal walls. It had cups on a belt that brought grain up to the top and then dumped it into silos. We went to the top, where there was a floor below a peaked roof. I tore out a few shingles to try to locate those screaming meemie guns to the north with my field glasses. I couldn't find them, so I said to my runner, Willy Hall, 'I haven't got time to stay up here. Here are my binoculars. You stay up here for a while and see if you can find out where that fire is coming from. It's not very far away.[4]

"I was walking back toward the railroad underpass when I spotted one of the 2nd Battalion company commanders walking back toward the east, away from his battalion front. Since I had previously commanded the 2nd Battalion, I knew all the personnel. It was Captain [Clyde R.] Russell. I asked him what he was doing there in the 1st Battalion area. The 2nd Battalion was still trying to press forward to take Le Ham. He should have been on the northwest edge of the village with his company. He said, 'I'm not going to stay up there with all those screaming meemies coming in.'

"I told him they were falling all over our area too, and talked to him for five or ten minutes, telling him that he was responsible for the welfare of his men. I gave him a break and sent him back to his company. I said, 'Russ, you're walking a dangerous line. I want you to go back up there, get with your company and get on with your attack.' I didn't tell Vandervoort at the time it happened, but I should have, when I knew one of the company commanders had walked away from them. Vandervoort did say later that Captain Russell became a fair company commander. [5]

"When I returned to the bridge area, Lieutenant Colonel Vandervoort was just about to put up a CP in the same house I had initially put mine in. I said, 'Van, I wouldn't do that. I was just in there and the Germans are firing direct on the house.'

"He said, 'You put your CP where you want, I'll put mine where I want.'

"I said, 'Okay, Van,' and walked off. But I watched.

"What was I going to do, argue with the guy? He was a great warrior and a hell of a good soldier, but as I said, he could be as hardheaded as hell. They were in there for about ten minutes before the Jerries started firing on it. Then they came pouring out of there like a bunch of bees from a hive. I laughed at him and I don't think he liked it. I've had to learn the hard way myself many times."

In Montebourg Station, Alexander had to reclassify "a 2nd Lieutenant, the nicest little guy you ever saw. But when the firing started, he would just shake. His company commander brought him to me and said, 'Colonel, what am I going to do here?' I felt his head to see if he had malaria, because a lot of our men got the shakes from it at one time or another. He wasn't feverish.

"I said, 'Send him back to the rear and I'll give you a note to explain the circumstances. We'll let them handle it.' I didn't have time to deal with it right then. I talked to the lieutenant a little and told him what I was going to do. I said, 'I'm going to send you back to headquarters and recommend you for some kind of administrative job, possibly in the States.' He wasn't happy about it, but agreed that maybe I was right. We sent him back and I never saw him again or found out what happened to him. Some people can control themselves under stress and others can't. Most of them did a noble job. They were all volunteers, for one thing. And a real test was when they went through parachute school and had to jump out of an airplane."

The fighting had stabilized by this point, so Alexander took a few men and headed back to the field his men had crossed under cover of the smoke screen. "After leaving that man in Arnone, I always tried to go back over an area and find anybody that got hit and left behind. Not very often, but every now and then, I found men that way. I usually took a medic or someone else with me.

"I was kind of scouting ahead a little bit. One of our lieutenants had been hit by artillery fire. He was lying on the ground out on the flank of our attack, where he had fallen as the attack moved past him. He kind of waved to me to get my attention. I went over and talked to him. He had been hit through the lungs and wasn't able to yell for help."

"I heard they brought up a stretcher and carried the wounded man away, but I didn't see him again until a veterans' reunion many years later. I didn't remember what I'd said when I found him, but he did. He said, 'I was lying out there and I couldn't move. You came along and had an orderly with you. There were no medics around because they were all on the other side of the village at the front. You told the orderly to go get a medic and bring him back there, even if he had to stick a bayonet in his ass and march him back.'"

By 9:00 p.m. there was less rifle and machine gun fire, but the screaming meemie bombardment continued. While some of his men slept and others remained on watch, Alexander was on the move. Disliking his executive officer duties, he thrived out in the field with the troops. He was dead on his feet because he had been awake for two days straight, but his responsibility toward his men was more important than sleep. "In battle, it is a 24-hour game," he explained, "and something's always happening."

Alexander's strong belief in personal reconnaissance included checking status after the fighting ended. This evening, he had patrolled his soldiers' positions and verified all was well. "I was returning to our CP when our supply officer for the 1st Battalion and his driver came down the road with a jeepload of ammunition. The jeep hit a mine and I saw them blown up in the air about 15 feet. I ran over. The driver had been killed and Lieutenant Donnelly was in bad shape and couldn't see. One of the other lieutenants and I carried him into the CP, gave him a shot of morphine and tried to comfort him. Although he could not see me he asked, 'Is that you, Colonel Alexander?' I assured him it was, and we would soon have him back with the medics. I thought he would be okay. [6]

The 1st and 2nd battalions were still way out in front of the 8th (on the right) and the 325 (back on the left). Alexander sent out patrols to monitor the 1,000-yard gap between the 505 and the 8th Infantry Division. [7] After checking his positions, Alexander "went back to the little house where I had established my battalion command post. There was a bed with a white cover on it in a bedroom. So I told my staff that I was going to try to get a couple of relaxing moments." I lay down with my clothes on and must have fallen asleep almost immediately. I have no idea how long I was out, but it couldn't have been very long, when a screaming meemie hit the corner of the bedroom. All the plaster was knocked off the ceiling and fell on my face. It felt like the whole building was falling in. Scared the crap out of me."

Instead of a little shut-eye, Alexander got what he later called his "biggest shock" of the war. So much for sleeping. He got up and checked positions again. Both the 1st and 2nd Battalions repelled multiple counter-attacks from enemy units of a platoon or less in size. [8]

The next day the 325 fought forward, coming up on the left flank and linking up with Vandervoort's lines. Le Ham remained in German hands. The 8th Infantry moved up to Alexander's right. "We stayed there that night and the next night were relieved by elements of the 8th Infantry. Our 1st and 2nd Battalions were moved to reserve in an area near Picauville. "As we were leaving, I heard that railroad gun back in action against the 325 as they fought to take Le Ham. After the artillery observer and I knocked it out, the Germans must have pulled it back and repaired it.

"I told them it was a boofer mounted on a railroad car and I thought they had pulled it back along the tracks a little further. But they couldn't locate it and shell it. Apparently the Germans working the gun had a direct shot at the 325, because I know a lot of good boys were hit bad there. It's a wicked gun against the infantry. I felt like I should stay there and find it for them because they were getting hit so badly."

Alexander remained in command of the 1st Battalion, while Lt. Col. Walter Winton filled in as executive officer of the regiment. "We stayed in reserve to the south of Ste. Mère-Eglise for a rest, and then moved to a position north of Etienville," Alexander notes. While in reserve, he finally had the chance to write a letter to his parents, reassuring them about the safety of his brother Ed, now assigned to the 82nd Airborne, and informing them that he had been given command of a battalion.

France
June 19, 1944

Dearest Mother,
This is "D" day plus 14 now and we have been in a reserve area for 2 days, and although occasionally we are shelled, we are in general getting a good bit of rest. Believe me, the boys have it coming to them. They have fought like demons and been invincible.

As I indicated in another letter, I am, by my own request, commanding a battalion again. On "D" day the Battalion Commander, his Exec, and the S-3 were all killed. The senior officer left was a lieutenant, so I asked to be allowed to take over the battalion. I really was not needed at Regiment HQ as Exec nearly as badly as here. So I am still Regiment Exec Officer in assignment, but actually have been commanding the 1st Battalion since "D" day. They needed me here, and between us, we have done a "hell of a good job" as quoted from a message sent to me by the commanding General, commending us for having held a vital river crossing in the face of superior enemy forces.

Well darling Mother and Dad, I love you both very much always.

Mark
I am sure Ed is still in England. He is assigned to my division now.

Alexander recounted the incident differently in later life, making it seem as if he had only been following orders, but the above and other letters make it clear that he volunteered on the spot at La Fière, asking permission to take over the 1st Battalion in the midst of the battle that S.L.A. Marshall called "probably the bloodiest small struggle in the experience of American arms."[9]

CHAPTER SIXTEEN

WESTWARD TO THE DOUVE: THE BATTLE OF ST. SAUVEUR-LE-VICOMTE

On June 15, the 325 GIR and the 505 PIR of the 82nd Airborne Division jumped off on an attack to the west. The objective was to drive roughly 15 miles to the Douve River to help cut off the peninsula and isolate Cherbourg. The 325 was on the left against the river. The Douve River crossed their path 15 miles ahead running north-south, then turned east, running parallel and just south of the 325. From the 505, Vandervoort's 2nd Battalion was just to the right of the 325. "My 1st Battalion sat on their right," Alexander recalled. "To our right was the 9th Infantry Division.

"In leading off, my battalion had to pass through the 60th Regiment of the 9th Division, which is really a pretty good division. But the regiment was bogged down, lying in rows along the hedgerow and getting shot to pieces by German mortar fire. I remember what a sad lot the 60th appeared as we passed through them like a dose of salts. Obviously, they would have been safer advancing or pulling back a little.

"My 1st Battalion was situated as such: Johnson's C Company on the left, Dolan's A Company on the right, and B Company in reserve. Our experienced battalion drove the Germans quickly back. The assault unit was led by 1st Lt. Mike Chester, a very aggressive combat leader."

Alexander had two pieces of heavy equipment normally worth their weight in gold to the lightly armed paratroopers, if only the terrain could accommodate them. "I had two tanks, but my battalion was in the woods right then and I couldn't very well use them there. Vandervoort's 2nd Battalion hit a heavily fortified farmhouse. Instead of wasting his men, he came over and said, 'You're not using them. How about giving me those two tanks?'

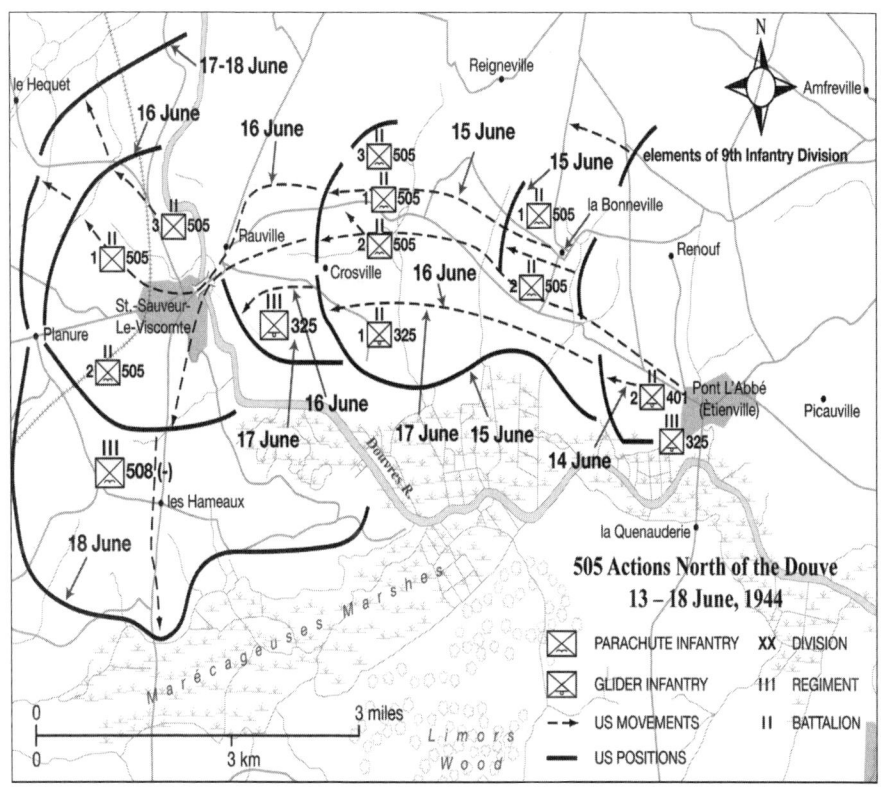

WESTWARD TO THE DOUVE: THE BATTLE OF ST. SAUVEUR-LE-VICOMTE

The Attack to the Douve River.

"'Take them,' I said, 'I'm getting out in front of you and I don't want to be out there.' So I gave them to him. The 1st Battalion was moving quickly forward. The 2nd Battalion on their left was stuck and not advancing. This left the 1st Battalion with an unprotected left flank. Once Vandervoort had the tanks, he could knock out the farmhouse and get his 2nd Battalion moving quickly forward again.

"When I gave Vandervoort the two tanks, he limped forward to where I was and asked me for them. He was on his crutches. He was being held up by a German strong point in two stone farmhouses and I figured he needed the tanks more than I did, as we were not confronted with the open field of fire that he was facing at the time. We were moving through trees and small fields with hedgerows." [1] "Then I never could get the tanks back. He already had them in action and wouldn't return them. He's a good friend of mine, but I was really teed off over that one."

Even on their heels, the highly disciplined German soldiers fell back in an organized manner, making the Americans work for every inch of ground. "I found one of my platoon commanders, Chester, behind a tree shooting at an 88 position. I tapped him on the shoulder and told him it was his responsibility to track and direct his men. In other words, don't get pinned down in the fighting when you are supposed to be the guy in charge.

"He said, 'Well, *you're* here.'" As in, you're here, so clearly you're taking care of that. He was joking.

They took the 88 without too much trouble and continued. True to style, Alexander was in almost constant motion, repeatedly moving to the front to check the status of his lead companies, helping them deal with any problems and returning to his staff to get the lay of things. "At one point I was on my way forward when I saw four people heading back towards me. It was the C Company commander, Lieutenant Johnson, another lieutenant and two German prisoners. Johnson was one of the guys with me a few days earlier when I received powder burns on my face and my runner got a big scoop taken out of his back.

"Johnson's a nice guy, but he was pretty mad right about then. He's also a big guy. As I came up, he had his pistol in his hand and was saying, 'I ought to pistol whip the shit out of you guys,' to these two Germans. I laughed a little bit, and Johnson said, 'No, I really feel like it.'

"Then I saw that he had a big piece of flesh ripped out of his side and I could see his ribs. The other lieutenant was a new replacement we had gotten during our stay in England. He had been shot through the knee. They were headed to the rear. Johnson took about a month to heal. I think they probably grafted some flesh on him to cover all of his ribs.

"As we continued, we experienced only sporadic resistance, mainly from a stone farmhouse and surrounding buildings. At dark, we arrived just short of the village of Crosville, and pushed on in the dark to a position about halfway to the Douve River." North and west of the little village, "we sat down for the night. The 60th Infantry Regiment from the 9th Division was supposed to be on our right, but they had fallen well behind. We had gone about seven miles. Lieutenant Dolan and his A Company had done very well that day, as had Johnson and C Company."

The attack resumed at dawn with Alexander's force more or less fanned out on either side of a dirt road. "At one point as we advanced, the Germans caught me out in the middle of a field when I was trying to take a short cut. They cut loose with a machine gun. It was kicking the dirt up right behind me. I ran like hell and dove in a hedgerow. I landed next to a sergeant with a big grin on his face. He said, 'Colonel, you sure can run fast!'

"We hit stiff resistance from an 88 gun emplacement on the hillside and had a pretty good shootout before taking it." By 2:00 p.m., however, Alexander's men had captured the gun and reached the road running along the Douve River. "I could hear the 2nd Battalion fighting astraddle the main road to the southeast. The regiment from the 9th on our right was far behind."

Because they were out front again, Alexander set up in a defensive position on the river road, defending from both directions. "We had not more than taken up our defense than a German command car with four occupants drove right into us from the north along the river road, not realizing we had advanced so far. Our men shot them to pieces. I don't know how it happened, but a German artillery major survived the incident with only scratches and bruises."

"Some Frenchman on a bicycle saw the action, turned around and pedaled madly back northeast on the river road. I'm sure he informed the Germans of our position." Alexander watched as the Frenchman rode off into the distance, approaching some panzer tanks about a mile away. "I had my artillery observer bring down a concentration of fire. When the smoke cleared, the tanks had gone and I saw no further German action in that area.

"The firing ceased in the 2nd Battalion area, leading me to believe that they had also reached the river. Leaving a platoon-sized roadblock on the river road, I gathered the battalion and started them moving toward the main road that crossed the Douve River in Vandervoort's area.

I went ahead of the battalion with my orderly and a radio operator. When I arrived at the bridge, Colonel Ekman, General Ridgway, General Collins, our corps commander, and General Omar Bradley, who controlled the entire U.S. First Army, were all already there." It was an awful lot of brass to check in on the work of a few battalions. Something was clearly afoot.

The original mission called for all three 505 battalions to advance to the river. The 1st and 2nd battalions of the 505 had already arrived, and the 9th Infantry was making its way. The 3rd Battalion, initially held in reserve, moved a little behind and to the right of the 1st Battalion on the last day of the attack toward the river. But when Vandervoort neared the bridge crossing into St. Sauveur-le-Vicomte, he discovered a massive German evacuation in progress in the streets of the town. Moreover, the Germans had made a major blunder by failing to destroy the bridge completely. If the Allies moved fast and hit hard, they could establish a bridgehead across the Douve more easily and earlier than anticipated.

The generals sped to the spot and Bradley put out the order to all branches of the American military. "Bradley approved us crossing the river. It had to be cleared by him. Before you cross a river, you better know that you're going to have support, or they'll chew you up if you get out there by yourself. We were sticking our neck out, but the General sure provided an opening barrage."

A massive naval, aerial and artillery TOT (time on target) bombardment on St. Sauveur-le-Vicomte preceded the attack across the bridge. The warships floating off Utah and Omaha beaches turned their big guns and let them loose. All army artillery within range opened fire as well as aircraft bombers, and all rounds fired hit the target at the same precise moment. The barrage was brief but devastating. A second barrage was called in after a brief adjustment, further laying waste to enemy guns, men and vehicles.

As the barrage lifted, Vandervoort's 2nd Battalion started down the slope in column formation. The 3rd Platoon led the assault, with Sergeant Spencer Wurst's 1st Squad in front. Wurst describes the action:

> We moved along the edge of the road, attempting to use the ditch as cover. We were taking considerable small arms fire [...]. The Germans had us in sight and were firing rifles and machine guns directly on us. About 150 yards from the bridge, we were also taken under very heavy direct artillery fire [...] most likely from self-propelled guns. These were HE—high explosive—shells, not anti-tank. The weapons were firing at point blank range or 'over the sights'—right over the barrel—and the shells were on us before we heard the report of the guns.
>
> The Germans had taken position on the other side of the river to our left and right front, on slightly higher ground. [...] We hit the dirt as the shells skimmed the top of the roadbed, passing over our heads by two or three feet. The best we could do was get the hell out of there as fast as possible. We had to jump up and run across the bridge. [...]

We lost a number of men on the rush across the bridge, but [Pfc. John] Corti [a BAR man] was the only one in my squad who was hit. The shells were coming heavily but still high, skimming the top of the road and hitting trees or the walls of houses scattered on the other side. They exploded far enough away that they didn't do much damage, at least to us. I read later that as we forged our way across in the middle of all that artillery, General Bradley, watching from afar with General Ridgway, complemented us on our work. "My God, Matt," he is reputed to have said, "Can't anything stop these men?" Reading this, I felt pretty good even fifty years after the fact. [2]

Alexander's 1st Battalion crossed right behind Vandervoort's men. "The last of the 2nd Battalion had crossed the half-blown bridge. Ekman ordered me to bring up the 1st Battalion. I told him they were already on their way and the lead elements began arriving as I spoke. I was to push on through and hold the high ground to the right. Ridgway informed me that he had 15 batteries of artillery to back us up if we needed them. That was rather reassuring.

"My 1st Battalion crossed the bridge immediately behind the 2nd Battalion without too much fighting. The bombardment had pulverized St. Sauveur-le-Vicomte. We took up a position on the high ground in the northeast part of the town and the 2nd Battalion was positioned straight ahead." Late that afternoon the 3rd Battalion moved into position to the right of the 1st Battalion. [3] "Soon the 508 was brought up and took up a position (to the left) in the southwest part of the town. A very firm bridgehead was established.

"While we were getting into position, I lost a lieutenant that I was pretty fond of. The Jerries were hitting us with some fire. They dropped a mortar shell very close to where we were. This lieutenant got hit and went down. He got a piece right in his shoulder and there was no place where it came out. The fragment must have gone into his body and bounced off a bone down into his chest. I think it did because there was no exit wound. You never know exactly how much damage is done, but I knew he was hit bad because he was turning yellowish gray. You can quite often tell when a guy's hit real bad. I gave him a shot of morphine and sent him to the rear, but heard that he died on the way. I believe it had gone into and ruptured his lung or maybe as far as his heart. But you never really knew for certain."

The following day, elements of the 9th Division crossed the bridge and in two days reached the west coast of the Normandy peninsula, cutting off any movement by the Germans from northeast to southwest or visa versa, and enabling General Collins and his corps to intensify their drive to the north to capture Cherbourg. Taking advantage of the enemy's failure to destroy the bridge and establishing a bridgehead greatly affected the fight for France.[4] Historians today believe that Cherbourg was taken two weeks earlier because of events at St. Sauveur-le-Vicomte. The early crossing, in turn, led to an earlier breakout of Patton's tanks into the heart of France. German forces trapped on the east side of the Douve River and the usable, although damaged, bridge demonstrate that the enemy was caught off-guard by the Americans' rapid advance.

The 505 and 508 PIRs held their positions in St. Sauveur-le-Vicomte for several days. "I set up my battalion CP in one of the undamaged farmhouses," Alexander recounts. "One of the headquarters men came up to me and said he was going to cook me a suckling duck dinner with potatoes and tomatoes from a garden and a duck from a nearby pond. That sounded great after eating army rations for so long.

My staff and I were sitting down at a kitchen table, prepared to eat our first hot meal in ten days, when right then, the field telephone rang. It was a call from Colonel Ekman. He said that General Ridgway had called and wanted me to report to and as executive officer of the 508th PIR as soon as possible, that they needed me there. A minute later, the telephone rang again and General Ridgway himself confirmed the order.

"I said, 'But Sir, I'm a 505 man.'

"He said, 'You *were*.'

"He wanted me over with the 508 right now. So I jumped into a jeep and left my suckling duck dinner to my replacement, Maj. Bill Hagen, and headed over to the 508, which was on the other side of the bridgehead." [5]

Alexander stood in command of the 1st Battalion, 505, for only ten days. In that time they accomplished much. Lieutenant Dolan later wrote, "Without exception, he was the finest battalion commander I ever served under," and he even named a son after him: Mark Alexander Dolan. [6]

CHAPTER SEVENTEEN

THE 508 PARACHUTE INFANTRY REGIMENT

WHEN ALEXANDER REPORTED AS THE new executive officer to Col. Roy E. Lindquist, the commander of the 508, he received a rather frosty reception. The senior officers of the 508 had been together for more than 18 months and Alexander was an outsider. Initially, Alexander had no idea why he had been transferred, but he soon learned that the 508 had undergone a shake-up in its command structure. Ridgway had relieved the executive officer (who had replaced Ekman when he joined the 505 several months earlier). It was found he disobeyed an order early in the morning on D-Day.

It seems that Alexander was used either directly or indirectly as a threat to take over the regiment if Lindquist didn't perform more in line with Ridgway's expectations. This was something Alexander gathered much later from a conversation with Ridgway. "Ridgway said the senior command of the 508 was not aggressive enough. They wanted me over there to try and fire them up a little bit. That's all I was ever told."

Once again, Alexander was back in the role he so disliked, that of executive officer, doing paperwork and running the headquarters. As General Gavin later noted, Roy Linquist was "a hell of a good administrator" who "kept records like I've never seen before," but when it came to leadership, he "was the very opposite of Rube Tucker" (the aggressive 504 PIR commander). [1] Alexander also thought Lindquist was probably "the best administrator in the division."[2] Linquist's records and paperwork were just the way he liked them and he would just as soon do the work himself. This no doubt suited Alexander, who greatly preferred to be out in the field.

This pairing had the potential to be one of the most effective

Colonel Roy E. Lindquist, the commander of the 508 Parachute Infantry Regiment throughout World War II. *Photograph courtesy of Bob Murphy*

regimental command structures in the war. Unfortunately and ironically, however, both Linquist and Alexander were serving in the wrong capacity. Alexander's drive, instincts, and "lead from the front" mentality suited him perfectly for combat leadership, while Lindquist's practice of relying on and tracking reconnaissance reports during combat, and his knack for paperwork gave him the perfect skill set for an executive officer. As Gavin later wrote, "I know Mark very well, having had him serve under me in various capacities in the regiment and in this division. His academic standing at school is somewhat understandable in view of his dislike for this type of work. For the same reason he has not been an outstanding staff officer. He is, however, a superior troop leader in combat. He is possessed with exceptional courage and performs brilliantly on the battlefield." [3]

The 508 and the 505 remained in place for 48 hours. During this time, Alexander learned that Colonel Batcheller, formerly commander of the 1/508 and regimental commander of the 505, had been killed when his field grave was located nearby. He and a planeload of men had been misdropped in the area, and he was killed leading an attack on a German position.[4]

On June 18, the 508 and the other regiments of the 82nd were deployed in a defensive position facing to the southwest. The 82nd, 101st and 90th divisions were strung across the peninsula to prevent German forces from moving further up into and reinforcing their isolated countrymen.[5] "This freed up General Collins, our corps commander, to go ahead and concentrate on capturing the deep water port of Cherbourg. They didn't want us to advance. They just wanted us to stay and hold the ground and protect Collins' rear while he took the port. It took about two weeks.

"In this defensive position, held from June 18 to the morning of July 3, not a great deal happened. We received infrequent incoming mortar and artillery fire. However, as XO, I had little to do and had Colonel Lindquist's approval to frequently check out the regiment's defensive positions." As airborne historian Guy LoFaro points out, "during this period of static warfare, aggressive patrolling and nightly inspections of the lines were crucial to ensuring the division retained its edge and that the troopers did not succumb to the allure of a few minutes of comfort at the expense of vigilance." [6]

Alexander's inspections and night patrols proved the necessity of such vigilance. "On one of these patrols I was with my new runner, Virgil McGuire. We were scouting ahead of our lines and went into a fairly substantial stone farmhouse through the back door. We entered that way from the woods because I knew we were getting close to the German lines. So we went in and peeked out the front window. There was a line of Germans coming, moving down the road and crossing in front of us. I counted them and then, as soon as they went by, we got the hell out of there. Not a great place to be."

This and other experiences with Alexander left a lasting impression on McGuire, who later paid him tribute: "He was absolutely fearless and didn't realize that senior officers could get killed. He went on reconnaissance patrols far in front of our lines. He packed a lot of living, and almost died, in the 11 days he was with the 508." [7]

"Most of the time when I was out and about I took McGuire with me, but sometimes I went alone," Alexander stated. "One evening I was restless. It was a very dark night with a cloudy sky and we were in a wooded area straddling a dirt road that ran into the enemy's positions. I decided to check some of our positions, one in particular that protruded out a ways. I quietly moved down the dirt road through the trees. All at once I realized I was hearing German voices on both sides of me."

Alexander very quietly retraced his steps. When he finally located the 508 roadblock position he was looking for, both men were asleep. "I kicked one of them real hard to wake him up. Scared the hell out of him. But I didn't turn them in or anything like that.

"Sometimes guys get over-tired and over-confident when they're in a defensive position. You've got to stay alert, which they were not doing. In fact, they left a hole for the Germans to come right in. They could have made an attack right through that area. That's why we had people awake at night, to make sure somebody like me didn't go probing in there. No one else was around, so I didn't do anything more about it. But I kept an eye on those two guys for the short time that I had left in Normandy.

"Another night I had been out checking our deployment and it started to rain again. I returned to our command post and my orderly McGuire had somehow procured a pup tent and two blankets. Alongside the tent he dug a trench, as we had been receiving occasional mortar fire in the bivouac area. There was mud at the bottom of the slit trench, so I crawled into the tent with my two blankets and was soon sound asleep." Alexander woke once to the sound of mortar fire and explosions, but was too comfortable to consider moving into the muddy hole. He quickly fell back to sleep. "We were so used to the shelling, it got so sometimes you almost ignored it."

Awakened again to the sound of nearby explosions, Alexander lay in the tent with his eyes open. "Another round landed very close, and with the next flash and explosion I could see four holes in the top of the pup tent. That convinced me. I got up, grabbed my two blankets and moved into the muddy trench.

"It was in July and it was pretty warm, but when you got wet, you got cold. I had a big ol' raincoat for when it rained real hard. There was a puddle at the bottom of the trench, so I threw a couple of branches in there with leaves on them. Then I kicked some more dirt in on top of it, making it dry enough to put my blanket on. It was muddy, but water wasn't getting around my coat or soaking into the blanket. I didn't get to sleep very long anyway. Shortly, the Jerries started dropping a lot more in the area."

The last group of German defenders at Cherbourg finally surrendered on June 29 and 30, bringing the entire peninsula into Allied hands. "Victory came at a high price," writes Normandy historian Dominique François. "The Americans lost more than twenty thousand troops in the battle for the Cotentin Peninsula. Although German losses, numbering fourteen thousand, were not as high, forty thousand men were taken prisoner. The harbor train station had been destroyed, and sunken ships obstructed the entrance to the port. It was necessary for the Americans to reconstruct the entire infrastructure of the port and clear the harbor of mines before it could receive convoys of matériel. The first shipment arrived on July 16." [8]

With the north of the Cotentin Peninsula liberated, "the Americans turned their attention to the southern part of the Manche, with the hope of rapidly breaking out of the hedgerows. [...] Since the capture of Carentan by paratroopers on June 12, frontlines in the sector had not budged an inch. The Americans had concentrated all their efforts on Cherbourg. Meanwhile, further east, troops who had debarked on Omaha Beach were ground to a standstill in the Battle for Saint-Lô." [9] Omar Bradley, frustrated with slow progress in all areas, decided to launch a massive breakout using all of his available forces. He set an attack across his entire front for the morning of July 3.

By this time, casualties for the entire 82nd were already above 50 percent, and they were even higher if headquarters troops were not included. The over-all mission of the airborne was to jump behind enemy lines, take key objectives and fight like hell until replaced by front-line or seaborne forces. Because airborne troops were so aggressive, leaving them in much longer raised the risk of incurring such high casualties that the recovery time before another combat jump could be as much as a year. A cadre of veterans was absolutely necessary to bring replacement troops into the fold effectively.

The commanders of two of Gavin's three parachute regiments protested when told they would again go on the attack. Lindquist showed character by pointing out to Gavin that in some cases his rifle companies were down to 50 men from 190. He wanted the 508 to be pulled off the line. Edson Raff, the 507 commander, told Gavin, "If we attack any more we won't have a cadre to make a regiment when we get back to England. I think we ought to be withdrawn." Gavin agreed and brought the protests to Ridgway. However, Bradley wanted the 82nd, the only division slated for the attack that had combat experience prior to D-Day, to participate. Ridgway agreed to one more attack. [10]

"Bradley launched his attack with vastly superior forces that seemed likely to crush the enemy quickly—at least on paper." Begun on July 3, the push to take the crucial towns of Lessay and Coutances became long and bloody. "To reach Coutances, the Americans first had to break the deadlock at La-Hay-du-Puits, whose surrounding hills the Germans had heavily fortified." La-Hay-du-Puits "was an important crossroads for routes to Cherbourg, Carentan, Barneville and Coutances. To the west of the city lay the estuary of Ay; to the east were the marshlands—both difficult terrains to master. Breaking the deadlock was thus first necessary to seize the high ground; this, in turn, would permit the southern passage for Patton's tanks over the valley roads." This battle lasted ten days, and the entire southward path of the Allies depended on it. [11]

For the 508 PIR, the first day's objective was to drive southwest about 6,000 yards, just short of the village of Blanchelande and clear the left slope of one of the monts, or hilltops, Hill 131. The 505 was assigned to take the rest of the hill. The following day, July 4, the 508 was to take Hill 95, about 4,000 yards southwest of Hill 131. The final objective for the division was to take Le-Haye-du-Puits, which sat just beyond Hill 95.

"On the morning of July 3, Colonel Lindquist gave me the attack order: the 505th on our right, the 325th on our left. Our 508 regimental alignment had 2nd Battalion on the right and 3rd on the left, with 1st Battalion following in close reserve. The attack went well until I heard over my radio a little before noon that Lieutenant Colonel [Thomas J.] Shanley, leading the 2nd Battalion, had tripped the wire to a bouncing betty and caught a ball in the back of his neck. The loss of Colonel Shanley was critical, leaving only an inexperienced captain, Chet Graham, to lead the battalion."

Knowing where he could do the most good, Alexander asked Lindquist if he could fill in for Shanley. Lindquist agreed. "I immediately went forward to the 2nd Battalion, which was involved in cleaning up a German defensive position. The battalion was unorganized and doing some looting of the captured Germans and their positions. Everybody was trying to get a pistol here or an insignia there and so forth, which is typical."

Lieutenant Colonel Shanley had several pieces of shrapnel in him and couldn't turn his head. Alexander sent him back to the medics and proceeded to get the battalion organized and moving up the grade toward the objective for the day. "We closed on it about an hour before dark.

"After our 2nd Battalion, my battalion at this stage, had proceeded about 1,000 yards short of our objective, I heard a hell of a firefight break out to our rear. I took one man with me to backtrack and see what was going on. As we took a bend in the dirt road and looked down the hill, we could see Germans in a deep drainage ditch firing at our oncoming 1st Battalion. My runner and I moved into a good position above them and poured it on from their rear, knocking off a couple of them. I know I got one because he slumped down when he was hit, and I think I hit a second. The others started crawling along the ditch to try and get away.

"I ran forward and grabbed the point rifle squad of the 1st Battalion, brought them around the retreating Germans and pinched off their escape. After a firefight, they waved a white handkerchief and surrendered. I put in a request verbally right there on site to get that young corporal who led the rifle squad a Silver Star. I don't think it ever happened. We captured 25 or 26 Germans led by an SS lieutenant. I still have his P-38."

Lieutenant Colonel [Shields] Warren, commander of the 1st Battalion, came up, saw the last of this action and remarked that Alexander would make a good platoon leader. Alexander directed Warren to follow closer to the lead battalion and not leave space for enemy troops to exploit. "I think the reason the Germans ended up behind us is because the 505 on our right ran into something pretty solid. As they broke it up, some of the Germans drifted laterally between our 508 battalions."

By the end of the day, the 505 had seized its objective, Hill 131, taking casualties and capturing German prisoners. Elements of the 508 took the southern slope. "They had a pretty good scrap taking Hill 131," as Alexander put it.

The next day the 508, primarily Alexander's 2nd Battalion, was to take Hill 95, after which their work in Normandy would practically be complete. This was the last real test before the division would be pulled off the line and sent back to England to recuperate. The finish was at hand. What could possibly go wrong?

Chapter Eighteen

Hill 95

Alexander saw that his battalion got into a good defensive position for the night, bivouacking behind "a small knoll between [his] battalion and Hill 95." With half an hour of daylight remaining, he set out to make a reconnaissance for the attack scheduled for the following morning, July 4, at dawn. "I always did that to figure out where in the heck I was going. I didn't want to go into something blind and lead my men into a trap.

"I found that there was an open valley between us and the Germans. If we went straight ahead, we'd have to cross that open area. I moved to the left-forward edge of a wooded area, crawled behind a stone wall and pulled a rock out of it. That way I could lie there and observe without being exposed. I was looking at the whole valley right up to the top of the hill. With my field glasses I spotted two German gun positions up on the hill. I think both of them were 88s. One of them might have been a 75mm mountain howitzer. They had quite a few of those, because we were facing part of a German mountain division.

"While lying there, I heard something behind me. I looked up and one of our young guys was walking down the knoll, out of the trees towards me. I yelled, 'Get down! Get down, dammit! The Germans can see you!' But he just kept walking. I didn't have to yell a second time though, because the Jerries saw him and zeroed in. Their shot was a little bit low. They put an 88 round in the rock wall directly in line with him. He took off running.

"Luckily, I was about twenty feet off to one side of the 88 round. I lay there for a little longer and figured out how I was going to attack with my battalion. I wanted to find out who that guy was, but I never could. I don't think he wanted me to know. He knew I was going to chew his ass."

When darkness closed in, Alexander left his observation post, crawling along behind the wall until he got back up in the woods. He returned to his CP, called Colonel Lindquist on a field telephone and told him how he planned to attack. Alexander reported he would move the battalion to the left into a tree-covered ridge that rose all the way to the top of Hill 95 and attack from there. He specifically said attacking straight ahead was a poor idea because of the open valley. "They're shooting right down our throats from up there," he told Lindquist.

"I had plenty of time to give the company commanders moving orders on how to proceed and the way I wanted them to go. I was going to put two companies in the lead if there was room in this wooded area. Going up in the woods is a hell of a lot better than out in the open where they can zero in on you with an 88 or a mountain howitzer. It was a hell of a lot better plan than going across that open valley."

Luck had definitely been on Alexander's side throughout the war. Any of his numerous close calls could have put him in a hospital, or more likely in a grave. His first brush with death came when his men almost pushed him out into the open sea on the Sicily jump. Then he narrowly avoided being raked by a German fighter aircraft as he hid behind a stump. Later in the same campaign, a shell landed next to him and Captain McRoberts, but turned out to be a dud. A falling flowerpot in Italy was seconds away from crushing his skull. Also in Italy, the Germans in the Arnone train depot mercifully chose to surrender instead of kill.

In Normandy, too, Alexander cheated death, caught in the middle of an open field by an enemy machine gun crew. And he walked up to a well concealed, dug-in fortification before seeing it. Fortunately, it was only manned by dead Germans. Finally, however, his luck ran short.

"I had no more than hung the phone back on the tree than the Germans put a round of 81mm mortar into the branches. I think I heard it coming but took a dive too late. I was hit in the back by two shell fragments. It felt like someone stuck a fence post in my back. All I could do was lie there and cuss and think of all the times they were shooting directly at me and missed. They finally blindly lobbed one over the hill in the dark and got me."

Alexander later said he believed the knoll they rested behind may not have been quite tall enough to totally conceal the battalion from Hill 95.

Perhaps the gunners saw someone light a cigarette and sent a shell in that direction.

"Doctor Montgomery and the medics got me right away," and quickly went to work. As Alexander struggled to breathe, air bubbled out of the open wound. Luck hadn't completely abandoned him, however. Two days earlier, the Surgeon General's office had released a directive: any wounded man with a sucking blowhole wound should be taped tight, right away. The medics did just that. "They put all kinds of tape on me, taped my chest tight, closing the wound so that I would not have a blowhole and collapsed lung." The new directive kept him alive.

"They called regiment for a jeep and put me in the front seat with the driver." As they sped toward the field hospital, the blood quickly soaked through Alexander's bandages and down into his seat. The cushion became slippery and he struggled not to slide off. "After about a mile, we stopped briefly at regiment CP and I had a few words with Colonel Lindquist, but I couldn't talk very well. And then they took me on in.

"It was rather foggy. I rode for about three hours it seemed, because it was just turning dawn when we got to this hospital tent. I put my foot down and started to dismount from the jeep. I remember two men with a stretcher coming out of the fog. When I saw that stretcher coming I thought, 'Well, I made it,' and passed out.

"The mind can do some strange things. I was able to stay conscious until I knew I was at the hospital tent. I've seen guys who were shot up really, really bad just hang on and keep living way after they should have died. And I've seen other people who died right away."

For the next several days, Alexander drifted in and out of consciousness. "The next thing I remember, two doctors were trying to take an X-ray of my chest. I was bare from my waist up, but still wearing my pants. I had the shakes and could not hold still for the X-ray. When I came to after surgery, Major General Ridgway was sitting on a stool by my cot holding my hand. He was talking to me, but I do not remember what he said, as I was only semiconscious.

"The next time I came to, Father Connelly was bending over me, praying. I remember telling him that I was not Catholic. He told me to just be quiet, that he was taking care of things. When I came to again, the nurse came to me, looked at my dog tags and said, 'Colonel, you are not registered as a Catholic.'

"I said, 'No, just a Christian.'

"She said, 'Well, you're a Catholic now. Father Connelly gave you the last rites.'"

Alexander continued to sleep a great deal while his body tried to recover. "I wasn't breathing too well about then. I can remember the day after the operation, I was trying to get some air. I didn't know it, but one lung had collapsed. The doctor got on it and had everybody going. He put a tube down through my nose. They splashed water in my face and kept me swallowing to get it to go down the right way and to the right place. They put it into my lungs and pumped in oxygen."

When Jack Norton heard that his old commander had been hit, he immediately drove out to see him, but Alexander has no memory of it. The nurses said he had numerous visitors, but he was sleeping or too groggy to remember many of them. Virgil McGuire brought Alexander's personal items to the field hospital and set them under his cot.

He was still doing badly, but after a few days he was able to stay awake longer and was much more coherent. His old runner Chick Eitelman came by for a visit. Fully recovered from his wounded knee, Eitelman was adamant that Alexander never would have been wounded had he been there to look out for him. "Chick, they dropped one on me in the dark of night. How could you prevent that?" asked Alexander. Eitelman was not persuaded, and years after the war, he still believed he could have prevented the harm.

The corporal also had something else on his mind when he came to see Alexander in the hospital. "Chick took care of my clothes and so fourth, but I didn't use him like some guys used their runner/bodyguard. Krause knew that I liked Chick, and that he was a damn good orderly and a good guy to have with you when you got in trouble. When I got shot up, it was clear I would be out of action for a long time. So Colonel Krause asked Chick to come over as his orderly."

"Krause wants me to be his orderly, but I don't want to be," said Eitelman. "What am I going to do about it?" Alexander replied, "Just tell him you don't want to be his orderly. That's all." Eitelman did, although certainly in a much more diplomatic fashion, and soon obtained a transfer to the regimental intelligence section (S-2 area). [1]

After he was hit on the early morning of July 4, Alexander was replaced by his battalion executive officer, Capt. Chet Graham. Graham had not yet led a battalion, but he had good instincts and know-how. According to Graham, the orders he received for the day were "to cross the open ground and take Hill 95, with no information given of enemy strength nor possible help from our artillery."

"I asked Colonel Lindquist, 'What about Colonel Alexander's plan to advance through the cover of the trees?' He said, 'You have your orders.'" [2]

Graham was shocked by the order. Battalion strength was down to 225, including only eight officers, from the 640 men who had jumped with the battalion on D-Day. A direct charge against the dug-in Germans backed by cannons would undoubtedly be costly to the remaining men. But, as Graham put it, "that was our job."

Graham placed D Company on the left, holding back one platoon as a reserve, and positioned E Company in the middle and F Company on the right. The right flank was secured by Krause's 3/505. Graham describes the attack: "We moved at 8:00 a.m. across the area with no cover and were shelled by 88s for most of the two miles. Our 3rd Battalion [3/508] didn't move until 10:00 hours and never contacted us. We had an uncovered [left] flank for three days. [3]

Graham's account continues: "[On our right flank] Colonel Krause, CO of the 505, 3rd Battalion, had sent out a patrol that was cut up by machine gun fire. The medic [Pvt. Merrill M. "Marty" Scherzer] who was sent out to help was killed by fire from machine guns." The medic was intentionally targeted, bringing the fighting to a very ugly level. Graham sent out a patrol that flanked the machine gun, bringing in the prisoners.[4] Sergeant Dwayne Burns, 2/508, recounts:

> F Company had captured a machine-gun emplacement on the way, which yielded four prisoners. [...] We marched the four down the road until we ran into the reserve unit and they said they would take the prisoners off our hands. [...] Just prior to noon, I had to go back to the rear [...]. Just outside the rear area, in a ditch alongside the road, I found the same four dead Germans. [...] Someone had used a machete on their heads and I thought I was gong to be sick. [...] They [the men who killed the prisoners] claimed it was the same machine-gun crew who shot down their medic while he was trying to help the wounded. They had demanded an eye for an eye. [5]

According to Graham's summary of the larger 2/508 picture, "D Company received mortar fire and lost six men, one officer and our S-3, Captain George Simons. D Company [...] held the left front of the hill, and E Company had trouble, but got where they were supposed to be. F Company was hugging the hill with open ground on its right and was being cut up."

The Germans and Americans were not the first soldiers to occupy this ground. Hill 95 had been an outpost of the Romans, who left a sheltered moat inside the perimeter circling the hill about ten feet wide. This worked in Graham's favor, for he was able to move troops under cover from one side of the battle to the other. Graham pulled F Company back out of the meat grinder, preparing to move E Company partially to the right.

"During this time, I was being called back to our big radio to converse with Colonel Lindquist. He told me to move F Company back, saying, 'We don't give up ground we have taken. Get them back.'" Graham explained the situation and his plan. Lindquist nixed it.

"I told him he should come and see for himself instead of second-guessing from a mile away," said Graham. "I was relieved of command on the spot. [Captain] Royal [R.] Taylor came down and followed the plan."

The 2nd and 3rd Battalions of the 508 and elements of the 505 continued the fight. The 2/508 managed to capture the crest of the hill, only to lose it to a vicious German counter-attack at 2:00 p.m. The paratroopers regrouped and re-attacked Hill 95, finally retaking the crest at around midnight, putting an end to the long, bloody day. "In twenty-four hours the 2d Battalion was commanded by four different officers. Shanley was wounded on July 3rd in the attack on Hill 30. Lieutenant Colonel Alexander was wounded during the night, and Captain Graham took temporary command until Captain Taylor arrived. During the night movement to the crest was initiated, and by 0500 Hill 95 was secured. This was one 4th of July that few men in the 508th could ever forget." [6]

Lenny Sacharoff, 3rd Battalion, HQ Company, gives a compelling eyewitness account of the aftermath of the battle: "The Americans did manage to take the hell, but the casualties were staggering. So many people were killed or wounded. It was terrible! I remember looking at the scene the morning after the battle, and these were trucks loaded high with piles of bodies, just like sacks of potatoes. Oh my god, it was awful! I had seen a lot of German dead, but when you see so many bodies with your uniform on, the insignia of your outfit, it hits a lot harder. So, now, on the fourth of July […] I think of that day!" [7]

Whenever Alexander spoke of friends he had lost, memories still brought up strong feelings of sadness, although he maintained a calm manner of speech. But the events on Hill 95 after he was wounded aggravated him like no other topic. The written version of his condemnation, as strong as it is, cannot convey the edge in his voice. "They went right across that open space and straight up the hill instead of taking advantage of the woods. There was no reason why they should go across that open valley. I knew if they did they would get their butts blown off. It shouldn't have been that way. They really got nailed and a lot of guys got killed.

"After the war, I asked Captain Graham, who took command of the battalion after I was hit, 'Why did you guys go across the open valley?'" He said, 'We had our orders to go straight ahead, so we did.'

"Lindquist stayed back in his CP and never even did come up before giving those orders, I found out afterwards. I know he didn't do reconnaissance himself while I was still kicking. I didn't like to go without a reconnaissance. It's foolish, in fact. But he was more of a guy that commanded from back a-ways. He always laid back and relied on information from others, and you generally can't do it that way and be successful. Can't do it.

"That operation always bothered me, because I know if I'd been there, a lot of these guys wouldn't have lost their lives. I had figured out how to go up that ridge in the trees. We had a much better chance that way than going straight up. They got their butts shot off.

"The 3rd Battalion, 508, was led by Lieutenant Colonel [Louis G.] Mendez. Lindquist ordered them to attack the hill. He was a good commander, but he almost got relieved too. He didn't want to make the attack because there was a lot of firepower up on that side of the hill and not much cover. He knew there would be a lot of men killed.

"Gavin had to call him over the field telephone, urging him to go on with the attack. And Mendez replied, 'You come up here and give the order.'

"Gavin said, 'Look, you're an Academy graduate. You're a military man. You go on and get that attack going.' Words to that effect. So he did, and he lost a lot of men. Really got pounded down." [8]

According to 82nd Airborne historian Phil Nordyke, "The attacks by the 82nd Airborne on July 4 resulted in over five hundred enemy killed and over seven hundred captured. But the division had suffered heavily as well, as courageous officers and men attacked a well-armed foe, dug in on high ground." On July 5, most of the division consolidated, while the 325 GIR made an assault on La Poterie, and division artillery fired nearly 3,000 rounds to break up enemy counter-attacks on 507 PIR positions in the area. For the next two days, the division maintained its positions on the high ground northeast of La Poterie, during which it assessed the heavy losses among both officers and men.

On July 8, the 8th Infantry Division passed through the 82nd and attacked La-Haye-du-Puits. "The 82nd was placed in corps reserve and all attached units were released from attachment. [...] On July 11, the entire division moved down to Utah Beach." The division had inflicted higher casualties on the German Army than they themselves had incurred, but the casualties of the All Americans were so appalling that battalions waiting to be loaded on LSTs for the trip to England were taken to be mere companies by fresh units still coming ashore. In all, only 17 LSTs were needed for the return.

Not surprisingly, infantry regiments had incurred the most tremendous losses: the three parachute infantry regiments suffered a 55 percent casualty rate, while casualties among the glider infantry were even higher, at 58 percent. Tellingly, the casualty rate of the division's officers was higher yet: of the 12 battalion commanders who jumped into Normandy on D-Day, only one, Lt. Col. Louis Mendez, DSC, emerged from the campaign without incurring a wound or serious injury. [9] Two of the 12 replacement battalion commanders were killed and four were wounded, Alexander among them. As Clay Blair grimly concluded after tallying up the casualty rate among senior 82nd Airborne infantry commanders in Normandy, "the toll of infantry battalion commanders may have been the heaviest for any division in a single campaign in the war. [10]

CHAPTER NINETEEN

RECOVERY, HOLLAND AND THE BULGE

A GERMAN SHELL LOBBED BLINDLY into the night on the eve of his regiment's final battle in Normandy robbed Alexander of doing what he did best—leading troops. He would never command a regiment in combat, a position for which he was surely destined by character, aptitude, training and experience. Yet the rest of his life, both in and out of the military, is best summed up in this motto: "You can take the paratrooper out of the fight, but you can't take the fight out of the paratrooper."

The serious wounds Alexander received at Hill 95 effectively ended his career as a commander of front line troops, but not surprisingly, he did not give up the effort to get back into battle. He petitioned his commanders to return to the front in both Holland and the Bulge, but his medical condition largely confined him to administrative posts. These included commanding camps for the 82nd Airborne at Suippes and Soissons, France, and running the Parachute School at Fort Benning. Despite their importance, these assignments still required pushing pencils and processing paperwork, tasks for which he felt no affinity, but to which he determinedly applied himself, continually pushing the limits of his endurance.

Alexander's no-nonsense temperament, his distain of army "chickenshit," and his natural leadership qualities all were manifest even in the surgical hospital, as he gradually came back to himself after a serious operation to remove the shrapnel from his lung. He first, however, spent several days in the medical tent near St. Sauveur-le-Vicomte. "I was hooked up with tubing in just about all of my orifices until the fifth day, at which time, thirty-four days after floating into Normandy on a parachute in the dark of night, I was put on a stretcher and carried by ambulance to a British hospital ship at Omaha Beach. We crossed the channel to Portsmouth, England, where I was loaded on a hospital train that carried me to a base hospital in central England. This was a surgical hospital.

"Each morning, the chief surgeon came by to make an inspection. The first two mornings he came in, one of his men yelled 'Attention!' and a bunch of guys stood up next to their beds.

"I said, 'What the hell is going on around here?'

"They said, 'Oh, the Colonel insists that everybody who is able stand up by his bed for inspection.'

"I said, 'Bullshit!' All these guys have been shot to pieces, and they're supposed to get up and stand by their beds. I said, 'Tomorrow morning, nobody's going to stand up. And if you have any trouble, blame it on me.'

"So the next morning, he had his man call twice for us to come to attention and nobody did. After that, the guys were left alone. I think the Colonel knew damn well he was wrong. You find guys like that, who throw their weight around unnecessarily. A lot of these guys hardly had the energy to get up out of bed, let alone stand there while he made his inspection.

"Then, to top it off—I think I'm a trouble maker—there was a guy there that had been shot through the hips and was in a cast clear up to his upper chest. He had been there about two weeks already and needed some encouragement. So I got hold of some crayons and drew a pair of breasts in the appropriate places on his cast.

"I was just two beds down from him and knew that every morning the old colonel came in and flipped his blankets back. That morning, he flipped the blankets back and didn't say a damn word. But I could see his face getting red. And everybody got a laugh out of that."

Alexander's recovery was slow. Surgeons had removed a large shell fragment during the operation in the field hospital in France, but a smaller one had gone unnoticed. Now, about a month later, four doctors stood around his bed discussing a possible second operation to remove the smaller fragment, located one inch to the left of his heart. "Two doctors were for operating and two for leaving the fragment in place. I was starting to heal and the fragment was cube-shaped and would not move.

"After listening to the doctors, I said that if they couldn't make up their minds, I sure could. 'Just leave that shell fragment where it is.' The doctors laughed and said, 'There's our answer.' I still have the Kraut steel in my lung.

"Another one of our 82nd Airborne boys, a lieutenant in the 325 glider regiment, had a small piece of shrapnel actually inside his heart. Fortunately, it was small enough that the wound in the heart clotted and healed. After a month and a half in the hospital, the shrapnel made its way to his right arm and they removed it from there."

After nearly 40 days in the surgical hospital, Alexander was transferred to a recuperative hospital facility near Portsmouth. A letter home, written July 27, 1944, shows a diagram of his wounds, describing his injuries and scars. He here notes he is coming along well, and has avoided a second operation. *However, as my lung was deflated and the nerves extending around my ribs to my lower frontal chest regions were severed, this business of getting my chest inflated and up to what it should be again is a very slow business and will take several months to return to normal. I am working at it each day [...].*

After a few days, Alexander was transferred to the 77th Convalescent Hospital, designed to get men back in shape for active duty. True to form, he again took issue with the way things were run.

"The first night there, I woke up to find men crawling across the support beams near the ceiling. The next day I found out that the Colonel had everyone restricted to 9:00 at night. The men would sneak

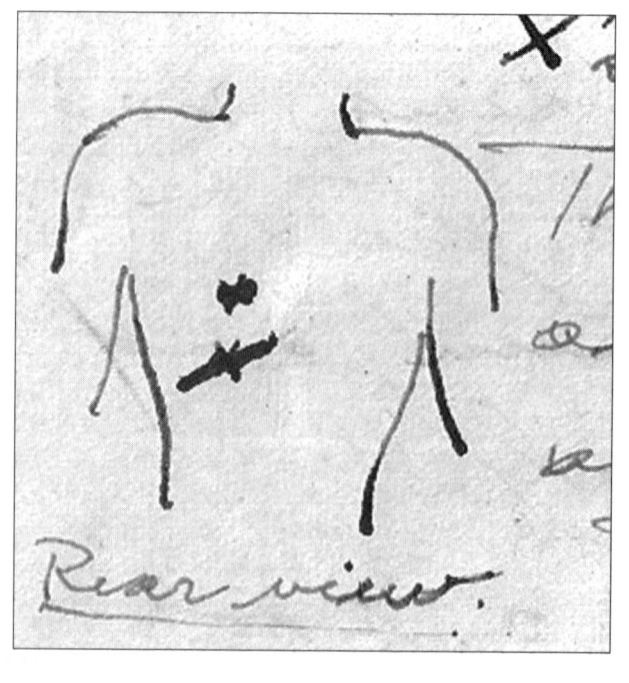

Alexander diagramed his wounds in a letter home to his parents. "I was hit where the Xs are by two shell fragments. The long, lower wound was an opening into my chest about an inch long, but also, I have the long incision as indicated where they cut in, removed portions of the two shattered ribs, and also sewed up two torn places in my lung."

out and had to return through a high window." Alexander was incensed and told the Colonel what he thought. He informed him that the men would be going out and remaining out after 9:00. "He said if we stayed out past curfew he was going to court-martial us. I said, 'Okay, I hope you do,' because his curfew rule was not a good one." The soldiers stayed out late and nothing ever came of it.

On September 10, General Gavin called the hospital and asked to have Alexander released. "The hospital commander came down and said, 'The General told me he's got a job for you where you're going to work only about an hour a day. I don't believe him and I don't think you're ready for active duty yet.' So he refused to clear me."

It quickly became clear why Gavin had called, instead of waiting for Alexander's release. On September 17, 1944, the 82nd and 101st Airborne Divisions along with the British 6th Airborne Division made a daring daytime jump into Nazi-held Holland in Operation MARKET-GARDEN. MARKET, the airborne phase of the plan, involved nearly 5,000 transports, fighters and bombers and 2,500 gliders; GARDEN, the ground phase, involved the British Second Army, whose tanks were massed along the Dutch-Belgian border. Under protection of artillery and fighter-bombers, these forces were to rush up through Holland on a narrow corridor cleared by the paratroopers, who were tasked to seize the ground and hold open the route. The American paratroopers were to capture Eindhoven and Nijmegen, wresting control of their crucial bridges so the English armored column could push north along the narrow, 60-mile highway to reach the 6th Airborne Division, which would jump near Arnhem to secure a Rhine River crossing.

Alexander was determined to get into the action. "When I learned about the Holland jump, I went to the hospital commander and told him I wanted out. Previously, I had weighed about 152 pounds, stripped. After getting hit, I got down to 130, but now was back up to 138. He didn't think I was ready, but I insisted. I told him I was leaving no matter what, so he might as well go ahead and release me. He did. I bummed a ride on a C-47 to Paris. And I knew a quartermaster there who gave me a jeep. Then I drove up the corridor."

Alexander arrived shortly after the 82nd Airborne had taken the railroad and highway bridge in an epic battle at Nijmegen. "In all, around two thousand Germans defended the two massive bridges," of whom 500 to 750 were positioned at the railroad bridge. Assigned to the highway bridge, among others, was Kampgruppe Euling, commanded by SS Captain Karl-Heinz Euling, whose 9th SS Reconnaissance Battalion was attached to the 10th SS Panzer Division. "The force consisted of part of the attached 9th SS Reconnaissance Battalion, one company of 10th SS engineers, and an understrength battalion of 10th SS panzer grenadiers." Other units importantly included "the 4th Company, 572nd Heavy Flak Battalion (with four 88mm dual-purpose guns and eight 20mm antiaircraft guns)."[1]

When Alexander arrived at the front, Montgomery's tanks were still fighting to link up with the British 6th Airborne at Arnhem. "The Allies had quite a hard time holding the corridor open, because it was a long corridor. Too far," he said. Montgomery, who had conceived the plan, had underestimated the problems in carrying out such a deep penetration on a very narrow front: as Browning famously protested to Montgomery during the planning phase, "Sir, I think we might be going a bridge too far." And indeed, the British armor ground to a halt about two miles past the city of Nijmegen.[2]

"Our 82nd people were very upset," Alexander stated, "because the 82nd had many losses securing the city." No one was more upset than Col. Rueben Tucker, commander of the 504 PIR, whose 3rd Battalion incurred very heavy losses. Crossing the Waal River in canvas assault boats under heavy German fire, the 3/504 successfully captured the north end of the highway bridge, but only at horrific cost: 46 men killed and over 50 wounded. When General Gavin met up with Tucker in his CP, "Tucker was livid" because the British armor had not yet started to move. "His first question to me [Gavin] was, 'What the hell are they doing? We have been in the position for over twelve hours, and all they seem to be doing is brewing tea. Why in hell don't they get to Arnhem?' I did not have an answer for him."[3]

Alexander's old battalion, the 2/505, selected to capture the south end of the highway and railroad bridges, also incurred tremendous casualties, especially in their assault on Hunner Park and the traffic circle leading into the immense highway bridge. The aftermath of the battle looked like a picture from hell. "The scene in Hunner Park and the traffic circle was ghastly. German corpses and mortally wounded were lying half in their trenches and foxholes where they had been bayoneted or shot. Wounded and dead troopers littered the landscape, with weapons and the debris of war strewn everywhere." By the end of the fighting, F Company had "lost seventeen killed and twenty-three wounded," and "Company E suffered nine killed and twenty-five wounded." Both the 3/504 and the 2/505 received a Presidential Unit Citation for their role in the battle.[4]

When Alexander reported in, it was very clear to all that he was in no condition for combat. The 82nd Chief of Staff, Colonel Wienecke, used him as an assistant for a few special projects, mostly back in England, while the 82nd Airborne remained in Holland until November 17, carrying out defensive operations. A letter written from England on October 5, 1944, informs Alexander's father that General Ridgway had recommended Alexander for reassignment to Fort Benning, but would meanwhile keep him in Europe on limited duty. *They are rather short on airborne field officers, particularly those with the experience I have had. [...] Saturday I am going to report back to headquarters and get busy at something. [...] The General was about to give me a regiment, and I hate going back to the Division in a limited capacity, not being able to lead troops in the field. [...] If I'm not able to do a good job of something, I shall ask them to send me back [home]. Right now I'm stymied, and shall be until I have a try at going back to duty.*

While the division slogged on in Holland, protecting roadblocks and dikes day after day in dreary, cold, rainy weather, Alexander was assigned to ready Camps Suippes and Soissons in France. Here the 82nd would return after being relieved from active duty, to rest, re-equip, and take on replacements. They would leave most of their everyday equipment and nearly all of the 75mm and 105mm howitzers, heavy machine guns, bazookas, mortars, and other heavy weapons they had brought to Holland for the replacement force, so plenty needed to be done. Once again, Alexander's nature was at odds with the administrative frame of mind.

"The two camps to house the 82nd were about 75 miles northwest of Reims. I mostly stayed at Camp Suippes, which was an old French Army camp used in World War I. To get the camps ready, I had some men destroy a few small buildings and change a few other things. I noticed a French soldier walking around with a clipboard. Whenever we would change something, he would start writing. It turns out his job was to write down everything we did to the camp. Later the French government was going to charge the U.S. government for it all. I thought that was crazy, since we were in the middle of a war. I made sure we didn't destroy or dismantle anything else."

As Alexander and his crew went about the business of preparing to house the entire division, "the Germans came over one night with that new jet that they had just developed, and bombed the camp. I was in a building and a cabinet fell off the wall. I had my helmet off and it put a nice cut right above my eye. It wasn't much of a wound and the medic pulled the cut together with butterfly tape.

"That would have been my fifth Purple Heart if I had taken all the opportunities I had to get one. I got knocked out when I landed in Sicily. That would have been one. I got hit on the shinbone in Italy with a spent piece of shell at Arnone. It just scraped my skin a little bit, but that would have been a Purple Heart, had I applied for it. Then I got hit twice in Normandy: first, my gun sight hit my chin on landing. But I didn't think any of those deserved a Purple Heart, and it was the same with the cut above my eye. A Purple Heart was quite an honorary deal to show that you got wounded during the war. But hell, you could fall down and scrape yourself as far as that goes." The Purple Heart that Alexander did receive was for the life-threatening wounds he incurred at Hill 95.

Alexander's work required trips between Camps Suippes and Soissons (also called "Sissonne"), which offered an opportunity he could not refuse when a pilot suggested he fly him in his Piper Cub. This was the same model two-seat aircraft Tommy Thompson had flown down inside the walls of the mosque in North Africa. Although Alexander's second experience was not as intentionally adventurous, it nevertheless almost turned out to be fatal.

"We got to Camp Soissons without incident, but on the flight back, low clouds covered the ground. We flew around for quite a while waiting for the ground to re-appear. I was sitting in the rear seat and noticed beads of moisture on the back of the pilot's neck.

"I said, 'Why are you sweating? Are you hot?'

"He said 'No, I'm scared.' I then discovered we were almost out of fuel and would be on the ground soon, one way or another.

"Finally, a little hole in the clouds opened up and he quickly put us down in a farmer's field. The farmer wasn't too happy about that."

One of the brighter notes while Alexander was in France was his reunion with his brother Ed, now assigned to the 307 Engineers, the engineering battalion attached to the 505. He had missed the Holland jump due to an injury to his hand, and arrived in camp early. Alexander was very pleased to see a family member after more than a year and a half.

Not knowing how to work at less than 100 percent capacity, Alexander became physically and mentally exhausted preparing for the arrival of the 82nd from Holland. Once it finally got to France, the demanding pace continued as he worked to keep up with the logistics and demands of housing and resupplying the seriously depleted division. Alexander's exhaustion colored his letters at this time: he spoke of depression in a letter to Mary, and a letter to his parents on November 8, written just after he heard the news of President Roosevelt's re-election, expresses impatience toward the Allied countries and the United States' role in the war. *Well, it's up to you fellows to carry the load on politics and police. All we can do is fight and hope that you back there will get us a square deal out of this whole mess.*[5]

The inability to moderate his activity aggravated Alexander's wounds, increasing his pain and causing him to cough up unusual amounts of blood. *I cracked into the hospital not long ago*, he wrote to his brother Don on December 8, 1944. *The old wound was giving me some trouble, and on the chief surgeon's recommendation, General Gavin is finally sending me back [for a position on the school staff at Fort Benning]. He personally contacted General Weems, Commandant at Benning, and everything is set up. All I'm waiting on now is my orders.*

Alexander's orders, however, were not to arrive for some time. On December 16, 1944, the Germans launched an all-out attack into the Ardennes, beginning of the Battle of the Bulge. Both the 82nd and 101st Airborne Divisions were virtually stripped, with very little equipment or winter clothing, waiting to be refitted in France. On the evening of December 17, a call from SHAEF described the situation on the front to the east as critical: "the airborne divisions were to be prepared to move twenty-four hours after daylight the following day."[6]

As Col. Bill Ekman, commanding the 505th, put it: "The equipment situation was critical. Many of the weapons were in Ordnance, and there were shortages in field rations and ammunition. All requests for such items had not been completely filled. Clothing was at the laundry, equipment was stored, and winter clothing had not been issued to the regiment. The personnel shortages were most serious in the case of specialists—particularly for crew-served weapons. The training program was not completely underway when the alert came; there had only been a week of serious training [...]. To complicate the personnel issue, at 03:00 on 18 December, after the alert for movement had been received, but before the regiment left Suippes, two hundred replacements arrived. This left no time to get them oriented, classified, or properly distributed and they were just thrown into the move."[7]

Shortly before the Holland mission, General Ridgway had taken command of the newly created First Allied Airborne Army, consisting of all United States and British paratrooper divisions; General Gavin, in turn, took command of the 82nd Airborne. When the fighting broke out in the Bulge, all the senior generals other than Gavin were attending a conference in London, and Ridgway could not be immediately contacted. Gavin thus found himself in charge of both the 82nd and 101st as the acting commander of XVIII Corps (Airborne). He "gave both divisions orders to prepare for immediate movement to the area of Bastogne, Belgium," Alexander stated. "The 82nd moved out that evening and the convoys returned to pick up the 101st.

"When the 82nd arrived in Bastogne, the corps commander directed them further north to stop German General Sepp Dietrich and Colonel Peiper's armored columns, which were driving toward Antwerp on the North Sea." Dietrich, commanding the greatest German force and the most tanks, sought to cut off the English and Canadian armies from the main Allied forces. "The 82nd had a front of about 15 miles wide," Alexander commented. "That's a hell of a front." The following day, the 101st deployed to Bastogne, a vital crossroads amid the mountains where all main routes converged. They had a hell of a fight coming their way as well. Both divisions went into defensive positions.

Alexander wanted to be with the division at the front, on the northern shoulder of the Bulge. "I asked Gavin to take me with him. He said, 'No, I need you here. You're still not in very good shape,' which I had to acknowledge. So I was base commander again and busy as hell trying to get our administration and base sleeping straightened out. Other divisions like the 11th Armored were coming through there too, and I had to set them up for about a week while they got ready to go up and join the fighting. The old Hun did surprise us with his offensive and we were hard pressed to stop his drive. The winter campaign was really rough going."

The freezing weather and snow-choked, rugged terrain of the Ardennes are now as legendary as the valiant actions fought in the Bulge. In particular, the drama of the "Battling Bastards of Bastogne" immediately seized the popular imagination as the 101st Airborne, completely surrounded, repeatedly staved off German attacks from December 20 to 27, when elements of Patton's Third Army finally came to their aid. No less gallant, yet less celebrated, was the immovable defense of the 82nd Airborne on the crucial northern shoulder of the

Recovery, Holland and the Bulge

Bulge, where airborne troops and the 2nd, 99th, 1st and 9th infantries held firm at St. Vith in a decisive stance that defeated the Germans' primary objective.

Always short on heavy weapons, the paratroopers were particularly disadvantaged in the Bulge, where they were thrown against Hitler's new Sixth Panzer Army, the reconstituted Fifth Panzer and Seventh and Fifteenth Armies. The situation was rendered further critical because weaponry and ammunition were both in short supply after 50 long days in Holland. The 505, for example, "went into battle with only three 81mm mortars and seven or eight 60mm mortars for the entire regiment." [8]

Gavin turned to Alexander, sending him on a vital mission. "Gavin assigned me an extra job, besides keeping command of the camp—to get 57mm anti-tank guns and deliver them to the 82nd. And if I could, some heavier stuff. The 57mm was the standard anti-tank gun for the British Army, and some were available in England. I made two trips to London, from where I had a bunch of 57s and some other things flown over to Paris. I had a convoy waiting for us there, and we took them over to where the 82nd was fighting in Belgium in the snow and cold, about 40 miles beyond the city of Liège, where I turned them over to our supply officer.

"If airborne troops are left in combat, sooner or later they hopefully will get some back-up with tanks or artillery. We had a regiment of artillery, 105s and a lot of 75mm howitzers. The 75s you could drop from an airplane. The 105s you could bring in a glider, but you couldn't drop them with a parachute. This was one reason we used gliders as much as possible, to bring in the big 105s. But of course, you also want someone to go in and clear the field for the gliders before they land."

Alexander made three supply trips in all. His third trip, taken around Christmas, allowed him a brief visit his brother Ed, serving with the 307 Engineers. "It was colder than hell, a lot of snow on the ground. So I found two sleeping bags and I took them with me. On our way up there, there was a lot of quail in the snow. And they wouldn't fly so much as they'd run. So I shot the heads off of 12 of them with my carbine and took them up to the General's mess. And then I stopped by the engineers' area and gave Ed the two sleeping bags. That was the last time I saw him overseas." As he put it in one of his final letters home, *Christmas for Ed and me was not pleasant, but that is war. Just to be alive these days is something to be grateful for, and we are that.*

CHAPTER TWENTY

RETURN AND TRANSITION

As THE BATTLE OF THE Bulge ground on through one of the coldest winters in European history, Alexander remained in France as commander of camps Suippes and Soissons. Not yet fully healed and continuing to spit up blood, he was ordered to the zone of the interior (United States) on January 20, 1945.

"I was lucky and caught a flight on an Air Force plane, arriving in New York City on January 22, 1945. Mary met me at a hotel and we

Mark and Mary Alexander celebrate at the Zanzibar Club in New York City on the evening he returned from Europe, January 22, 1945.

The Alexanders pose for their first family portrait at Mary's parents' home in Pennsylvania, where Alexander first met his two-year-old daughter.

went out that evening to celebrate at the Zanzibar Club. Mary was thin, but looked ever so good to me. From New York we went to Easton to Mary's old home for me to meet my beautiful, blonde daughter of almost two years. I had never seen her, as she was born while I was in North Africa. Mary Jo was beautiful and very active. It took us some time to get acquainted. We stayed in Easton with Mary's parents for a few days and then took a train to Lawrence, Kansas, for a brief visit with my parents before I reported for duty at Fort Benning, Georgia."

Both General Ridgway and General Gavin had written Alexander letters of recommendation, and he was able to choose from several assignments: instructor at the Command and General Staff School, a post at Army Headquarters at the Pentagon, or instructor-administrator at the Parachute School at Fort Benning. Wary of his health, and responsible for a young family, for once in his life Alexander played it a little safe.

"I needed to take it easy for a while, so I chose the familiar background at Fort Benning," he recalled. "Mary, Mary Jo and I arrived there in February. As I was a lieutenant colonel, we rated on post quarters, and had a big two-and-a-half-story house just across the street from the parade grounds. Mary Jo liked to watch the parades and flag raising ceremonies. My first assignment was as director of advanced training, and later I became the director of training for the entire Parachute School."

Alexander was surprised at Fort Benning to find himself again working with Paul Woolslayer, the captain he had relieved of duty early

Parachute School, Fort Benning, Georgia, 1945. Gen. Ridgley Gaither, Jr. takes the podium, backed by his director of training, Lt. Col. Mark Alexander.

in the war. "After Sicily, they didn't bust him. They shipped him back to the States. I was more surprised when I found out he had been promoted to major. I asked General [Ridgley] Gaither [Jr.], my new boss, why they had promoted him. He said, 'because you gave him a *superior* rating.'" Alexander said unequivocally that he did no such thing.

Puzzled, Gaither retrieved Woolslayer's records and they had a look. The only signature was the initial "A" on the left of the form in question. "He had indeed been given a superior rating. But it was someone else's 'A' on there. It wasn't mine. So after I sent him back to the rear because he wasn't doing his job in Sicily, he was shipped back to the States and given a promotion!" At the Parachute School, however, Woolslayer was back in his element. He performed as a tough but effective trainer, and chose to make a career in the army after the war.

By the end of January, German gains in the Ardennes had all been lost again to the Allies. Over the next few months, Hitler's army, on its heels, was progressively pushed back into the German interior. The defeat of Germany was near at hand, but training continued at a rapid pace at Fort Benning. "We carried on with intensive training," Alexander recalled, "fully expecting to be sent to the Pacific Theater to carry on with the fighting against the Japanese."

Every trooper who ever came through the Parachute School heard the joke the jump instructors told about the erstwhile recruit who never quite figured things out. Alexander liked to tell it this way:

"The new recruit asked, 'What's going to happen, Sir?'

"The officer said, 'The plane will take off. You're going to line up, hook up, and when you get to the door, you jump. If you have any problem, the jump sergeant will help you get out the door. When you get in the air, if your parachute doesn't open after you count 1,000, 2,000, 3,000, you open your reserve. If you get hurt, when you get down to the ground there will be an ambulance waiting for you.'

"So the guy hooks up and gets to the front where the sergeant immediately kicks him out the door. As he's falling, he counts 1,000, 2,000, 3,000. The parachute doesn't open, so he pulls his reserve, and the reserve doesn't open either. He looks down at the ground and says, 'I bet those lying bastards haven't even got that ambulance down there.'"

Alexander continued his hands-on approach at the Parachute School, leading by personal example. "Often when I was training director, I'd go up in the aircraft and watch them jump and see that everything was going all right. I'd jump out last. I can remember one day

I was standing up in the front of the airplane near the door. A couple of them jumped and the third man slipped. Another guy fell on top of him. Real quick, there were five guys piled up. The jumpmaster and I sprang on top of them and held them so they couldn't get out. They were all tangled up by that time and somebody would have gotten killed. They were kicking and yelling, they were so excited to get out the door.

"We also trained glidermen because they were going to use them in a couple of outfits that were going to cross the Rhine River, and they also wanted them for the invasion of Japan. I decided to take the glider course and went to school for two weeks. I learned about gliders, how to load them and various other things. I didn't learn how to fly one, but to be a soldier that rode in one. I always said to myself, 'God help me if I ever have to go into combat in a glider.' I didn't want any part of that. They vibrated all the time like they were going to fall apart. They were made out of steel, aluminum and canvas.

"I knew a guy named Jack Watson who went through the training the same time that I did. He would get deathly sick every time he was up in a glider. He always carried a bucket with him.

"I said, 'Why don't you quit this business?'

"He said, 'No, god dammit, I'm not going to quit. I've made up my mind that I'm going to stick it out.' And he did."

As commander of the jump school, Alexander had a variety of unusual experiences, some of which had political overtones. "The politicians would come down to the school to watch the jumps and the demonstrations, but none of them ever jumped." One of Alexander's most interesting (and to him, amusing) assignments occurred when "Chiang Kai-shek sent two of his generals over with 40 or 50 men, to have them trained as paratroopers. These two generals came along kind of for the ride, but they didn't want to jump. I have a picture of the two of them in the plane with me. They look scared. I was talking to them, and they looked like they thought I might push them out of the plane."

Another unusual assignment, this time highly honorific, occurred when President Roosevelt died in office on April 12, 1945. "When Roosevelt died, I was assigned to command half the honor guard in Hot Springs, Georgia. I got a beautiful letter of accommodation on that from the major general in charge. Half of the honor guard was mine and half went to the infantry school, because they had a band but we didn't have one at the airborne school. There was a lot of formality involved with every part of it: getting on the train, and escorting the train and the president."

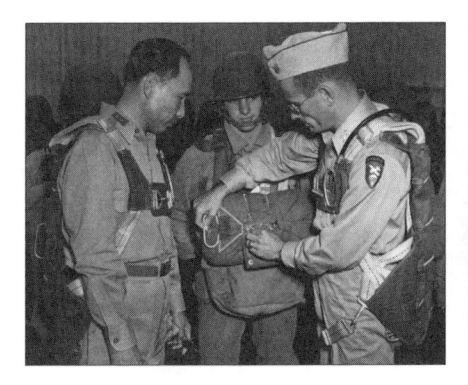

Above: Chiang Kai-shek, the leader of free China, sent 40 of his men and two generals to the United States for jump training at Fort Benning. Alexander here demonstrates how a reserve parachute is opened. Both "free" and communist Chinese were still fighting the Japanese at this time. After Japan's surrender, they would fight each other for control of Mainland China.

Above right: Two of Chiang Kai-shek's generals watch American paratroopers exit a C-47 aircraft during a training jump at Fort Benning, Georgia.

Right: Chiang Kai-shek's generals appear a little wary.

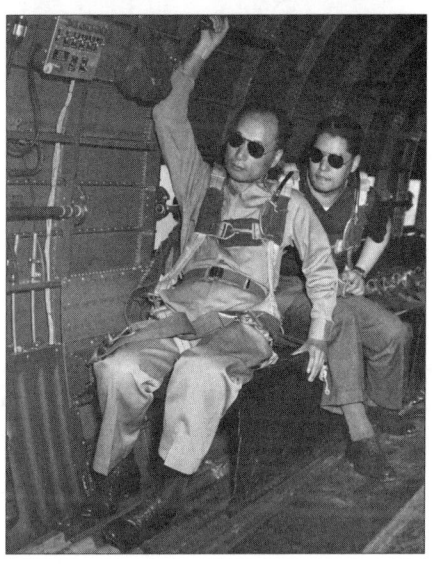

The text from the commendation reads as follows:
To: *The Commandant, The Parachute School, Fort Benning, Georgia.*
1. *The troops at Fort Benning who were granted the memorable privilege of serving as an escort to the remains of the Honorable Franklin Delano Roosevelt, President of the United States, at Warm Springs, Georgia, 13 April 1945, performed their duties in a praiseworthy and commendable manner, which I greatly appreciate.*
2. *The appearance of the men, their soldierly bearing, and their alert and respectful demeanor were a great credit to the Army of the United States on this eventful and sad day in the history*

of our country.
3. Members of the 2nd Parachute Training Regiment, ably commanded by Lieutenant Colonel Mark J. Alexander, Infantry, were among the troops who gave an outstanding performance on this solemn and momentous occasion.

/s/ Fred L. Walker
FRED L. WALKER
Major General, U. S. Army
Commandant

On May 8, 1945, the Allies formally accepted the unconditional surrender of Germany. Hitler's Third Reich and the war in Europe were finally at an end. Victory in Europe Day (VE Day) brought millions of people into the street to dance in celebration. The war in the Pacific had yet to be won, however, and the United States shortly took new and drastic measures. On August 6 and 9, 1945, atomic bombs were dropped, respectively, on Hiroshima and Nagasaki. On August 15, Emperor Hirohito announced the surrender of Japan in a radio address to his stunned and devastated nation. When news of the surrender hit the United States, the country again erupted into jubilant celebration.

Like thousands of other servicemen, Alexander sought to continue a military career, but this was not to be. In the transition to a peacetime army, almost any permanent medical issue was enough to flush one out, a rule that especially applied to officers. The United States military was just too large to maintain in a time of peace. "I applied for regular army and passed the written exams," Alexander explained, "but about 30 days later the Surgeon General turned me down because of the lung wound and the piece of shrapnel still lodged in my left lung. General Gaither offered to have me assigned for one year to attend the top military school in Great Britain. I thought someone staying in the service should have the assignment and turned it down. I later regretted my decision, as it would have been a great experience for Mary and me. After I was discharged, I tried again for a regular army commission, but was again disqualified by the Surgeon General of the Army."

Never one to abide army "chickenshit," Alexander was initially taken off guard by the pettiness and greed he encountered in civilian life. Nothing surprised him more than the discovery that some of his fellow Americans would purposely take advantage of veterans in order to cheat them out of their money. This discovery started on a well deserved 90-day paid leave before Alexander was discharged from active duty. During this time, he and his budding family moved to Lawrence, Kansas, and then set off for vacation in Arkansas. "My dad went with us for part of the trip," Alexander recalled, "and we did some fishing on their beautiful rivers. I was still in uniform because I was officially on leave.

"Dad and I were going to fish one morning. We went to a bait shop to get some bait, rent a canoe and buy fishing licenses. The guy behind the counter told me I didn't need a license in Alabama, since I was in the military." That sounded good to Alexander. He and his father got in their canoe and headed down river. "As soon as we got around the first bend, a police officer standing on the side of the river waved us over. He wanted to see our licenses.

"I said, 'I was told I didn't need a license if I was in the service.'

"He said, 'Oh no. Everyone must carry a license,' and wrote me a $25.00 ticket.

Upset by the injustice, but realizing there wasn't much he could do about it, Alexander made his way to the local courthouse. The judge handling the ticket said, "That'll be $25.00 for the ticket and $15.00 for lawyer fees."

"I said, 'Lawyer fees? I don't have a lawyer!'"

"Do you want me to reopen the case?"

Wanting to avoid any further fees, Alexander paid the $40.00 to be done with it.

"Another day during this same vacation, Mary and I went out to eat. The waiter came over and said, 'We have a bologna sandwich, or a chicken dinner for $3.50.' Mary ordered the dinner, but I didn't want much to eat, and I thought I'd save some money by getting the sandwich. When we got through, he charged us $3.50 for the chicken dinner and $3.50 more for the sandwich. I complained about the price of the sandwich, but he said, 'No, I told you, it was all the same price: a bologna sandwich or chicken dinner for $3.50.'

"He did, really. We were sitting ducks. It's pretty funny to think about it now."

Alexander's leave came to an end, and he was discharged from the military in December 1945. Like millions of other returning veterans, he found it difficult to acclimate to civilian life. After being so long overseas, after killing so many men and seeing so many friends die in the service of their country, he was particularly angered to hear people brag they had managed to outsmart the draft.

"I think the maddest I got was back in Lawrence. There was a guy there who had a little hardware store and stayed there although he was eligible for the draft. What got me was when he bragged about how he stayed home while stupid guys like us went overseas and got wounded or killed. And he had $250,000 in the bank. I almost hit him in the mouth, but instead I just turned around and walked off."

Few people were so rude or oblivious, yet even decades later, similar instances still aroused Alexander's annoyance, although he had learned to temper himself. He particularly recalled meeting an old acquaintance, the captain of his college football team, who boasted about how he had not gone overseas because he had himself assigned as a physical trainer. "Two or three people I've bumped into have boasted like that. And I never say anything. I just let it ride. But I don't think they should be bragging about it. If everybody acted like that guy in the hardware store, fighting for your country wouldn't be worth doing."

By the beginning of 1946, Mary was well into her second pregnancy and the Alexanders had the itch to relocate. Alexander set off on an exploratory drive through the West and Southwest to find a town with prospects of good growth and a healthy environment in which to raise a family. "I was supposed to get back to Kansas before Mary gave birth, but I didn't make it. In Lawrence, on March 13, 1946, Mark James Alexander Jr. was born. Mary delivered a fine son." Alexander returned to find mother and child both doing well.

After fully discussing their options, the Alexanders decided to move to San Jose, California. Here, Alexander shortly met a former paratrooper named Bill Young. "He said, 'We're burying a paratrooper here the first of the week,' and asked if I would serve as a pall bearer." Of course Alexander agreed.

During the service, the minister read a report on how the soldier had died. His commander had been killed the night before. That morning, his unit attacked a hill and suffered heavy casualties. Before the funeral, Alexander had known nothing about the solider, but the details of his story quickly led to the fight for Hill 95. Only one detail was incorrect: the death of the commanding officer. The funeral was for Capt. George Simons, S-3 of the 2/508 in the battle for Normandy. The "dead" commander was Alexander himself.[1]

CHAPTER TWENTY-ONE

YOU CAN TAKE THE PARATROOPER OUT OF THE FIGHT, BUT...

SAN JOSE TURNED OUT TO be a wonderful place to raise a family. The Alexanders put down roots and never left. Mary was especially pleased to establish a home after so many years of packing and moving here and there while her husband had been in the military. Mary Jo and Mark Junior soon were joined by little brother Don, born in 1951.

For Alexander, the initial years in San Jose were dominated by the desire to establish a business of his own. A natural leader with an entrepreneurial spirit, he was continually frustrated by a lack of funds. Several opportunities presented themselves, but like many others of his generation who had struggled through the Great Depression, Alexander was loath to put his family at risk by going into debt to finance an uncertain future. As he succinctly phrased the question always on his mind, "What could I get into where I worked on the other man's money?"

Moving to San Jose before he'd found employment, Alexander worked a series of short-term jobs, followed by a stake in a taxi company, before he moved on to become a sales supervisor at Royal Crown (R.C.) Cola. Here, his paratrooper training and fighting instincts, notoriously difficult to quantify in civilian life, stood him in very good stead. "I had six drivers in San Jose, five in Redwood City, and three in Salinas. I had to go around to the various areas, and discovered that a big guy up at Redwood City was bullying the other guys all the time.

"I warned him, 'You're going to have to lay off of these guys. You're getting them upset and they're all going to quit.' And he poo-poo'd me for it.

"I talked to the manager up there and said, 'Why don't you let him go?'

"He said, 'I'm scared to.'

"So I said, '*Ooookay*,' and knew I would have to take care of it."

To pay employees, Alexander stood behind a counter with a swinging door. "When it came time to pay off on Friday evening, I had his check ready for him. I told him it was the last he would be getting from me.

"He said, 'You can't do that.'

"I said, 'I told you before, you had to quit picking on these guys. I'm going to have to let you go.'

"He said, 'You can't do that!'

"I said, 'Well, there's your last check and you're through as of tonight.'

"I guess he couldn't think of anything else to say. Again he repeated, 'You can't do that!' and charged me. But I didn't wait on him. I hit him coming through the swinging door, and got in two shots on him. The first one cut him up on his mouth, and he later said I knocked two teeth loose. I got in a second punch and hit him in the gut as he came in that swinging door.

"Then all the guys grabbed us. I was tickled to death they broke it up. He wanted me to go out in the yard and fight with him. I said, 'They don't pay me enough to go out in the yard and fight with you and roll around in the cinders, but if you find me someplace, sometime, and you want a bite of me, go ahead and try to take it.' And he finally left. The next day I had a knot on the back of my neck where I got inside of a punch, and I had a bump on my tailbone where he pushed me back against a desk.

"I worked at R.C. Cola for about a year, found no future there and quit. The franchise holder for the 15 western states offered me the Hawaiian franchise and said they would finance me, but I would have been in hock for many years, and we really did not want to leave the mainland."

Less than five years after the end of World War II, the Korean War began. By this time, Alexander had joined the reserves, and had been promoted to full colonel. When the commander of the United States Eighth Army died, Ridgway headed to Korea to take command, passing en route through San Francisco. Alexander recalls: Ridgway left "a note in red pencil with the Chief of Staff to call me back to active duty. The Chief of Staff called and gave me the word, 'Be prepared.'

"I asked how long I had, and he said '30 days.' So I started getting ready for it.

"In about two or three weeks, he called me again. He said, 'Colonel Alexander, the war department has decided not to call any more full colonels. Would you take a shake down to lieutenant colonel?'

"I said, 'Let me think about it.'"

Alexander was now confronted with one of the toughest decisions of his life. The Eighth Army had been on its heels for months. Ridgway had replaced many of the commanders with fresh, aggressive men. Alexander certainly fit that bill, and almost certainly would be given command of a regiment.

As hard as it was, he sat this one out. "Mary didn't want me to go. I had three kids by that time. I had to give it a lot of serious thought, but I called Ridgway's Chief of Staff back and said, 'No, if you can't take me as a full colonel, leave me alone.' So they did."

Not long afterward, Alexander had his first contact since World War II with his old friend Jack Norton. Norton had stayed in the military, and served as aid to the Secretary of the Army in the 1950s.

"They came to town one morning to tour the Food and Machinery (FMC) plant where they built a lot of tanks. Norton said, 'Come on, go through with us.'

"I said, 'I'd like to, but I haven't got a clearance.'

"He said, 'You won't need it.'

"When we got there, one of the guys tried to stop me at the door. Norton told him, 'He's with us. He's going through.' That cleared me. There was enough brass to get me anywhere. The security agent at the gate was kind of upset that they had taken me in."

Alexander also renewed ties with another old friend from the army, his right-hand man Chick Eitelman. Wounded twice in the war, Eitelman lived in Portland, Oregon. His work as a truck driver often allowed him to spend the night at the Alexanders' when he was in their area. Mary and the kids thought the world of him. "He was still doing barbells and working out a lot, but he died of a heart attack in 1956," Alexander reports. "Sometimes these big, powerful guys who have built up so much muscle don't do so well in old age. I don't know. I got a letter from him about two weeks before he died, and he was still lifting weights." This time, Alexander had lost Chick for good.

During the Korean War, Alexander worked at the U.S. Tire Company. After five years, he walked away from the offer of franchises in Fresno and Chico, which both involved him going into debt, to pursue a career in real estate. "I had only $15,000 in cash and a home I had purchased with a loan from Bank of America. I studied real estate law for three weeks, took the real estate examination, and passed as a salesman. One year later, as allowed by law, I took and passed the broker's examination." At last, Alexander had found his civilian career.

Many of the houses he sold were newly built. He bought one himself and moved the family to Campbell, a suburb of San Jose, where he sold a few more houses on the same street. "I sold one near mine to a Japanese man who had fought for Japan in World War II. In 1957, many Americans still had hard feelings about the Japanese. The woman across the street and the woman next door to the house for sale came over and said, 'You can't sell that house to a Japanese.'

"I said, 'Why can't I? The builder wants to sell it to him. He's offered the full price.' The old gal across the fence from him came over to see me another time to complain. Boy, she was adamant as hell about it. I said, 'I can't do anything about it, and I wouldn't even if I could. The war is over. Let's try to forget about it.' And that man still lives there today."

Just at the point his business was gong well, Alexander had one more invitation to get back into military matters. "My old 2nd Battalion master sergeant, Tommy Gore, stayed in the military and worked for a while as a courier out of Washington. I never figured out what department he worked for, but he brought me an application one time. I swear, it must have been about 15 feet long there were so many pages. This took place when we were having trouble with China, and the application was for a CIA assignment. They wanted me to train some of our local Chinese to jump. They would then drop them in China so they could work their way into the population and send out reports. I turned it down. Mary wasn't interested in my going and I wasn't either."

In October 1959, Alexander developed serious health issues, resulting in an operation for cancer and financial setbacks. "The illness came at a bad time. I had had three small subdivisions going and had to dump them all. Gradually, over a 17-month period, I went back to work. I decided I would work alone and set my own pace."

During this period of recuperation, Alexander unexpectedly had to call on his paratrooper fistfight skills when he and Mary attended a major real estate dinner at a local county club. All the agents from the area were there, including Harold Sparry, the father of the young man whom Mary Jo, now 19, was seriously dating. Although Mark and Harold had met, the mothers of the dating couple had not, and they now introduced themselves to each other since their children were dating. During the dinner, a cantankerous agent claimed that Alexander had cheated him out of a real estate deal. "He also thought that a fellow named Baroski, who worked at the title company, was partly responsible. But he wasn't. It was my deal."

The angered agent was physically a very big guy. "He caught Baroski going back to the men's room and threw him down on the floor. Then he knocked and rolled him around, tore his shirt, pulled his jacket off and stuffed it in the trash can." When word of the fight got to Alexander, he confronted the other agent. "What really made me mad was that Baroski wouldn't swat a fly, he was that nice. I said, 'You shouldn't be picking on Baroski. He's a mild-mannered guy. He didn't have a damn thing to do with that problem you and I had.'

"Well, he took a swing at me. I got under it and hit him with a left. It straightened him up and then I hit him again, knocking him down and breaking his nose. I always figured when you fight a bigger guy, you've got to get the first shot in. And get it in the right place. If I figured a guy was going to take me on and there was no chance to talk my way out of it, I didn't wait.

"The fight took place right beside the bar. I stepped over into the open space where I had room to move around, because he was a 200-pounder. A guy of 150 pounds doesn't want to be in close quarters with him. He got up and came at me again. I got in one shot and hit him in the ear before the guys grabbed us and broke us up. I was tickled to death they did. I didn't want to fight.

"I was embarrassed as hell for Mary afterwards. And I think the Sparrys were wondering what kind of a family their son was getting involved with. I had quite a reputation for a while after that dinner. Two or three guys came up to me at different times, saying, 'I wanted to meet the guy that busted that asshole's nose.'

Alexander remained in real estate until 1983, eventually transitioning to developing and selling land, which led to a chairmanship of the industrial committee for the San Jose Chamber of Commerce. His old jump injury, hurting him off and on, finally led to two hip replacement surgeries, the second of which was a complete success. In retirement, Alexander enjoyed fly-fishing and took up painting again after a hiatus of many years.

Another sustaining interest to which Alexander devoted a great deal of time in later years was the World War II Association of his old 505th

Mark Alexander, Chairman of the San Jose Chamber of Commerce, and his daughter Mary Jo greet Richard Nixon during his run for governor of California in 1962.

Alexander tried his hand at painting after giving it up for nearly 45 years. He here stands next to one of his landscapes in 1992.

You Can Take the Paratrooper Out of the Fight, But...

Houston, Texas, August 1981. Col. Alexander (left), Gen. James M. Gavin (center) and Col. Bob Piper (right) at a 505 RCT reunion.

Fort Bragg, North Carolina, May 1989. Alexander speaks to active-duty 82nd Airborne paratroopers and guests at All American Week, while an alert trooper stands at the ready. During the 1980s and 1990s, he returned to Fort Bragg almost every year, where he often had question and answer sessions with active-duty officers and NCOs.

Fremont, California, 1994. Fifty years after D-Day, two paratroopers and a glider pilot prepare to march in a parade. Left, Colonel Alexander; center, Sam Butler; right, unidentified glider pilot.

Parachute Infantry Regiment. "The loyalty and love for many of my wartime comrades will never die; we went through so much together." Alexander had always felt a deep bond with, and sense of responsibility for the men he had led in combat. This commitment continued throughout his life, extending to veterans he had never known, and to the families of those who had not been so fortunate as to survive the war.

Beginning with his command of Company 2 of the Parachute School at Fort Benning, Alexander received and responded to hundreds of letters from the families and friends of veterans seeking information about their loved ones. The first letter of the sort, dated June 27, 1945, was written by the father of William H. Neuberger, MIA, a private in D Company, 505 PIR. Neuberger was listed as missing in action since D-Day, and had recently been declared dead after the requisite year and a day. *Was the entire group that jumped with him out of the same ship [plane] lost or did some of them return, and could some of his buddies, perhaps through you, give us a little more detailed information of how and where he was lost?* the distraught father inquired.

Alexander took the question to heart, and responded from 82nd Headquarters on July 10: *Your son was a member of my regiment, the 505, to which I served as Regimental Executive Officer. I remember his name and face very well, but due to our many losses and that we were very hard pressed during the initial phase of the Normandy invasion, I am not acquainted personally with the manner in which your son was lost.*

Alexander answered the Neuberger inquiry after several days of thorough research. He provided the names of two former members of D Company then serving at the Advanced Training Division of the Parachute School who, like Neuberger, had been captured by the Germans and held at a hospital in Cherbourg. He details the place and time of the battle where Neuberger was captured, the nature of his wounds, and his probable fate when the Germans evacuated Cherbourg, and forwards the name and address of a sergeant who was with Neuberger at this time, suggesting the parents contact him.

As thorough and personal as this letter was, Alexander closes with the wish to do more: *I am indeed sorry that I can give you no further information. I myself was seriously wounded on July 4th in Normandy, and later evacuated. Eventually I was sent back to the United States to a limited duty assignment. If I can possibly secure additional information I will notify you immediately.*

These words not only serve as a gracious closing to Alexander's first letter to a grieving parent, they also perfectly encapsulate the care with which he responded to the many inquiries he later received for information on dead or missing veterans. Even in his final years, between 2001 and 2004, while he was making the recordings on which this memoir is based, people seeking information continued to contact him, and he continued to respond. By this time, of course, they were no longer the parents, and only rarely the siblings, of the veterans in question. They were instead sons and daughters, nieces and nephews, and increasingly, the grandchildren of servicemen in World War II.

In 2004, Mark Alexander passed away two weeks before the sixtieth

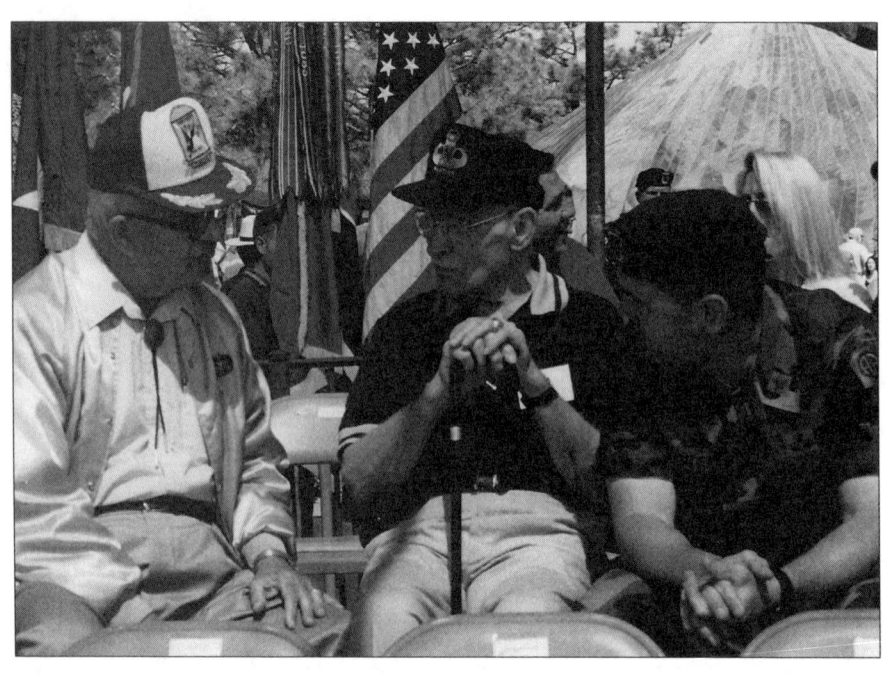

Old friends and fellow soldiers Lt. Gen. Jack Norton (left) and Col. Mark Alexander (center) speak with an active-duty 505 paratrooper general on a visit to the 82nd Airborne Division during All American Week in 1999.

Col. Joseph Anderson, 2nd Battalion, 505, shown here with his staff in front of a portrait of Alexander in the Sicily campaign.

anniversary of D-Day. Five months later, his old friend Jack Norton followed. Mark and Mary Alexander were married for 51 wonderful years, raising three kids, enjoying eight grandkids and, in turn, great-grandchildren. Mary is still going strong, and remains an inspiration to the entire family. She is, in addition, the strongest writer of the brood, and her diaries of the war years are a family treasure.

As for Alexander's last brawl, at the bar of that real estate dinner, Mary indeed was mortified. Not only did her husband get in a fight at a formal dinner, he did so in front of all his colleagues, including the parents of their potential son-in-law. No harm, it turned out, was done, except for busting a big bully's nose. Mary Jo and Harold Sparry's son John married in 1965 and had two sons. Their firstborn is the author of this book.

October 1986. Mark Alexander, 75,
and his wife Mary, 71 years of age.
They enjoyed 51 years of marriage.

Note to Veterans

If any veterans would care to write to me with comments on this book, your own service, or anything else, I would love to hear from you. All duties and branches of the military are equally welcome. I appreciate your service. After all, it's people like you that allow our country to be great. Please send correspondence to: John Sparry, 1821 South Bascom Avenue, #105, Campbell, CA 95008, or email me at jrsparry@aim.com.

Mark Alexander and John Sparry at Fort Bragg, All American Week, 1999.

Editor's Note

It has been a pleasure to work with John Sparry to bring his grandfather's World War II experience to light in this co-authored book. John spent many hundreds of hours taping Colonel Alexander's memories of the war, and many hundreds more transcribing, compiling, editing and researching the material that forms the basis of *Jump Commander*. He also conducted numerous interviews with 82nd Airborne veterans who served with his grandfather in World War II, traveling to regimental reunions in the United States and commemorative D-Day jumps in Normandy. The resulting book, part biography, part memoir, features as much as possible Colonel Alexander's own words, as well as other eyewitness testimony by men who served under his command in the 505th and 508th Parachute Infantry Regiments.

Before he was seriously wounded late in the Normandy Campaign, Colonel Alexander had the rare experience of making the first three of the 505 PIR's four combat jumps, dropping in Sicily, Italy and Normandy, and had led no less than three battalions—the 1/505, the 2/505 and the 2/508—in front-line combat. His book is a significant contribution to the eyewitness literature of World War II, and further fulfills a wish of his son (and John Sparry's uncle), Mark Junior, that his father set pen to paper and publish his account of the war.

If we are to have many more first-person World War II accounts—or indeed eyewitness accounts of combat in Korea or Vietnam—it will be increasingly up to the children, grandchildren and other younger relatives and friends of our veterans to gather and preserve these experiences for the historical record. In this, *Jump Commander* is part of a growing trend of co-authored works, as a glance at the bibliography will confirm. To this trend we must add the increasing number of divisional and regimental combat histories largely based on extensive veteran interviews and unpublished memoirs, complied by historians concerned to preserve the "I was there" experience of everyday life at the front, as seen from the bottom up.

As editor, I have silently corrected the spelling of the accounts cited herein, but have not attempted to render consistent the abbreviations, punctuation and other conventions of published sources, wartime letters by the Alexander family, or official documents. All expository notes are by John Sparry; editorial comments appear in the text in brackets.

This book has been the work of many hands. Before his death in 2008, Bob Murphy (*No Better Place to Die*, Casemate, 2009) willingly offered to provide photographs for the upcoming publication. A pathfinder in A Company, 1st Battalion, 505, Bob served under Alexander's command at La Fière, and the two men later became fast friends. Phil Nordyke, the official 505 PIR historian (*Four Stars of Valor*, Zenith, 2006), also graciously provided photos and maps. Spencer F. Wurst (*Descending from the Clouds*, Casemate, 2004), a member of F Company who served under Alexander in the 2/505 in Italy, stood by to advise on regimental and battalion history. Barbara Gavin Fauntleroy (*The General and His Daughter*, Fordham University Press, 2007) and Dan Roper (another former 505er) tracked down the sources for troublesome citations. It is a blessing to have such family and friends. It is thanks to you, too, that this book has come to be.

Gayle Wurst,
Princeton International Agency for the Arts,
April 2010

NOTES

Chapter 1: Learning to Fight
1. Major General James M. Gavin. Letter to Lieutenant Colonel Jack G. Cornett (Command and General Staff School, Fort Leavenworth, Kansas), February 2, 1945.

Chapter 2: Preparing for War
1. If Alexander had stayed with the 35th Division, he would not have seen combat until July 10, 1944. On the day his old outfit first met the enemy, he had already made three combat jumps, led three different battalions in front line battles, and lay near death in a Normandy field hospital.

Chapter 3: Early Days in the 505 Parachute Infantry Regiment
1. Colonel Haugen later got shrapnel in his abdomen just outside of Manila, as the U.S. took it back from the Japanese. Placed on a hospital ship, he died on the voyage home. Alexander visited Haugen's grave in San Francisco for many years.

2. Phil Nordyke, *Four Stars of Valor: The Combat History of the 505th Parachute Infantry Regiment in World War II* (St. Paul: Zenith Press, 2006), p. 34.

3. Ed Ruggero, *Combat Jump: The Young Men Who Led the Assault into Fortress Europe, July 1943* (New York: HarperCollins Publishers, 2003), p. 76.

4. Ibid., p. 352.

5. Phil Nordyke, *All American All the Way: The Combat History of the 82nd Airborne Division in World War II* (St. Paul: Zenith, 2006), p. 25.

Chapter 4: North Africa
1. One parachute battalion, the 509th, deployed before the 505 PIR. Designated as Company D, 509th Parachute Infantry, it spearheaded the Allied invasion of North Africa on November 8, 1942, where it successfully made three combat jumps. The unit was reorganized and redesignated as Company A, 509th Parachute Infantry Battalion,

and recognized as an independent unit in December 1943, and continued to operate throughout World War II.

2. Goods were said to be "short-stopped" when someone got their hands on them in transit and kept them for himself. After the Sicily and Italy campaigns, Alexander sent several hundred pictures, various souvenirs and two pairs of long underwear to his parents in Kansas. When the two suitcases arrived, they contained nothing but the long underwear. Everything else had been short-stopped along the way.

3. Allen L. Langdon, *Ready: A World War II History of the 505th Parachute Infantry Regiment* (Indianapolis: Western Newspaper Publishing Co., Inc., 1986), p. 9.

4. Len Lebenson, *Surrounded by Heroes: Six Campaigns with Division Headquarters, 82d Airborne Division, 1942–1945* (Philadelphia: Casemate Publishers, 2007), pp. 41-42.

5. Langdon, *Ready*, p. 12.

6. Ibid., p. 15.

7. Freeland and Balis were later killed in action. Sergeant Gavin returned to Fort Benning for Officers Candidate School and eventually returned to the 505 as a 2nd lieutenant.

8. Ed Ruggero, *Combat Jump: The Young Men Who Led the Assault into Fortress Europe, July 1943*. (New York: HarperCollins Publishers, 2003), p. 111.

9. Otis Sampson, Interview with Author, 505 Regimental Combat Team Reunion, San Antonio, Texas, August 2007.

10. Phil Nordyke, *Four Stars of Valor: The Combat History of the 505th Parachute Infantry Regiment in World War II* (St. Paul: Zenith Press, 2006), p. 49.

11. Ruggero, *Combat Jump*, pp. 117-18.

12. Ibid., p. 120.

13. Nordyke, *Four Stars of Valor*, p. 49.

14. Barbara Gavin Fauntleroy, *The General and His Daughter: The Wartime Letters of General James M. Gavin to His Daughter Barbara* (New York: Fordham University Press, 2007), p. 37.

15. Langdon, *Ready*, p. 17.

16. Clay Blair, *Ridgway's Paratroopers: The American Airborne in World War II*

Notes

(Garden City, NY: Dial Press, 1985), p. 85.
17. Langdon, *Ready*, p. 17.

Chapter 5: Sicily: From the Jump to Biazzo Ridge

1. For LeRoy Leslie's account, see Ed Ruggero, *Combat Jump: The Young Men Who Led the Assault into Fortress Europe, July 1943* (New York: HarperCollins Publishers, 2003), pp. 188-89.

2. Otis L. Sampson, *Time Out for Combat* (Charlestown, South Carolina: Book Surge, LLC, 2005), pp. 57-58.

3. Clay Blair, *Ridgway's Paratroopers: The American Airborne in World War II* (Garden City, NY: Dial Press, 1985). p. 98.

4. Sampson, *Time out for Combat*, p. 63.

5. For the move to high ground and information about prisoners, see Guy Anthony LoFaro, *The Sword of St. Michael: The 82nd Airborne Division in World War II.* (Doctoral Thesis, Stony Brook University, 2007), p. 141. http://dspace.sunyconnect.suny.edu/bitstream/1951/43104/1/103772725.sbu.pdf_

6. Ruggero, *Combat Jump*, p. 364. Measuring the survival instinct and the duties of an officer, Alexander stated, "I had the normal animal instincts to take a dive, and run when you needed to run, but I had a system. I put my men ahead of everything else. And I was concerned about keeping my men out of trouble. Then you don't worry about yourself." He demanded no less of the officers under his command.

7. A letter Alexander wrote to Mary from Sicily expresses a similar estimation of the enemy's fighting spirit (or lack of it): *The natives of Sicily are very small and dark. They want peace and readily accept us Americans as friends. The Italian soldiers here fight fiercely, but when beaten readily submit to being stripped of all arms and are apparently glad to be out of the war. Most of them hate Mussolini. They think he has betrayed Italy to her enemies.*

8. LoFaro, *Sword of St. Michael*, p. 141.

9. Alexander's father, without word of his son's mission, wrote to Mary on July 15, 1943, expressing the anxiety the family, like thousands of others, felt during the long wait for news. *Well my girl, how are you and the baby by now? Mary Jo must be a fine baby from what you say and we are all anxious to see her. The last week has been anxious times for me. I read so much about the paratroopers, I picture Mark in the thick of it. [...] I don't know if he is with the 505 or not as that cannot be published. I am anxious to know what Army (7th or 8th) he is attached to, then I would know just what battles he is taking part in. Just as soon as you get word from Mark, please let us know of anything you find out. Of course we cannot expect to receive letters while they are advancing. [...] Well dear, we are all pulling for Mark and I hope Edwin is right in saying "He's too tough for anything to happen to*

him." Please keep us informed as to any word received. Love to you and the baby.
10. From the beginning, Alexander always got along well with General Ridgway on the rare occasions they met in Alexander's early carrier. This camaraderie grew over the coming years and continued long after the war. Although Ridgway was 48 years old at the time of the Sicily jump, he lived to the ripe old age of 98. He and Alexander periodically wrote to each other until Ridgway's death in 1993.

11. The fighting at Biazzo Ridge and Gavin's report to Ridgway are reported in Phil Nordyke's 82nd Airborne and 505 Parachute Infantry Regiment histories. See: *All American All The Way: The Combat History of the 82nd Airborne Division in World War II* (St. Paul: Zenith Press, 2005), pp. 73-80, 89, 91; *Four Stars of Valor: The Combat History of the 505th Parachute Infantry Regiment in World War II*. (St. Paul: Zenith Press, 2006), pp. 81-95.

12. See Nordyke, *All American*, pp. 87-89, and *Four Stars*, pp. 79-80 and 90-92, for an account of the battle, including Sayer's actions and Gorham's death. The Alexanders were close to the Gorhams; Mark's letter to Mary telling her of Gorham's death greatly affected her, as she expressed to her in-laws: *He also told me of several officers I knew who were killed or wounded. I'm so happy that Mark's still all right I could cry, but I feel badly about the people he mentioned. One was a Lieutenant Colonel whose wife had [their] first baby while we were at Fort Benning and they were so thrilled about the child and so much in love. War is horrible but I pray it will be over soon and that Mark will be all right.*

Chapter 6: On to Trapani
1. Allen L. Langdon, *Ready: A World War II History of the 505th Parachute Infantry Regiment* (Indianapolis: Western Newspaper Publishing Co., Inc., 1986), p. 28.

2. Lt. Gen. John Norton, Interview with Author, Ste. Mère-Eglise, France, June 7, 2004.

3. Among the German forces leaving Sicily across the straight of Messina were two armored divisions, including the Herman Goring Division that fought against the American landings. This tactical blunder was a significant failing; the Allies would see these divisions in battle again.

4. Like many soldiers who came down with malaria during the war, Alexander had some trouble with the disease later in life. "I had a repeat once when I got back to the States at Fort Benning, a mild attack," he stated. "You'd shake and shiver."

Chapter 7: Return to North Africa and Preparations for Italy
1. Clay Blair, *Ridgway's Paratroopers: The American Airborne in World War II* (Garden City, NY: Dial Press, 1985), p. 102.

2. Ibid., p. 98.

3. On a personal note, Alexander wrote, *I am afraid that little girl of mine will be walking and talking by the time I see her.* He also sent greetings to various family members and informed his father that he was sending him a beautiful shotgun he picked up in Sicily as well as a Beretta, *a nice little shooting piece and just pocket size,* that an Italian colonel had surrendered to him at Trapani. He hoped his father would use the shotgun in the fall. *If Mary comes to visit you I would like to have her try it. I'm sure that some day we'll all go hunting together and it will be just about right for her.* (Mary was up for many of life's adventures; hunting, however, was not one of them.) A later letter reveals that Alexander did not send the Beretta after all: *I learned that all small arms would be confiscated by customs officers, so shall have to bring it or send by some convenient friend. Of course we would like best if eventually I could bring it to you.*

4. Alexander's description of the men's homesickness also seems designed to convince his brother Don to remain in the States as long as possible, especially as his brother Ed would be deploying to Europe. *I am very glad to hear from Don and wish to put in a paragraph for him here. Don—I enjoy your letters a great deal. [...] Hope things are going O.K. at Leavenworth. Recommend you stay there as long as you can. You have a job to do there and it's an important one. Don't let anyone talk you into wanting to leave it. Ed will be over here soon and two Alexanders are quite enough over here in this bedlam. Have for sure had some interesting experiences, but they are not worth the risk one takes getting them. The greatest thing I have learned over here is how wonderful a place America really is. [...] Give my regards to those at Fort Leavenworth, especially Colonel Harvey.*

5. Blair, *Ridgway's Paratroopers*, p.151.

Chapter 8: From Salerno to Naples

1. Frank Spence's story cited from the home page of author Ed Ruggero's website, http://edruggero.com/index.html.

2. Len Lebenson, *Surrounded By Heroes: Six Campaigns with Division Headquarters, 82d Airborne Division, 1942-1945* (Philadelphia: Casemate Publishers, 2007), p. 71.

3. Clay Blair, *Ridgway's Paratroopers: The American Airborne in World War II* (Garden City, New York: Dial Press, 1985), p. 151.

4. Spencer F. Wurst and Gayle Wurst, *Descending from the Clouds: A Memoir of Combat in the 505 Parachute Infantry Regiment, 82d Airborne Division* (Havertown: Casemate Publishers, 2004), p. 97.

Chapter 9: To the Volturno: The Battle of Arnone

1. Years after the war, Alexander recalled Corp. Fred Freeland as "one of the men who helped me parachute a mule out of a C-47 in North Africa. He was a nice young guy, maybe 19 years old. He had the beginning of a college education and was very talented. He was a good artist and he could write calligraphy. His future was bright,

but he went on patrol one night in Holland and the Germans shot him. I can think of a lot of them that we started out with that we didn't end with. A lot of them just got wounded, but plenty of them got killed."

2. Captain Sayer returned to the 505 later in the war and would also very successfully command a battalion in Korea.

3. Phil Nordyke, *Four Stars of Valor: The Combat History of the 505th Parachute Infantry Regiment in World War II* (St. Paul: Zenith Press, 2006), p 108.

4. Darrell Whitfield, Interview with Author, Ste. Mère-Eglise, France, June 5, 2004.

5. Otis L. Sampson, *Time Out For Combat* (Charleston: Booksurge, 2005), pp. 104-05.

6. Norton observation referenced in Guy Anthony LoFaro, *The Sword of St. Michael: The 82nd Airborne Division in World War II*. (Doctorial Thesis, Stony Brook University, 2007), p. 235. http://dspace.sunyconnect.suny.edu/bitstream/1951/43104/1/103772725.sbu.pdf

7. Ibid.

8. Spencer F. Wurst and Gayle Wurst, *Descending from the Clouds: A Memoir of Combat with the 505 Parachute Infantry Regiment, 82d Airborne Division* (Havertown, Pennsylvania: Casemate Publishers, 2004), p. 87.

9. Wurst and Wurst, pp. 89-90. Spencer Wurst, p. 77, also credits the Italian Campaign, and Arnone in particular, with giving the 2/505 experience that would make a vital difference in Normandy: "We still didn't have too many battle-wise, seasoned veterans in the 2d Battalion. [...] This situation was partly due to the fact that the 1st and 3d battalions had seen most of the heavier fighting in Sicily. In combat everything depends on the factors of a *particular* action. You can't always follow the rules. Arnone, especially, gave us the chance to learn to adapt our tactics in the heat of battle, with relatively little loss of life. But Italy served as one big training experience for the entire 505, not only for the 2d Battalion. The whole 82d Airborne was very fortunate to have experienced combat prior to Normandy.

10. LoFaro, *Sword of St. Michael*, p. 235.

11. During the Great War, the Americans lost 130,000 men, but the British lost a million. In other words, eight percent of Britain's population was killed or wounded, compared to one third of one percent of Americans. At the beginning of World War II, the United States had over three times as many people from which to build its fighting forces and had far greater industrial strength, allowing tanks and equipment to quickly roll off assembly lines. The British had been at war for several years before the United States got involved in late 1941; especially early in the war, it was paramount for them

to protect their heavy weaponry, but they were never able to replace their weaponry as quickly as the Yanks could. They hence threw their resources forward less hastily and usually put as many strategic pieces as possible into place before advancing. While this could provide the enemy time to prepare or recover, British soldiers were less likely to blunder into a trap, and the command of overwhelming numbers and firepower often resulted in fewer casualties per attack than the Americans experienced.

12. Wurst and Wurst, p. 86.

Chapter 10: Duty in Naples
1. Turk Seeley, Interview with Author, Ste. Mère-Eglise, France, June 6, 2004.

2. One of the dentists carried a Pinochle board with him and claimed he made more money betting on his Pinochle games than he did from his wages. He was later hit with an 88 and killed in Holland while riding in a jeep with a red cross on it.

3. Another letter written shortly before the 505 left Italy ends with an underlined sentence mentioning Alexander's cousin, who had an affinity for Ireland: *Nella would like to know where I think I shall be going very soon.* The regiment was soon to move to Northern Ireland, where it would refit and train in preparation for its next mission.

4. Mary's letter also represents the feelings of many wives of soldiers at the front, expressing her longing to see her husband and her tenderness for her infant daughter, and the hardships on the home front. *Sometimes I want Mark to see Mary Jo so badly that I don't know what to do. She's so adorable and she's growing so fast [...] I told Mark she'd be eating steaks by the time he gets home if the war doesn't soon. She can splash water far and wide during her bath and she spits cereal with amazing nonchalance and then laughs. Today for the first time she tried to crawl on the floor. I imagine it will be quite a while 'til she accomplishes that, but when she does, I'm going to need four hands to keep her from tearing down the place. She certainly has Mark's energy. We had a lot of excitement here Sunday. A huge gas tank blew up killing 3 and injuring 35. A thousand people were evacuated from their homes temporarily and all gas is shut off. People are cooking in furnaces, jack stoves and coal stoves. We have a little old fashioned coal stove in which it takes me three times longer to make Mary Jo's formula than it did by gas. We're lucky. I don't know how I'd sterilize bottles in a furnace.*

Chapter 11: Northern Ireland
1. Allen L. Langdon, *Ready: A World War II History of the 505th Parachute Infantry Regiment* (Indianapolis: Western Newspaper Publishing Company, 1986), p. 35.

2. Twenty years after the war, a veteran whom Alexander could not quite place approached him at one of the regimental reunions. Alexander admitted he knew the man's face, but couldn't remember his name. The other man replied, "Well, I sure remember you, because you gave me 30 days in the stockade for going AWOL." He laughed and said, "I don't hold it against you. I had it coming." He was a repeat

offender, and Northern Ireland was the third time he had taken an unauthorized leave.

Chapter 12: England
1. Allen L Langdon, *Ready: A World War II History of the 505th Parachute Infantry Regiment* (Indianapolis: Western Newspaper Publishing Company, 1986), pp. 35-36.

2. A letter from Mary to Alexander's parents, dated February 16, 1944, expresses the excitement, pride, and also fear the family felt on learning the news: *This is going to be a quickie, for if you haven't already heard the news, I can't wait for you to get it, and I'm too excited to make much sense anyway. Mark received the "Silver Star" medal for gallantry in action at a division review on Feb. 4th. He and five others were awarded the medal. He was not allowed to send the citation or to discuss it but he says, "Well, the only things your Mark did were in the line of duty. It embarrasses me to think of the way it was written up and to think of the men who really deserve awards for gallantry in action and didn't get them." [...] I'm babbling over, but when I think of what he must have gone through to be cited I get chills. Nonetheless, so far we've been very fortunate and I'm counting on it lasting. Mary Jo is proud too. I could tell by the way she acted when I told her. Mark is sending his medal to me to keep for him, so I'll bring it to Kansas when I come.*

3. After more than five grueling years of war, the King's piggy bank held more dust than money. Great Britain was forced to borrow so much capital, the last repayment to the United States was not made until 2006, more than sixty years after the end of hostilities. The Allies' ace in the hole was the United States' industrial and economic power. Yet many Americans, and very likely congress as well, would eventually become resentful if consistently huge sums of cash kept flowing out of the U.S. into British coffers. Intelligent minds on both sides of the Atlantic developed a plain and *nearly* invisible solution: rent and maintenance of camps and equipment served as another cash flow conduit.

4. Spencer F. Wurst and Gayle Wurst, *Descending from the Clouds: A Memoir of Combat in the 505 Parachute Infantry Regiment, 82d Airborne Division.* (Havertown, PA: Casemate Publishers, 2004), pp. 111-112.

5. Don McKeage, Interview with Author, 505 Regimental Combat Team Reunion, Fort Bragg, South Carolina, September 2007.

6. In conversation with John Sparry, Jerry Colombo, 3rd Battalion 505, stated that the officers hated Krause, but the enlisted men like himself loved him. This did not necessarily extend to all of the NCOs, as noted in Ed Ruggero, who reports that most of the men hated Krause for his abusive ways and "chicken shit" antics; that is, projecting power through overly emphasizing the ridiculous, minute duties and regulations of army life. Ed Ruggero, *The First Men In: U.S. Paratroopers and the Fight to Save D-Day* (New York: HarperCollins, 2006), p. 145; *Combat Jump: The Young Men Who Led the Assault into Fortress Europe, July 1943* (New York: HarperCollins, 2003), p. 83.

7. Clay Blair, *Ridgway's Paratroopers: The American Airborne in World War II* (Garden City, NY: Dial Press, 1985), p. 198.

8. Langdon, *Ready*, p. 41.

9. Ibid.

Chapter 13: D-Day: June 6, 1944
1. Richard Natkiel, *Atlas of 20th Century Warfare* (New York: Gallery Books, 1982), p. 166.

2. Clay Blair, *Ridgway's Paratroopers: The American Airborne in World War II* (New York: Dial Press, 1985), p. 218.

3. On this topic, Alexander also related an amusing story told by Lt. Joseph Myers of the 3rd Battalion: "We did have one guy, Joe Myers, who dropped behind the Germans on D-Day and got captured. He says, 'For two days, they had me in a barn along with some other prisoners. The Jerries brought us a barrel of wine. We all got drunk, and finally got the sentry to drink some too. And you know, I wandered off that night. I wandered for two days and finally made it back to our lines.'"

4. For an account of the 2nd Battalion's change of orders and perimeter defense of Ste. Mère-Eglise, see: Spencer F. Wurst and Gayle Wurst, *Descending from the Clouds* (Havertown, PA: Casemate Publishers, 2004), pp. 129-131.

5. Blair, *Ridgway's Paratroopers*, pp. 260 and 234, respectively.

6. Robert M Murphy, *No Better Place To Die. Ste. Mère-Eglise: The Battle for La Fière Bridge* (Philadelphia and Newbury: Casemate Publishers, 2009), p. 150. Murphy, a pathfinder from A Company, 505, has published the definitive eyewitness account of the 1/505's role in the battle for the Manoir and La Fière Bridge. Included are numerous eyewitness testimonies by members of the 507 and 508 PIRs, the 325 GIR and detailed accounts by key defenders from the 505, including "Red Dog" Dolan. A good friend of Murphy, Alexander contributed the foreword to the book.

7. Alexander comments: "The 57mm was one of the early anti-tank guns developed by the British, so we adopted it and built a lot of them in this country. But we later found it was really too light to damage most tanks, so they jumped up to 75s."

8. All four men of the bazooka teams earned the Distinguished Service Cross for their actions defending La Fière Bridge. See Murphy, *No Better Place to Die*, p. 231.

Chapter 14: La Fière Bridge and Causeway
1. Robert M Murphy, *No Better Place To Die. Ste. Mère-Eglise: The Battle for La Fière Bridge* (Philadelphia and Newbury: Casemate Publishers, 2009), p. 94.

2. Bob Murphy, Interview with Author, Commemorative Drop at La Fière Bridge, France, June 6, 2004.

3. Murphy, *No Better Place to Die*, p. 96.

4. Ibid, p. 98; for eyewitness details of the entire battle, see p. 91 and following.

5. Clair Blair, *Ridgeway's Paratroopers: The American Airborne in World War II* (Garden City, NY: Dial Press, 1985), p. 270.

Chapter 15: Montbourg Station
1. Phil Nordyke, *All American All The Way: The Combat History of the 82nd Airborne Division in World War II* (St. Paul: Zenith Press, 2005), p. 342.

2. Allen L. Langdon, *Ready: A World War II History of the 505th Parachute Infantry Regiment* (Indianapolis: Western Newspaper Publishing Co., Inc., 1986), p. 74. Langdon states that Colonel Ekman *proposed* having the 1st Battalion 505 circle around the 2nd Battalion 325 through the 8th Infantry Division's area, but does not mention that it actually happened. Alexander makes it clear that the next morning, the 1st Battalion did exactly that, moving through ground previously covered by the 8th Infantry before the 8th backed off for the night.

3. The Allies were the first to develop proximity artillery shells, which exploded 50 or 100 feet off the ground. Then the Germans got them, but at the time their ordnance would not explode until it came in contact with something. If they shot directly at a man, they might miss and it would sail on by. They aimed for trees because shrapnel from the explosion spreads out in a wider, more complete pattern than if it hits the ground. "They learned to target trees." Alexander commented. "We learned to stay out and away from trees in a lot of cases."

4. After the war, Alexander saw this runner at various reunions. Once at a regimental dinner back at Fort Bragg, the runner said, "There's always been something that I felt like I should tell you. I didn't stay up in that mill after you left. I was scared to." They both had a good laugh.

5. Alexander reports that he never told anyone of the incident with Captain Russell until years later when he and his wife were visiting the Vandervoorts at their home in South Carolina. Vandervoort replied: "You did him a hell of a favor. And that explains something. I believe that's one reason we got hung up that day on our advance toward Le Ham." According to Alexander, "another reason they got held up of course was because they were about half an hour late coming through, and they gave the Germans a chance to get set into strong positions. If you give them a chance to get set, they're going to get in a good position where they have a good field of fire and they can cover your approach. And that's what they did. The 2nd Battalion didn't make any further advances until the next day. They got held up solid."

NOTES

5. "I didn't learn that he lived until, not long ago, I talked with his wife in Pennsylvania. She said he had always suffered from disabilities, but had led a rather normal life and raised a family. He died in 1991." Over 50 years after the end of the war, Alexander remembered fine details about many of his men who had been wounded, but still did not know whether they had survived. He himself suffered a shrapnel blast through his back and into his lungs in Normandy, and it was a long time before he could seriously think of tracking anybody down. Those that died or were left as question marks under his watch vividly stuck with him for the rest of his life. He knew fighting meant scores of good men would die, especially given the nature of the elite troops of the day and the paratroopers' assignments against dug-in enemy positions, but he never took a life for granted.

7. Langdon, *Ready*, p. 76.

8. Ibid.

S.L.A. Marshall, *Night Drop: The American Airborne Invasion of Normandy* (New York: Jove Publications, Inc., 1984), p. 45. Originally published in 1962.

Chapter 16: Westward to the Douve: The Battle of St. Sauveur-le-Vicomte
1. Mark Alexander, Letter to William B. Breuer, May 12, 1983.

2. Spencer F. Wurst and Gayle Wurst, *Descending from the Clouds: A Memoir of Combat in the 505 Parachute Infantry Regiment, 82d Airborne Division* (Havertown, PA: Casemate Publishers, 2004), pp. 148-149. Ridgway is further reported to have replied to Bradley, "Sir, I would rather have a platoon of those men than a battalion of regular infantry." See Allen L. Langdon, *"Ready": The History of the 505th Parachute Infantry Regiment, 82nd Airborne Division, World War II* (Indianapolis: Western Newspaper Publishing Co., Inc., 1986), p. 80. For the assault on St. Sauveur-le-Vicomte, and especially action by the 1st and 2nd Battalions, 505, see Phil Nordyke, *All American All the Way: The Combat History of the 82nd Airborne Division in World War II* (St. Paul: Zenith Press, 2005), p. 379 ff.

3. Phil Nordyke, *Four Stars of Valor: The Combat History of the 505th Parachute Infantry Regiment in World War II* (St. Paul: Zenith Press, 2008), p. 212.

4. Nordyke, *Four Stars*, p. 213; Dominique Francois, *Normandy: Breaching the Atlantic Wall. From D-Day to the Breakout and Liberation* (Minneapolis: Zenith Press, 2008), p. 204.

5. Bill Hagen was the man who put on the handcuffs that had no key back at Fort Bragg. He finally got even with Alexander by eating his duck dinner, and always kidded him about it afterward.

6. Robert M Murphy, *No Better Place To Die. Ste. Mère-Eglise: The Battle for La Fière Bridge* (Philadelphia and Newbury: Casemate Publishers, 2009), p. 152.

Chapter 17: The 508 Parachute Infantry Regiment.
1. Clay Blair, *Ridgway's Paratroopers: The American Airborne in World War II* (Garden City, NY: Dial Press, 1985), p. 194.

2. Ibid., p. 293.

3. Major General James M. Gavin. Letter to Lieutenant Colonel Jack G. Cornett (Command and General Staff School, Fort Leavenworth, Kansas), February 2, 1945.

4. Allen L. Langdon, *Ready: A World War II History of the 505th Parachute Infantry Regiment* (Indianapolis: Western Newspaper Publishing Co., Inc., 1986), p. 80.

5. Blair, *Ridgway's Paratroopers*, p. 288.

6. Guy Anthony LoFaro, *The Sword of St. Michael: The 82nd Airborne Division in World War II* (Doctoral Dissertation, Stony Brook University, 2007), p. 373. http://dspace.sunyconnect.suny.edu/bitstream/1951/43104/1/103772725.sbu.pdf, p. 373.

7. Virgil McGuire cited in Zig Boroughs, *The Devil's Tale: Stories of the Red Devils of the 508 Parachute Infantry Regiment 82nd Airborne Division in World War Two* (n.p. Zig Boroughs, 1992), p. 133.

8. Dominique François, *Normandy: Breaching the Atlantic Wall. From D-Day to the Breakout and Liberation* (Minneapolis: Zenith Press, 2008), p. 217.

9. Ibid., p. 233.

10. Blair, *Ridgway's Paratroopers*, pp. 291-93.

11. François, *Normandy*, pp. 233-34.

Chapter 18: Hill 95
1. Eitelman remained in this post until he was wounded again in Holland.

2. Graham cited here and below in Dominique François, *508th Parachute Infantry Regiment: Red Devils* (Bayeux, France: Heimdal, 2003), p. 60-63. Frank McKee, F Company, 508 PIR, also states in François they went across open ground, p. 58.

3. William G. Lord II, *History of the 508th Parachute Infantry*, (Washington: Infantry Journal Press, 1948), is an excellent early regimental history which nevertheless contains some factual errors and discrepancies. The map on page 36, for example, incorrectly shows F Company 2/508 on the *left* flank and D Company on the right. The text correctly states that F Company advanced on the right and D Company on the left. Phil Nordyke, *All American All the Way: The Combat History of the 82nd*

Airborne Division in World War II (St. Paul: Zenith Press, 2005), p. 398, confirms this point and that the objective of the 3/508 was to attack the high point of the ridgeline that sat southeast of Hill 95. Graham may not have known this. After attacking heavily fortified positions, the 3rd Battalion was forced to return to the line of departure to regroup, which also could have contributed to the 2nd Battalion's open left flank.

4. This patrol is detailed in Phil Nordyke, *Four Stars of Valor: The Combat History of the 505th Parachute Infantry Regiment in World War II* (St. Paul: Zenith Press, 2006), p. 219.

5. Dwayne T. Burns and Leland Burns, *Jump into the Valley of the Shadow: The World War II Memories of a Paratrooper in the 508th P.I.R., 82nd Airborne Division* (Philadelphia: Casemate Publishers, 2006), p. 73. For the 505 account of the medic's death as well as Burns' story, see also Nordyke, *All American All the Way*, pp. 397-98.

6. Lord, *History of the 508th*, p. 37. The most complete oral history of the role of the 508 on Hill 95 remains Zig Boroughs, *The Devil's Tale: Stories of the Red Devils of the 508 Parachute Infantry Regiment 82nd Airborne Division in World War II* (n.p. Zig Boroughs, 1992), pp. 114-20. For eyewitness accounts of the battles for Hill 95 and La-Hay-du-Puits from a 505 perspective, see Nordyke, *Four Stars of Valor*, pp. 218-21.

7. Sacharoff cited in François, *508th Parachute Infantry Regiment*, p. 65.

8. For Mendez's personal account, see Patrick K. O'Donnell, *Beyond Valor: World War II's Ranger and Airborne Veterans Reveal the Heart of Combat* (New York: The Free Press, 2001), pp. 172-174.

9. Nordyke, *All American All the Way*, pp. 406-407.

10. Clay Blair, *Ridgeway's Paratroopers: The American Airborne in World War II* (New York: Dial Press, 1985), p. 295.

Chapter 19: Recovery, Holland and the Bulge
1. Phil Nordyke, *Four Stars of Valor: The Combat History of the 505th Parachute Infantry Regiment in World War II* (St. Paul: Zenith Press, 2006), p. 258.

2. Cornelius Ryan, *A Bridge Too Far* (New York: Popular Library, 1974), p. 159.

3. James M. Gavin, *On to Berlin* (New York: Viking Press, 1978), pp. 181-82. Alexander also recounted a lighter story about Colonel Tucker in Holland, which Tucker told him at Camp Suippes. "We sat at the bar in that little French training camp and had a drink together. And he was telling me, 'Up in Holland, Ridgway came up with Gavin and they wanted to check my position with me. We started crossing an

open field and soon the Jerries began throwing 120mm rounds in there. They were coming pretty close, so I took a dive in a shell hole. I looked up and those two damn generals were still walking. So I resolved that I was going to walk all the way across to the trees, even if the Germans put one in my pocket. I walked clear across without looking back. I finally get to the other side and turn around, and they're both taking cover in my shell hole!'

4. Nordyke, *Four Stars*, pp. 304, 305. For an extended eyewitness account of the 3/504 assault across the Waal River, see James Megellas, *All the Way to Berlin: A Paratrooper at War in Europe* (New York: Ballantine Books, 2003), pp. 119-140. For a first-person account of the 2/505 assault in Hunner Park, see Spencer Wurst and Gayle Wurst, *Descending from the Clouds: A Memoir of Combat with the 505 Parachute Infantry Regiment, 82d Airborne Division in World War II* (Havertown, PA: Casemate Publishers, 2004), pp. 179-197.

5. *Rain has been falling steadily for three days now and I am even damp in spirit. [...] I am glad to see Roosevelt stay at the helm until we have finished this war. [...] It will take a forceful and dominant man such as Roosevelt to hold his own with such cagey old foxes as Churchill, Chang Chi Check and others. Right now, I can't see where America is going to get a damned thing out of this European war. England, France, Russia and several of the small countries will make tremendous gains. However, we of the U.S. get nothing other than a meager bit of help in the Pacific [...]. The U.S. should have a definite understanding that she will have possessions and bases in the Pacific before this European war comes to a close and we lose our present [negotiating] power over England and France, in that we are winning the war for them in Western Europe. It is common knowledge that we are furnishing about 75 percent of the troops involved in the campaign.*

6. Phil Nordyke, *Four Stars*, p. 258.

7. Ibid., p. 587.

8. Ibid.

Chapter 20: Return and Transition
1. Dominique François, *The 508th Parachute Infantry Regiment: Red Devils* (Bayeux: Heimdal, 2003), p. 63, reports that Captain Simons was killed by a mortar round. Alexander regularly visited Simmons' grave for the rest of his life, and his children and grandchildren continue to place flowers on his grave.

Bibliography of Cited Sources

Blair, Clay. *Ridgway's Paratroopers: The American Airborne in World War II*. Garden City: The Dial Press, 1985.

Boroughs, Zig. *The Devil's Tale: Stories of the Red Devils of the 508 Parachute Infantry Regiment 82nd Airborne Division in World War Two*. n.p.: Zig Boroughs (privately published), 1992.

Burns, Dwayne T. and Leland Burns, *Jump into the Valley of the Shadow: The World War II Memories of a Paratrooper in the 508th P.I.R., 82nd Airborne Division*. Philadelphia: Casemate Publishers, 2006.

Fauntleroy, Barbara Gavin. *The General and His Daughter: The Wartime Letters of General James M. Gavin to His Daughter Barbara*. New York: Fordham University Press, 2007.

François, Dominique. *508th Parachute Infantry Regiment: Red Devils*. Bayeux, France: Heimdal, 2003.

———. *Normandy: Breaching the Atlantic Wall. From D-Day to the Breakout and Liberation*. Minneapolis: Zenith Press, 2008.

Gavin, James M. *On to Berlin*. New York: Viking Press, 1978.

Langdon, Allen L. *Ready: A World War II History of the 505th Parachute Infantry Regiment*. Indianapolis: Western Newspaper Publishing Co., Inc., 1986.

Lebenson, Len. *Surrounded by Heroes: Six Campaigns with Division Headquarters, 82d Airborne Division, 1942–1945*. Philadelphia: Casemate Publishers, 2007.

LoFaro, Guy Anthony. *The Sword of St. Michael: The 82nd Airborne Division in World War II*. PhD diss., Stony Brook University, 2007.

Lord, William G. II. *History of the 508th Parachute Infantry*. Washington, D.C.: Infantry Journal Press, 1948.

Marshall, S.L.A. *Night Drop: The American Airborne Invasion of Normandy.* New York: Jove Publications, Inc., 1984. Originally published by Little, Brown and Co., 1962.

Megellas, James. *All The Way to Berlin: A Paratrooper at War in Europe.* New York: Ballantine Books, Presidio Press, 2003.

Murphy, Robert M. *No Better Place to Die. Ste. Mère-Eglise: The Battle for La Fière Bridge.* Philadelphia and Newbury: Casemate Publishers, 2009.

Natkiel, Richard. *Atlas of 20th Century Warfare.* New York: Gallery Books, 1982.

Nordyke, Phil. *All American All the Way: The Combat History of the 82nd Airborne Division in World War II.* St. Paul: Zenith Press, 2005.

_____. *Four Stars of Valor: The Combat History of the 505th Parachute Infantry Regiment in World War II.* St. Paul: Zenith Press, 2006.

O'Donnell, Patrick K. *Beyond Valor: World War II's Ranger and Airborne Veterans Reveal the Heart of Combat.* New York: The Free Press, 2001.

Ruggero, Ed. *Combat Jump: The Young Men Who Led the Assault into Fortress Europe, July 1943.* New York: HarperCollins Publishers, 2003.

_____. *The First Men in: U.S. Paratroopers and the Fight to Save D-Day.* New York: HarperCollins Publishers, 2006.

Ryan, Cornelius. *A Bridge Too Far.* New York: Popular Library, 1974. Originally published by Simon and Schuster, 1974.

Sampson, Otis L. *Time Out for Combat.* Charlestown: Book Surge, 2005.

Wurst, Spencer F. and Gayle Wurst. *Descending from the Clouds: A Memoir of Combat in the 505 Parachute Infantry Regiment, 82d Airborne Division.* Havertown: Casemate Publishers, 2004.

Index

1st Battalion, 58, 87-88, 124, 173, 179-181, 185, 188-189, 195-196, 199-200, 202-207, 210-213, 216-218, 224-225
1st Infantry Division, 13, 63, 88
10th SS Panzer Division, 238
11th Armored Division, 242
12th Infantry Regiment, 199
15th Panzer Army, 243
101st Airborne Division, 172-173, 186, 190, 221, 237, 241-242
137th Infantry, 43
137th Infantry Regiment, 30
22nd Infantry Regiment, 199
2nd Battalion, 10, 13, 38, 52, 54, 62, 67-71, 77, 79-81, 83, 87, 90-92, 94, 96, 98, 100, 107-109, 111, 113-115, 120-124, 127, 133, 136, 139, 141-143, 148, 161, 168, 173, 176, 181, 185, 199, 202-203, 205-208, 210, 212-213, 215-217, 224-225, 256, 262
3rd Battalion, 69, 80, 87, 94, 108-109, 112-113, 147, 168, 173, 181,185, 191-192, 196, 199, 215, 217, 230-232, 238
3rd Infantry Division, 90
35th Division, 30, 32, 35, 40, 44, 266
307th Engineering Battalion, 58, 110, 193
320th Field Artillery Battalion, 183
325th Glider Infantry Regiment, 54, 116, 165, 170, 182, 195-196, 199, 200, 202, 204, 206-207, 210, 212, 232, 236, 275- 276

45th Infantry Division, 63, 86, 87
456th Field Artillery, 80
52nd Group Carrier Wing, 176
501st Parachute Battalion, 165
504th Parachute Infantry Regiment, 48, 54, 71-72, 80, 86, 89-90, 103, 109-110, 112, 116, 154, 165, 170, 172, 177, 219, 238, 282
505th Parachute Infantry Regiment, 10, 12, 48, 51-52, 54, 56, 59, 60, 64, 71-72, 78, 80, 83, 86-92, 94, 102, 104-105, 107, 109-110, 116, 122-124, 137-139, 141, 143, 146, 150, 153-156, 161, 163, 164-166, 170, 172, 173-174, 176, 178, 180, 182, 184-185, 189, 191-192, 195, 196, 199, 200-203, 206, 210, 212, 215, 218-220, 224-225, 230, 231, 240, 243, 259-262, 266-267, 269, 271-276, 278, 280-282
507th Parachute Infantry Regiment, 165, 170, 181-182, 189, 190-192, 196, 198, 223, 232, 275
508th Parachute Infantry Regiment, 16, 165, 170, 181, 186, 191, 217, 218, 219-225, 230-232, 252, 275, 279-281, 283
511th Parachute Infantry Regiment, 48
572nd Heavy Flak Battalion, 238
64th Troop Carrier Group, 13, 64, 71, 80
7th Panzer Army, 243
77th Convalescent Hospital, 236

79th Armoured Division, 178
8th Infantry Regiment, 199, 200-202, 206, 210, 233, 276
80th Anti-aircraft Battalion, 182
82nd Airborne Division, 9, 12, 54, 56-60, 63, 70-71, 86-88, 90-91, 94, 104-105, 107, 109, 115-116, 154, 165, 172-173, 182-184, 197-198, 211-212, 221, 223, 232-234, 236-243, 259, 261-262, 266, 268-269, 272, 276, 278-281
9th Infantry Division, 212, 214, 217
9th SS Reconnaissance Battalion, 238
90th Division, 197, 221

A Company, 88, 124, 188, 189, 193, 194, 212, 214, 275
Alexander, Donald, 15, 17
Alexander, Edward, 15, 18, 132
Alexander, Edward Ethen, 15
Alexander, Edwin, 15
Alexander, Harold, 15-18, 20-22, 60, 256, 263
Alexander, Ruby, 15, 18, 20, 22
Alexander, Virginia, 15
American Express Company, 16
Anderson, Colonel Joseph, 262
Ardennes, 241-242, 247
Arkwright, Brig. Gen. H.R., 120, 130, 132, 134-135, 138-139, 142
Arnhem, 237-238
Arnone, Italy, 107, 120-121, 123, 125, 128-135, 138, 141, 209, 227, 240, 271- 272

B Company, 31, 33, 34, 36, 189, 192, 196, 212
Barker Brothers, 24
Barneville, France, 224
Bass, Captain Hubert, 96, 125
Bastogne, Belgium, 242
Batcheller, Lieutenant Colonel Herbert, 123, 142-143, 156-159, 164-165, 170
Batchelor, Colonel, 220
Belfast, Ireland, 154, 156
Biazzo Ridge, Italy, 89
Blanchelande, France, 224
Boyd, Captain, 130
Bradley, General Omar, 100, 197, 215-217, 223-224, 278

British 22nd Armored Brigade, 120, 122, 161
British 6th Division, 173
British Eighth Army, 106-107
British Second Army, 237
Brooke, Sir Alan F., 162
Butler, Sam, 260
Byers, Kelly, 7, 56, 191-192

C Company, 189, 191, 202, 212, 214
Camp Edwards, Massachusetts, 30, 56- 57, 153, 281
Camp Quorn, 161, 166
Camp Robinson, Arkansas, 30
Campbell, Beth, 21
Cancello, Italy, 120, 129, 133
Capri, Isle of, Italy, 150, 152
Carentan, France, 223, 224
Casablanca, Morocco, 58-60, 62
Castel San Lorenzo, Italy, 112-113
Cauquigny, France, 187, 189, 193, 196-198
Cerny, France, 71, 80
Chef-du-Pont, France, 186, 190-192
Cherbourg, 179, 185, 197, 199, 212, 218, 221-224, 261
Chester, 1st Lieutenant, 212
China, 155, 256
Citadel, The, 47
Clark, General Mark, 107, 109-110, 113, 122, 154
Collins, General, 197, 215, 217, 221, 266-267
Collins, Mary, 7, 39, 40-44, 46, 50-52, 57, 59, 68, 97, 105, 153, 172-173, 241, 244-246, 250-253, 255-258, 263, 268-270, 273-274
Colorado River, 23
Comiso, Italy, 108
Command and General Staff College, 50
Conchello, Italy, 107
Connell, Lieutenant, 77, 126, 130
Connelly, Father, 142, 228-229
conservatists, 41
Cotenin Peninsula, France,173
Cook, Lieutenant, 31
Cooperider, Lieutenant Claiborne, 207
Coutances, France, 224
Czechoslovakia, 29

INDEX

D-Day, 10, 81, 86, 154, 161-162, 175, 188, 198, 219, 223, 230, 233, 263, 274-275, 278-279
60th Anniversary of, 10
Darnell, Captain, 31, 32, 33
Dednum, Sergeant, 159, 160
Desert Rats, 135
Dietrich, General Sepp, 242
Doc Clee, 76, 80, 84
Doc Stein, 80, 84, 85, 89, 98, 136, 137
Dolan, Lieutenant John "Red Dog", 188-191, 193, 195, 212, 214, 218, 276
Dole Pineapple Company, 24
Donnelly, Lieutenant, 210
Douve River, France, 212, 214-216, 218, 278

Eaton, Colonel 182
Eddy, Lieutenant General Manton, 162
Eider, Corporal, 76-77
Eindhoven, Holland, 237
Eisenhower, General Dwight D., 58, 103, 161-162, 176
Eitelman, Corporal Chick, 89-90, 92, 117-118, 128, 130-131, 149, 180, 185, 229, 255, 279
Ekman, William "Bill", 164-167, 176, 180-181, 185, 196, 200, 203-206, 215, 217-219, 241, 276
Emmanuel III, King Victor, 110
England, 154, 161, 166, 167, 170, 171, 172, 173, 178, 206, 223, 225, 233, 273, 282
Etienville, France, 211
Euling, SS Captain Karl-Heinz, 238

Fifth Panzer Army, 243
Ford, Henry, 101
Fort Benning, Georgia, 38-40, 44, 52, 105, 157, 177, 190, 234, 239, 241, 245-247, 249, 260, 267, 270
Fort Bragg, North Carolina, 54-57, 105, 137, 259, 274, 277
Fortress Europe, 12, 268, 275
France, 10, 29, 154, 161, 177-178, 181, 218, 234, 241, 270-271, 273, 276, 280, 282
Franco, Dr. Robert, 137
François, Dominique, 223, 279, 280

Freeland, Corporal Fred, 64, 76-77, 124, 267, 271

Gaither Jr., Ridgley, 246-247, 250
Garber, Lieutenant Dick, 175-176
Gavin, Colonel James M., 12, 14, 48, 49-53, 56, 63-64, 68-70, 72, 84, 87-88, 94, 99-100, 103-105, 114, 139, 143, 161, 162-164, 169, 190-192, 196-198, 205, 219-220, 223, 232, 237-238, 241-243, 245, 259, 266-269, 279, 281
Gela, Sicily, 13, 63, 72, 81, 85, 86, 88
George VI, King, 161
Germany, 29, 39, 155, 174, 247, 250
Gibbons, Captain, 176, 178
Gold, James, 58
Gore, Sergeant, 133, 256
Gorham, Lieutenant Art, 87
Gorham, Lieutenant Colonel, 48, 58, 76, 80, 131-132, 181, 192, 195, 202, 208, 214, 218, 224, 250, 266, 269, 279
Gorman, D. L., 67
Graham, Captain Chet, 7, 224, 229, 230-232, 280
Grand Canyon, 23
Granville, France, 196
Gray, Major, 54, 57, 59, 64, 66, 68, 88, 116
Great Britain, 29, 250, 274
Great Depression, 15, 16, 18, 19, 253
Gregory, Sergeant, 130
Griffith, Mel, 19, 23
Guernsey, Isle of, U.K., 177

Hagan, Captain William, 54, 218, 279
Harden, Colonel Harrison, 80-82, 104
Haugen, Lieutenant Colonel Orin D., 48
Hitler, 12, 29, 41, 96, 149, 243, 247, 250
Holbert, Percy, 178
Holland, 234, 237, 239-240, 242-243, 271, 273, 279, 281
Holmes, Brigadier General Julius, 162

Ireland, 154, 156-157, 159-161, 167, 273
isolationists, 41

Japan, 39-40, 248, 250, 256
Jeffries, Charlie, 21
Jeffries, Nella, 21, 273
Jersey, Isle of, U.K., 177

285

Johnson, Lieutenant Gerald "Johnny, 202, 212, 214
Johnson, Wilton, 7, 76
"Jonnie the Jumper", 59

Kairouan, Tunisia, 70-71, 102, 105-106
Kai-shek, Chiang, 248-249
Kampgruppe Euling, 237
Kansas City, Kansas, 19, 24
Kaster, Colonel, 42
Keerans, General, 87, 143
Kellam, Major Fred, 179, 180-182, 185, 189-190
Kesselring, Field Marshal Albert, 108, 110, 122
Klondike Gold Rush, 16
Korean War, 254-255
Krause, Colonel, 80, 87, 108, 147, 168-170, 181, 192, 199, 229- 230, 274

La Fière bridge, 173, 179, 180, 181, 185, 186-187, 190, 192, 196-197, 211, 275- 276
La Poterie, France, 232-233
La-Hay-du-Puits, France, 224, 233, 281
Landes, Dr. K. K., 23
Lawrence Golf Club, 16
Le Ham, France, 200-201, 203-204, 206, 208, 210, 277
Lebenson, Len, 61, 267, 271
Leicester, England, 166
Leicestershire, England, 161
Leigh-Mallory, Sir Tafford, 162, 163
Leslie, LeRoy, 75
Lessay, France, 224
Lindquist, Colonel Roy E., 219-221, 223-224, 227-228, 230-232
LoFaro, Guy, 221
Long, Captain Talton, 124, 126-127, 129

Mall, Lieutenant, 31
Maloney, Lieutenant Colonel, 190
March, Colonel, 182
Marina di Ragusa, Italy, 81, 85
Matterson, Sergeant Robert M., 194
McGinity, Captain James, 105, 124, 127, 185
McGuire, Virgil, 221-222, 229, 279
McKeage, Don, 7, 167, 274

McRoberts, Captain, 92, 93, 123, 129, 133, 227
Memphis, 25, 34, 42
Mendez, Lieutenant Colonel Louis G., 232-233, 281
Merderet River, France, 173, 178-179, 187, 189, 199
Messina, Sicily, 89, 96, 270
Montebourg, France, 199-201, 203, 206-208
Montgomery, Field Marshal Bernard, 100, 107, 228, 238
Moor, Jimmie, 17
Moore, Dr. Raymond C., 23
Murphy, Bob, 7, 183, 188, 194, 195, 276
Mussolini, 110, 268

Naples, Italy, 107, 113, 115-116, 118, 120, 137, 139-143, 145-147, 150, 156, 271, 273
National Guard, 14, 30, 32-33, 36, 50, 88
Neuberger, Private, 261
Neuville-au-Plain, France, 173, 178
New Orleans, Louisiana, 24, 25
Nijmegen, Holland, 237, 238
Nixon, President Richard, 258
Nordyke, Phil, 8, 232, 266-267, 269, 271, 276, 278, 280-282
Normandy, 9-10, 142, 153, 172, 174, 177-178, 183, 186-188, 197, 217, 222-223, 225, 227, 233-234, 240, 252, 261, 266, 272, 278-279
North Africa, 12, 58-59, 70, 76, 78, 95, 98, 103, 105-106, 135, 154, 156, 170, 240, 245, 266, 270-271
Norton, Captain John "Jack", 7, 69, 75-78, 83-84, 89, 94, 99, 102, 104, 110, 133, 143, 158, 165, 176, 180-181, 185, 203, 229, 255, 262-263, 270, 272

O'Neal, Sergeant Russell, 194
Oakley, Second Lieutenant, 193-194
Omaha Beach, 203, 223, 235
Operation AVALANCH, 107
Operation HUSKEY, 12, 63, 68
Operation MARKETGARDEN, 237
Operation NEPTUNE, 12, 63, 68, 107, 174

INDEX

Operation OVERLORD, 174
Oujda, Algeria, 60-62, 67, 70, 80, 106

Paestum, Italy, 110
Palermo, Sicily, 89, 90
Palma di Montechiaro, Sicily, 90
Panama, 105, 165
Patton, General George, 87, 89-90, 100, 103, 135, 161, 218, 224, 242
Pinckney School, 16-17
Piper, Colonel Bob, 242, 259
Point Vito, Sicily, 91, 99
Pointeck, Lieutenant, 55, 66
Poland, 19, 29
Presidio, the, 43-44

Rae, Captain Robert, 191
Raff, Edson, 223
Ragusa, Sicily, 89, 104
Ramee, Colonel Per, 33-34
Renth, Jr., Ed, 30
Renth, Sr., Colonel Ed, 30, 32
Rhine River, 237, 248
Rice, Captain Casey, 124
Ridgway, General Matthew, 54, 61, 63, 72, 87-89, 97, 104, 110-111, 113, 157, 164, 169-170, 174-175, 182, 184, 191, 192, 196-197, 203, 215, 217-219, 223, 228, 239, 242, 245, 254-255, 268-271, 275, 278-279, 281
Rome, Italy, 109, 111, 153
Rommel, General Erwin, 60, 187
Roosevelt, President Franklin D., 36, 41, 241, 248
Roundtree, Lieutenant, 47
Royal Engineers, 178
Roysdon, Captain, 185
Ruggero, Ed, 55, 271
Russell, Captain Clyde, 62, 81, 96-97, 116, 142, 147, 208, 277

Sacharoff, Lenny, 231
Saint Louis, Missouri, 24
Saint-Lô, France, 223
Saint-Sauveur-le-Vicomte, France, 216-218, 234, 278
Sainte-Mère-Eglise, 173, 178-181, 185, 191-192, 196, 201, 211, 270-271, 273, 275-276, 279

Salerno Bay, Italy, 107
Salerno, Italy, 107, 110-111, 122, 140, 154, 271
Sammon, Pinky (Charles), 55
Sampson, Otis, 7, 67, 76, 132, 267
San Louis Obispo, California, 40
Sanders, 13, 73, 75, 126, 130
Santa Croce Camerina, Italy, 86
Sayer, Captain Ed, 88, 124-125, 269, 271
Sciacca, Sicily, 90
Scoglitti, Sicily, 63, 87
Scymkowicz, Lieutenant Frank, 83
Seeley, Private Turk, 113, 140, 273
Shanley, Lieutenant Colonel Thomas J., 224, 231
Sicily, 12, 63-65, 68-73, 80-81, 87-92, 94-97, 99-100, 102-105, 108-111, 124, 143-144, 156, 165, 170, 172, 177, 185, 194, 227, 240, 247, 262, 267-270, 272
Sixth Panzer Army, 243
Snyder, Bill, 35
Soissons, France, 234, 239-240, 244
Sprinkle, Lieutenant, 78-79
Stilwell, General Joseph, 33
Suippes, France, 234, 239-241, 244, 281

Taylor, Captain Royal R., 57, 59, 104, 231
Tedeschi, Richard, 138
Thompson, Jack "Beaver", 95
Thompson, Lt. Col. Tommy, 13, 64-65, 71, 73, 103, 105-106, 111, 176, 240
Trapani, Sicily, 91, 94-96, 102, 104, 270
Truman, General Ralph, 32-33, 36-37
Truman, Harry, 32, 36, 37
Tucker, Colonel Rueben, 238

U.S. Eighth Army, 254-255
U.S. Fifth Army, 107, 109-110, 112, 122, 154
U.S. Geographical Survey, 23
USS *Frederick Funston*, 154
Underwood Feed and Grain Mill, 16
United States, 12, 29, 30, 31, 40, 72, 94, 101, 170, 242, 249, 250, 261, 272, 274
United States Army, 12, 31
USS *Monterey*, 57, 59
Utah Beach, 187, 191, 196, 233

Vandervoort, Major Ben, 108, 143, 168, 181, 203, 206-208, 210, 212-213, 215-217, 277
VE Day, 250
Vittoria, Sicily, 86
Volturno River, Italy, 107, 109, 120-123, 129, 131, 138, 140-141, 161, 271

Wancio, Edwin F., 194
Warren, Lieutenant Colonel Shields, 225
Watson, Jack, 248
Weems, General, 241
Wehrmacht, 174

Weidman, Pee-Wee, 20
West Point, 50, 69, 105, 164
Whitfield, Private Darrell, 129, 271
Wienecke, Colonel, 239
Wilson, Lieutenant William, 77
Winton, Colonel Walter, 171, 211
Wood, George, 142
Woolslayer, Captain Paul, 55, 65, 77-79, 83-84, 246, 247
Wurst, Private Spencer, 7, 116, 133, 138, 216, 272, 282

Young, Bill, 252